The Siege of
VIENNA

The Siege *of* Vienna

THE LAST GREAT TRIAL BETWEEN
Cross & Crescent

John Stoye

PEGASUS BOOKS
NEW YORK

THE SIEGE OF VIENNA
THE LAST GREAT TRIAL BETWEEN CROSS AND CRESCENT

Pegasus Books LLC
45 Wall Street, Suite 1021
New York, NY 10005

First Pegasus Books cloth edition 2006
First Pegasus Books trade paperback edition 2007

Library of Congress Cataloging-in-Publication Data is available.

ISBN: 978-1-933648-63-7

10 9 8 7 8 6 5 4 3 2 1

Printed in the United States of America

Contents

Illustrations

The following authorities have kindly given permission for the reproduction of these plates: The Trustees of the British Library for nos. I–IV, VI, VII, IX–XI and XIV–XV, the Kunsthistorisches Museum, Vienna, for no. V, the Curators of the Bodleian Library for no. viii, and the Ashmolean Museum for nos. XII–XIII

Maps and Plans

Some of the
Principal Personages

Mehmed IV, *Sultan*

Kara Mustafa, *Grand Vezir*

Michael Apafi, *Prince of Transylvania*

Serban Cantacuzene, *Prince of Wallachia*

George III Duka, *Prince of Moldavia*

Murad Ghiraj, *Khan of the Crimea*

Imre Thököly, *'King' of Hungary*

Louis XIV, *King of France*

John III Sobieski, *King of Poland*

Charles XI, *King of Sweden*

Leopold I, *Emperor*

Eleanor of Pfalz-Neuburg, *Empress, Leopold's third wife*

Eleanor of Mantua, *Dowager Empress, Leopold's step-mother*

Eleanor, *Leopold's half-sister, who married Charles Duke of Lorraine*

Frederick William, *Elector of Brandenburg*

John George III, *Elector of Saxony*

Max Emmanuel, *Elector of Bavaria*

Charles V, *Duke of Lorraine*

Herman, Margrave of Baden, *President of the War Council in Vienna*

Lewis of Baden, *his nephew*

Philip William, *Count Palatine of Pfalz-Neuburg*

Ernest Augustus, *Duke of Hanover-Calenberg*

George Frederick, *Count Waldeck*

Abele, *President of the Treasury in Vienna*

Borgomanero, *Spanish ambassador in Vienna*

Buonvisi, *Papal Nuncio in Vienna*

Caplirs, *Vice-President of the War Council*

Caprara, *Leopold's envoy to the Sultan*

Königsegg, *Imperial Vice-Chancellor*

Kuniz, *Leopold's envoy to the Sultan*

Lamberg, John Maximilian, *a senior court official in Vienna*

Lamberg, John Philip, *his son, Leopold's envoy to Berlin and Dresden*

Montecuccoli, *President of the War Council until 1680*

Nostitz-Reineck, *Bohemian Chancellor*

Pallavicini, *Papal Nuncio in Warsaw*

Rébenac, *French ambassador in Berlin*

Schwarzenberg, *President of the Imperial Council*

Sinelli, *Bishop of Vienna*

Sinzendorf, Hans, *President of the Treasury until 1680*

Starhemberg, Conrad, *Statthalter of Lower Austria*

Starhemberg, Ernest Rüdiger, *his son, commander of the Vienna garrison*

Stratmann, *Austrian Court-Chancellor*

Zierowski, *Leopold's ambassador in Poland*

Zinzendorf, Albert, *a senior court official in Vienna*

To Catherine
for withstanding the siege

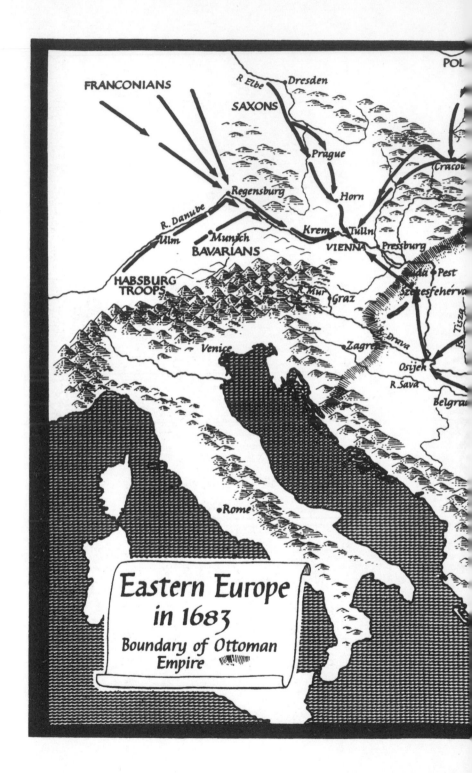

Eastern Europe in 1683
Boundary of Ottoman Empire

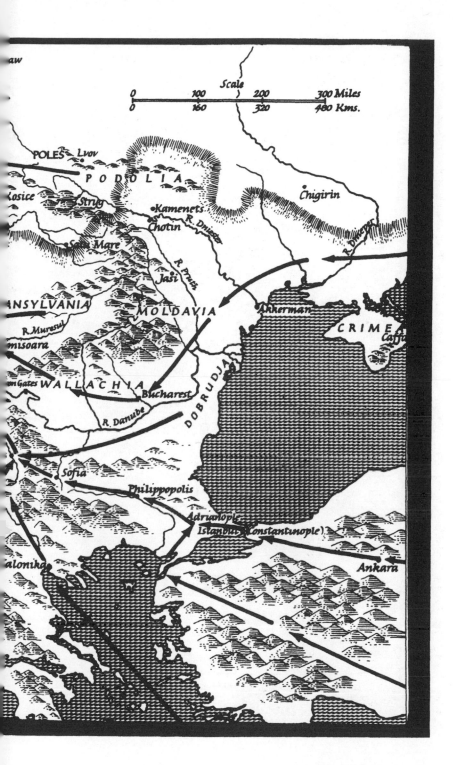

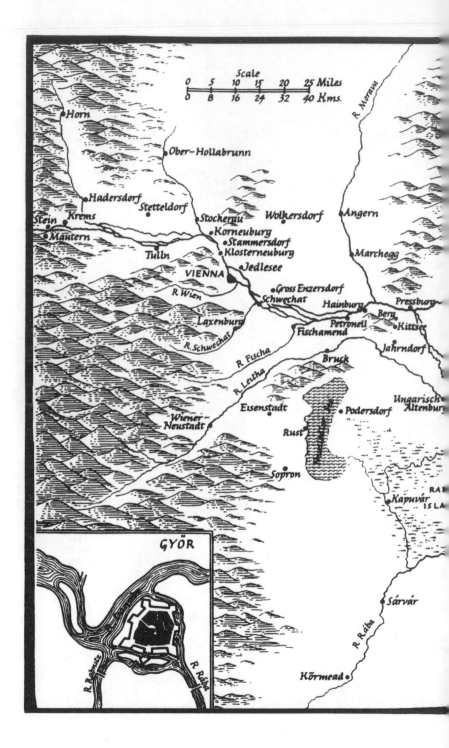

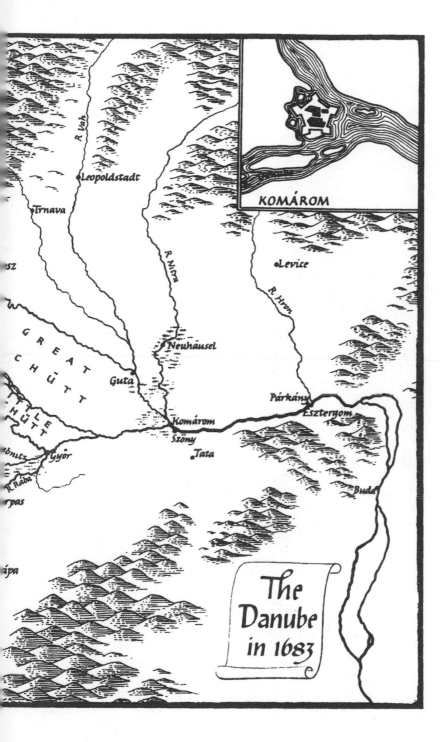

KOMÁROM

R. Vah

Leopoldstadt

Trnava

R. Nitra

Levice

R. Hron

G R E A T

C H Ü T T

Neuhäusel

Guta

L E

H Ü T T

Komárom

Szöny

Tata

Parkány

Esztergom

Györ

R. Raba

Buda

The
Danube
in 1683

1

The Origins of the
Ottoman Attack

I

On 6 August 1682, an important meeting took place in Sultan Mehmed IV's great palace in Istanbul. The highest officers of his government were present, and those among them who opposed the Grand Vezir Kara Mustafa for personal reasons, or deplored his aggressive statesmanship, had been silenced. They now agreed to disregard the existing treaty of peace with the Emperor Leopold I, which was not due to expire until 1684, and they recommended a military campaign for the year 1683, to be mounted in Hungary with the maximum armament of the Sultan's empire.

In fact, these dignitaries were formally accepting the Grand Vezir's decision to intensify a policy already in operation; but they could hardly fail to realise how much depended on the bigger scale, and therefore on the scope, of his new proposal. In 1681, a number of the Sultan's troops stationed north of the Danube had been sent to help Imre Thököly, the Magyar leader in rebellion against Habsburg authority in Christian Hungary, that part of the country which the Turks themselves did not occupy. Early in 1682, more troops were drawn from an even wider area, including Bosnia and Serbia, for the same purpose. Their commander, old Ibrahim, the governor of Buda, gave Thököly powerful assistance and some useful Habsburg strongholds in Slovakia were captured. Up to, but not beyond this point, the policy was flexible. It could be modified or even reversed. But now the Sultan, inspired by the Grand Vezir, went decidedly further. He recognised Thököly as 'King' of Hungary under Ottoman protection. He instructed his own court, and in addition the full complement of his household troops, to winter in Adrianople. He began to summon other contingents from his more distant provinces. It was soon understood that they were all to move northwards during the early months of the following year to Belgrade, the general rendezvous for an immense concentration of forces.

Five days later, on 11th August 1682, at Laxenburg near Vienna, Leopold I received the opinion of his counsellors on the question of peace or war with the Turks.[1] They unanimously advised him to try to renew his treaty of peace. These statesmen paid far too little attention to the gloomy dispatches from the Habsburg envoys in Istanbul, George Kuniz and Albert Caprara, or to the threatening situation in Hungary. They were almost all preoccupied by the recent aggressions of Louis XIV in Flanders and Germany and Italy, and by Leopold's and Louis' rival claims to succeed Carlos II of Spain if he died childless. They considered that the ambitious foreign policy of the French court had gained rather than lost momentum since the treaties signed at Nymegen* in Holland, in 1678 and 1679, put an end to seven years of public warfare in western Europe. They believed that Louis XIV was more to be feared than Mehmed IV. They argued that further concessions to France would prove fatal to Habsburg power and reputation, while possible concessions to the Sultan might be retrieved in due course. They appeared to have in mind, not an immediate order to Caprara to make a positive offer to the Turks (this they had always refused to contemplate), but a further dragging out of discussion between their envoys and the Grand Vezir; if necessary, somewhat later, they would consider the surrender of a few fortified points in the area between Habsburg Pressburg and Turkish Buda. The Sultan, after all, had not stirred in the critical 1670s when Christian Hungary was in a state of mutiny against Leopold. They tried hard to convince themselves that he would not stir far in the 1680s.

The Austrian counsellors were mistaken, but the westward orientation of Viennese policy was an obstinate tradition of long standing. The dominant idea, at least since the early part of the century when the Ottoman power was relatively quiescent, had been to deal gently with the Moslems in order to spare the maximum force required to oppose Christian enemies in western Europe. This was the tactic in 1664, after the great victory of St Gotthard on the banks of the River Rába, when the Habsburgs made concessions (unnecessarily, it seemed to some critics) in order to secure the twenty years' truce due to expire in 1684. 'The Crescent Moon (of Islam) climbs up the night sky and the Gallic cock sleeps not!' was a popular German saying of the time. Leopold 1 in the Hofburg heard clearly the crowing of the French court and, with the majority of his statesmen, disliked Louis XIV intensely; but for him, the moon rose in comparative silence and the Sultan represented the principle of evil in a somewhat remote sphere, at least in the years before 1682 and 1683. A strong clerical interest at his court, which argued the merits of defending or

---

*Louis XIV here concluded separate treaties with his principal adversaries, the Dutch, the Emperor, and the King of Spain – who ruled over the Spanish Netherlands, Luxembourg, Franche Comté (which he lost by the terms of this agreement), Milan, Naples and Sicily.

expanding Christendom, battled in vain against the traditional emphasis in the complex system of Viennese diplomacy.

In August 1682, therefore, the Turks decided on an ambitious military attack against the Habsburg at an early date; and the Habsburg decided to try to avoid war. It is a coincidence which helps to explain why twelve months later the armies of the Sultan were camped round the walls of Vienna itself. In fact, the Habsburg government was not caught completely off its guard, as other evidence will show. But a fundamental underestimate of Turkish striking power continued to bedevil its general policy.

An official ceremony in Istanbul, the mounting of the Sultan's insignia – the *Tugh*, or horsetails – outside the Grand Seraglio, publicly proclaimed his intention of leaving the city in the near future. As so often in past years, no doubt, it seemed that he would hunt during the autumn and then go on to Adrianople. Indeed, he left on 8 October,[2] after the fast of Ramadan and the feast of Bairam were over, hunted at leisure through various tracts of countryside, and reached Adrianople early in December. His harem and household followed him. But observant men were on the watch for a great deal besides the usual paraphernalia of a despot's private pleasures. They saw the different sections of the Sultan's permanent army, usually stationed in and near Istanbul, now assembling outside the walls of the city around his gorgeous ceremonial tent, the movable headquarters and symbol of his government: the Janissaries and auxiliary infantry units, the Spahis and other household cavalry, and a host of technicians and tradesmen required for the service of the troops. Although a marvellous cavalcade had ushered the Sultan out of the city with traditional Moslem emphasis on the importance of such an occasion, the majority of the soldiers left a week later, moved forward without stopping long anywhere, and reached Adrianople before him. Here they remained for four months, the core of an army which expanded rapidly as additional detachments kept coming in; for messengers had gone out to the farthest edges of the empire in Asia and Europe, and also to Egypt. The *beylerbeyis*, or governors-in-chief, were instructed to bring with them the contingents for which their revenues made them liable, and to see that the lesser provincial officials, the *sandjakbeyis*, and the landowners large and small, who held land on military tenures, did likewise. Gradually, these forces began to make their way to Adrianople, Belgrade or to points on the road between them.

Meanwhile Kuniz and Caprara had both been brought from Istanbul, and the representatives of other rulers arrived at the temporary centre of government where the Sultan and Grand Vezir resided. One came from Moscow, and the treaty made in 1681 with the Czar of Muscovy was ratified, which ensured peace in a vast area north of the Black Sea. The envoys of the Prince of Transylvania were for once well and lavishly entertained: the Ottoman government hoped to make certain that Prince Michael Apafi sent his forces to join the army, and paid his tribute punctually in the coming year, at the same time acting as a counterweight to Thököly, the new 'King' in Hungary. A conference with Caprara took place, in which arguments aired at earlier meetings between the Austrian and the Turkish statesmen were repeated. It was a farcical occasion, because Leopold had made no fresh offers, and because Kara Mustafa was determined not to commit himself until the weight of the army to be assembled in Hungary had given him an overpowering advantage. Caprara learnt now that the price of peace was the surrender of Győr, a fortress of the greatest importance to the Habsburg defences, situated on the Danube, fifty miles south-east of Pressburg. The Turks realised that he had no authority to agree to this; he was already that familiar phenomenon in the history of Ottoman relations with the Christian states, a captive diplomat, detained for possible use by the Turks at their discretion. As a matter of much greater immediate importance, at Adrianople the Sultan willingly agreed with his counsellors that he should lead the army to Belgrade, while thereafter the Grand Vezir exercised supreme military command as his deputy.

For some time attention had been given to the condition of the route through the Balkans. The repair of bridges across the Maritza and the Morava was taken in hand. Unfortunately, exceptional rains increased abnormally the weight of water flowing off the Rhodope and Balkan mountains. The passage of the foremost troops inevitably churned up the road, to the disadvantage of men, carts, and beasts coming up behind them. On 30 March the vanguard of Janissaries set out, to be followed soon afterwards by the Sultan and his household with the main body of troops, the ambassadors of Austria and Poland, and all the rag-tag and bobtail that accompanied a court or an army on the move at this period. Perhaps 100,000 persons were trekking forward.

Caprara's secretary has left an account of what took place on the road to Belgrade in April, 1683.[3] Some parts of the army marched or rode by day, but when the secretary tried to sleep at night he woke to hear other troops, advancing through the darkness by the flare of countless torches. Carts and wagons of every description went along with, or followed, the different detachments; often they got lost, or lagged behind. Great flocks of sheep and herds of cattle formed the basis of the victualling system, and Caprara guessed that 32,000 lbs. of meat and 60,000 loaves were consumed daily.[4] Prices fluctuated as rival commissariats bid against one another to supply their men. Privileged persons went by coach, and coaches stuck in the mud. The rains were shocking. If most men slept in tents, the more exalted (among whom the Austrian diplomats were still lucky to count themselves) sometimes found accommodation in the hospices which generations of wealthy and pious Moslems had built at intervals along the road. Sometimes there were halts of a day, or two days, when cities like Philippopolis and Sofia were reached; the army camped outside, and only civilians and grandees were allowed to pass the walls. Otherwise, there was nothing to be done except to go patiently forward after the vanguard – the indispensable vanguard of Janissaries which led the way, marked out the distances, and prepared the ovens every evening for those who followed them. Behind the Balkan troops, the men of Anatolia and Asia were now coming up. At Niš the other great route was joined, from Salonika, down which were moving the men from the Aegean and the men of Africa. The main body finally reached the outskirts of Belgrade on 3 May. A little earlier, officers had been sent ahead to close all the wineshops. A little later, the Sultan's entry into the city was of great ceremonial magnificence. The season of war and serious business approached with the spring, though spring itself, and the indispensable growth of fresh pasture for the innumerable livestock of this army, came late.

At Belgrade the Danube meets one of its largest right-bank tributaries, the Sava. Across the Sava stands Zemun, where the enormous camp was set on 4 May. More troops came in daily from different directions. The artillery was reviewed, though a Turkish account suggests that it did not include more than sixty guns and mortars. Munitions and provisions were loaded on 150 ships, for dispatch up the Danube. Every day the Sultan rode out from Belgrade on tours of inspection, and on 13 May he solemnly entrusted the sacred standard of Islam, 'the Flag of the Prophet', to the Grand Vezir, appointing him generalissimo for the campaign. Between 18 and 20 May the governor of Mesopotamia arrived with his men. The Janissaries marched out of camp, and a few days later the Grand Vezir followed with most of the remaining troops. The Sultan and his court stayed on at Belgrade with a small but adequate guard.

The pace of the Turks' advance was still slow, and they did not reach Osijek until 2 June. Two things held them back, rain, and the knowledge that their great bridge over the River Drava, another major tributary of the Danube, was not yet in a proper state of repair. For at Osijek, the route into Hungary crossed the Drava by a long pontoon bridge and then, a little way upstream, another bridge – constructed of massive timbers, with spectacular wooden towers placed at short interval – traversed the marshes for a distance usually estimated at five miles or 6,000 paces. Throughout a chequered history of decay and renovation since Suleiman the Lawgiver's reign, this formidable engineering work was the main gateway into Hungary from the south. Croats and Magyars had tried more than once to destroy it, and Caprara's secretary in 1683 noticed the scars surviving from a brave effort to burn down the bridge in 1664.[5] According to their own accounts, the Turks had been engaged on repairs during the previous six months; even so, they were too slow not to delay Kara Mustafa's army. While the work was hurriedly completed, Osijek itself hummed with business. Troops arrived from Albania, Epirus, Thessaly and even Egypt. The pasha of Veszprém had come southwards and reported for duty with his men. Above all Thököly himself appeared, to be greeted royally.

On 14 June the army began to leave Osijek. Most of the European, Asiatic and African contingents had now arrived, and once past the bridge a stricter order of march was enforced. The vanguard, led by Kara Mehmed of Diyarbakir, with 3,000 Janissaries, 500 Cebecis (also footsoldiers) and the cavalry of Diyarbakir, Aleppo, Sivas and Egypt, was 20,000 strong, and subsequently increased by some 8,000 Tartars who were then riding across Hungary to the Danube. Next came the main body of troops, followed by a powerful rearguard; but for neither of these are firm figures available. On they tramped, or rode. Instead of the rains, they complained of lack of water, and retailed the usual story that enemy agents were poisoning the wells. Prince Serban Cantacuzene, the tributary ruler of Wallachia, now appeared with his due contingent of men and wagons, to be employed by the Turks to strengthen their inadequate commissariat. Ten days later, Székesfehérvár was reached. A final decision on the future line of march had to be taken at this point, where the itineraries diverged towards alternative objectives on the long frontier between the Christian and the Moslem worlds.

On Saturday 26 June the Grand Vezir held a council.[6] Its discussions have been unreliably reported but there is no doubt about the immediate result. On 29 June the Turks entered enemy territory to the north-west, and moved towards the Habsburg citadel of Györ. Prisoners disclosed the concentration of strong hostile forces, and once again the commanders checked the order of march. Tartars, and other irregulars, fanned out ahead. Then came the vanguard, then various troops normally stationed in Hungary. The main army itself was divided into three distinct columns: on the right the Anatolian cavalry, on the left the cavalry of Europe, with the mass of infantry and artillery in the centre. The baggage followed. The rearguard kept its distance well behind. On Thursday 1 July, the Turks reached the right bank of the River Rába, not far from the town and fortifications of Györ. Soon all Europe hummed with the news of their advance, and it was realised that the days of reckoning were at hand.

This short chronicle of events between August 1682 and July 1683 is based on good evidence. The history behind the chronicle at once appears much more obscure. It is one thing to describe the movement of these massive forces across the Balkan lands, quite another to show why they took this course, and at this date. Ottoman history in the seventeenth century, in spite of some heroic inquiries, has still to be written. There remains in Istanbul a forest of administrative records to be explored for this period, but in any case the Moslem cultural and political tradition never gave the Sultan's greater office holders the impulse to compose state-papers and diplomatic instructions on the western model, or to write their memoirs in order to explain and justify their actions. Even Alexander Mavrocordato, the Greek dragoman who accompanied Kara Mustafa to the gates of Vienna, educated at Padua and a keen collector of western books, preferred to commit to paper only the most meagre account of what occurred in 1683.[7] Yet no man was better placed to observe and to judge the secret course of Turkish politics at Istanbul, Adrianople, and in the gorgeous tents which were the headquarters of the Grand Vezir.

II

One or two far-seeing Moslem writers of the seventeenth century contrasted unfavourably the working of contemporary Ottoman institutions with what they believed was the sounder practice of earlier periods. It is more important to take into account the conventional opinion of their day. For the plain man, accepting without debate the structure of human society as it existed, the frame of government provided by the great empire of the Ottoman Sultan seemed indestructibly part of the nature of things. Its splendour, and strength, far overshadowed the current tribulations of humanity within it. Anyone who cares to browse, for example, through the writings of the traveller Evliyá Chelibí,[8] son of a prosperous Istanbul goldsmith who crossed and recrossed the Moslem world in a long sequence of journeys between 1640 and 1670, will be left with a vivid impression of his complete sense of confidence. No city, in Evliyá's experience, could approach the magnificence of the Istanbul he so lovingly describes: its palaces and places of worship, its educational establishments and hospitals, its plethora of the guilds of skilled craftsmen. Nothing could detract from the glory of those marvellous conquests which the sultans of his own day, Murad IV and his two successors, had made in various parts of the world. They were worthy of Selim the Cruel and Suleiman the Lawgiver. Look up his account of the gun-foundry and its workmen in the capital, and of the *topjís*, or artillerymen: who could doubt that both were incomparable in their own line of business? Read his description of the siege by the Turks of Azov in 1640: the reader must believe that such a partnership of Moslem courage in battle with massive military organisation was, and would always be, superior to the efforts of any enemy. Besides, victories brought their due advantage to the brave adventurer. Evliyá tells of the booty distributed, of his own share of slaves and furs and other valuables; it was the traditional, practical motive for Ottoman militancy from the Sultan or Vezir down to the dingiest camp follower. In this valuable and conventionally-minded author there is not the slightest hint of a 'failure of nerve', no inkling of living mainly in the shadow of past Moslem achievements.

Against Evliyá it must be said that the armed forces, and the structure of government, were no longer based on the practice which made possible Ottoman expansion in earlier days. Apart from Murad IV, the sultans of the seventeenth century retreated to the hunting-lodge or the inner household of the palace. Their fear of rivals led them to refuse political and intellectual education, or any exercise of authority, or even personal freedom, to other members of their own family. This defect became the more glaring when a rule was established in 1617,[9] in order to avoid the alternative dangers of a minority, that the vacant throne must always pass to the eldest surviving prince of the imperial house: a man, therefore, who had spent his earlier life 'caged' in the palace for the greater security of his predecessor. Power was still the Sultan's, but responsibility increasingly rested with a sequence of Grand Vezirs whose

tenure of office depended on the Sultan's good will, susceptible in turn to
secret intrigue within the palace or hunting-lodge. The men who made the
crucial political decisions were vulnerable in a way that Selim and Suleiman
had never been in the previous century.

Nor was the standing army any longer so compact, highly trained, or
dependent on the Sultan and independent of everybody else. The Janissaries,
who were the infantry, and some of the *ojaks* or regiments of Spahis who
were the household cavalry, had been normally recruited in the past from
Christian populations in the Balkans; so also were the more talented men who
became high officers of state. Educated as Moslems, drafted into the army or
the administration, they were the well-paid servants who upheld the supreme
power in its miraculous, isolated splendour. They were themselves cut off
from the social order which they helped to control. Already in the sixteenth
century, the Moslem populations began to react against this dominance, of
a permanent military force and a brilliantly organised government, both
manned by converted Christian 'slaves'. Many of the leading statesmen and
commanders had left behind them children who were Moslem-born, and who
naturally reinforced the pressure in defence of their own obvious interest.
The Janissaries were recruited increasingly from the sons of former Janissaries
and from the Moslem population, particularly in Istanbul itself and other
large cities like Cairo. They broke the old rules which forbade them to marry
before retirement, or to trade; while married tradesmen, and others, purchased,
the privileges of 'veteran' Janissaries. These tendencies were noted by foreign
observers before the close of the sixteenth century. Then, gradually, the élite of
the recruits which was educated in the schools of the Seraglio, was also taken
from influential Moslem families.[10] It amounted to a fundamental alteration in
the personnel of the governing class, and of this the famous Köprülü dynasty
of Vezirs forms a conspicuous example. The chances that Mehmed Köprülü's
sons and nephews would enjoy either affluence or influence were not much less
than those of Le Tellier's or Colbert's family in France.

One result of this change was the greater sensitivity of the régime to the
religious problems of the Moslem world. The inevitable tensions between the
sects and orders of dervishes, and the representatives of orthodoxy, involved
the army because the Janissaries were deeply influenced by the great sect of the
Bektashi. The link between them received official sanction in 1594. Fifty years
later the Mevlevi, another sect, certainly had influence in high places. The
views of the Bektashi and the Mevlevi, on a wide range of subjects, from the
veneration of saints to the drinking of wine, and their intermittent sympathy
with Christian ideas, tended to meet with the strong disapproval of the
orthodox. At the same time the Janissaries of the capital interfered increasingly
in politics, partly in order to insist on the payment of full wages while the
value of the currency steadily depreciated. Strife broke out between them
and rival contingents in the standing army. They learnt to ally with opposite
parties at court, and there were occasional periods of complete anarchy in the

headquarters of the empire. Then Mehmed Köprülü obtained full powers as the Grand Vezir in 1656. His rule could not restore the old structure of the state, but it did reinforce orthodoxy in religion. For the time being the more radical sectaries were suppressed, and the Janissaries and other paid troops were reduced to order. One of the most powerful allies of Fazil Ahmed, the second Köprülü, was Vani the stern preacher who denounced all dervishes and wine-drinkers.[11]

A further consequence of this reviving orthodoxy may well have been increased hostility to the Christian churches. While the Orthodox Christian clergy tended to look to the Ottoman government for protection against the encroachments of Roman Catholic missions, and were much alarmed by the multiplication of Uniate churches in communion with Rome, some of them had responded to this Catholic threat by a vigorous movement of reform under Patriarch Cyril Lukaris (executed in 1638). They also began to look with growing attention and sympathy towards the Orthodox Czar and Church of Muscovy, then coming more closely into line with Greek religious practice thanks to Nikon, Patriarch of Moscow (until 1657) and other reformers. The Orthodox rulers of the Romanian principalities, Wallachia and Moldavia, over which the Sultan claimed sovereignty, also occasionally looked to Muscovy (and to Catholic Poland) for support. But these developments simply strengthened the Istanbul government's determination to control its Orthodox subjects with the utmost rigour. Meanwhile, economic pressure by the Christian states of western Europe increased in the Ottoman lands. If an old tactic of the Turkish rulers consisted in playing off the envoys from Protestant Holland and England against the ambassador of Catholic France, and it was often profitable, there could be no doubt that the 'capitulations' of these countries with the Sultan formed the basis of their growing commercial supremacy in the Levant. Moslems rightly mistrusted wealthy alien merchants who imported debased currency, manufactured in the west for use in the Turkish dominions.[12] Foreign Christians tended to do business, first of all, with the native Christians, and this was a further cause of offence.[13] Dislike and alarm were naturally to reach new heights when the French admiral Du Quesne and his ships burst into the Aegean on the prowl after pirates in June 1681, and remained in those waters for nine months. 'The Gran Visir thunders amongst us,' the merchants from the west complained, but he had good reasons for doing so.

The state was becoming more obstinately Moslem in personnel and outlook. This is one comment that may be made on old Evliyá's view of the Ottoman empire's continuing glory. Other fundamental changes, which he could hardly be expected to grasp, were also taking place.

When the masterful Murad IV died in 1640, a strongly entrenched party of courtiers in the palace soon realised that warfare was the simplest means of keeping the standing troops otherwise quartered in or around Istanbul at arm's length. This helps to account for the prolongation of the desultory war against Venice, begun in 1645 for the conquest of Crete. But rivalries at court then tended to make each faction exploit the sympathy of rival contingents in the standing army. It was found that a naval war against Venice involved the defence of the Dardanelles, and of Istanbul itself, so that large numbers of soldiers had to be kept close to the vital centre of government. They were still on the spot to be used by, or to use, the factions. The Grand Vezirs, who often had a clear notion of their imperial responsibilities, sometimes tried to employ the troops against the court, and sometimes regarded military disorders as the primary evil to be stamped out first. Alternatively, without troops they could not hope to repress the mounting tumult in parts of Asia Minor. A final and most important element in an anarchic situation was the temperament of the Sultan: 'mad' Ibrahim (1640-7) made courtiers and politicians fearful for their personal safety, and was therefore responsible for kaleidoscopic changes of front, and reversals of alliance by all the interests involved. The minority of Mehmed IV (born in 1640) had very much the same effect on the situation. During this period two main parties, patronised by the mother of Ibrahim and the mother of Mehmed respectively, fought one another to a standstill – the older lady was slaughtered in 1651 – but the boy Sultan was so much under the influence of his immediate entourage that the foothold of successive Vezirs was correspondingly weak. Sivash, in office in 1651, and Ipsir, who was Mehmed Köprülü's patron, were without doubt men of ability.[14] Later on the Sultan had grown older and surer of himself, and his determination to maintain the Köprülüs in office as the responsible Grand Vezirs did more than anything else to restore stability while this stability made it easier to increase the revenue of the state and to pay the troops, whose discipline improved accordingly.

The first Köprülü ferociously repressed most of the elements of disorder: the influence of household politicians in court and harem, the perpetual rumbling of stipendiary troops in the larger cities, and the incendiarism of dervishes. His success vindicated Evliyá's faith in the structure of Ottoman dominion, even if that structure was insensibly changing.

When Mehmed Köprülü died in office in 1661 his son Fazil Ahmed succeeded him unopposed, and ruled fifteen years. He too died in office and Kara Mustafa, a son-in-law, took his place in 1676. This long span of time, hardly interrupted by such easy transfers of power, gave a continuity and firmness to the central authority which made it more formidable than at any period earlier in the century. Much depended on the Sultan's willingness to tolerate Vezirs who acquired greater effective power the longer they remained in office. But Mehmed IV, like his exact contemporary Louis XIV, had endured years of misery during his minority, and unlike Louis he never dreamt of being his own first minister. The development of court protocol, with its deliberate denial of an education in politics to members of the ruling house, made this improbable in any case. Only someone of exceptional quality could break down such a barrier, and Mehmed's virtues as a prince were the simple ones:

to survive his minority, to prefer hunting to politics, and not to die for many years. His vices were said to be avarice, and occasional fits of acute jealousy.

The Köprülüs, father and son, were not the men to elaborate a system. They felt their way, a step at a time, but recognised with great perceptiveness the unalterable facts of their situation. In consequence they were remarkably consistent statesmen. It was necessary to satisfy the Sultan, and this meant giving him funds enough to lead the easy, expensive life he craved, dedicated above all to the pleasure of hunting on a fabulous scale. It was necessary to tame the capital city, and the unruly elements there which had supported so many palace upheavals in the past; significantly Mehmed IV did not visit Istanbul once in ten years (1666–76).[15] Finally, the Köprülüs had to accept the whole burden of empire, to keep in due subordination the provincial pashas, the tributary rulers along the frontiers, and neighbouring princes who threatened the frontiers. All these needed resolute and aggressive statesmanship. Under Fazil Ahmed, himself an administrator rather than a military commander by training, it became clear that intensive military activity presented the most reasonable answer to this threefold problem.

Warfare was expensive, but it justified heavy taxation from which the Sultan took his full share. It beat the big Moslem drum against the non-Moslem world, which helped to control the religious fervour inspiring ordinary public opinion at a time when tension between orthodoxies and heresies kept such fervour at a high pitch. War likewise drew off troublesome forces from the capital, both the Janissaries and the tradesmen who worked for them. More important, campaigning on a large scale justified enlarging the army to a maximum, and within this expanded force it was easier to contrive a balance of power which subdued the more refractory elements. Even among the standing troops the Köprülüs checked the Janissaries and the cavalry (these Spahis, recruited from the household pages, had been one of the most uncontrollable bodies of men in the 1650s) by careful attention to the separate cadres of gunners and armourers. All these units were counterweighted again by the fiefholders and their contingents summoned from the provinces, by other groups of paid soldiery, and by the increasingly large personal followings of provincial governors. By his emphatic and peremptory summons the Grand Vezir rallied the empire's military resources. All together, if the giant Ottoman armament wasted the many areas through which the contingents passed on their way to the allotted theatre of war, it also maintained stability and discipline by an approximate internal balance of power. Of course, the manoeuvre roused grumbling. The more closely many *ortas*, or companies, of Janissaries became associated with the guilds and the artisan population of Istanbul, the more they aspired to be civilians with the privileges of soldiers, and the less they liked a summons to war which seemed partly designed to decimate them. The more the old fiefs (the so-called *timars* and *ziamets*) tended to become negotiable sources of revenue for courtiers and politicians, the less enthusiastically many fiefholders obeyed the same summons. Yet, for the government, the policy justified itself, forcing the old military institutions to continue functioning, with some benefit to the empire.

Distant warfare strengthened the Grand Vezirs at court. Mehmed IV had now realised that his own interest required a strong chief Vezir to govern for him, but he could hardly help hearing the whispered hints of his household servants, or realising that the Köprülüs enjoyed a power which might be said to rival his. Intrigue always continued, and there was a danger that the Sultan would one day be tempted to depose the man who was nominally the Sultan's 'slave'. At court, also, the Vezir was overshadowed by the Sultan's precedence. Almost paradoxically he became stronger *in absentia*. Whatever his enemies might suggest to discredit him, it was on balance dangerous to tamper with his appointment in the course of a military campaign. Then, if he concluded it successfully, it seemed senseless to try and depose him at a moment when victory enhanced his prestige. A little later was too late: campaigning had already recommenced, so that the cycle of events which left the Grand Vezir in power, and his enemies partially silenced, began again.

III

The assault on Vienna was therefore only one of a long series of campaigns, all caused in part by the special character of Ottoman court politics. But its timing and direction owed even more to the complex history of the Ottoman frontier lands in Europe. These stretched in a wide arc for 1,200 miles from the Adriatic to the Sea of Azov, combining military strongholds with an amazing variety of political checks and balances. They were the outworks in Dalmatia, Slavonia, Hungary, Transylvania, Moldavia, Podolia, the Ukraine and the Crimea, which protected the inner Balkan lands and the Black Sea. They confronted the enemy states of Venice, Austria and Poland, as well as the Cossacks and the Muscovites; they confined, and helped to control, the Christian populations under the Sultan's rule. From one point of view Kara Mustafa inherited and exploited a remarkable system of defence, which the Ottoman government had built up in Europe after two centuries of experience. From another he mishandled and perverted it, thereby compelling the Poles and the Austrians to unite against him.

In Hungary direct occupation of the frontier had existed since 1541. The pashas of Bosnia and Kanisca faced a miscellaneous array of forces, garrisons, irregular bands and noblemen's troops nominally subject to the government of Inner Austria at Graz, or to the Ban (the Viceroy) of Croatia. The pasha of Buda kept watch over the Habsburg citadels on or near the Danube below Pressburg, as well as over the mountainous territory north and north-east of Buda. The pasha of Timisoara meanwhile governed an inner part of this broad frontier zone, and with other commanders in the Tisza valley safeguarded the Ottoman interest in Transylvania, lying east of Hungary.[16]

The forces controlled by a man like the pasha of Buda were usually a match for the local Habsburg commanders, or for Magyar raiders along the middle Danube. Yet this was a remote frontier, close to one of the stronger Christian states. Larger armaments were needed from time to time. In such an emergency the standing troops of the Sultan, and the enormous reserves of manpower available in the empire, could be moved up from the Balkans and Asia to Belgrade and Buda. His permanent military strength distinguished the Sultan's dominion from almost every Christian government until the mid-seventeenth century, and the campaigns in Transylvania and Hungary between 1659 and 1664 showed that it was still effective.

Moreover, the Turkish administration had now lasted so long in Hungary that the subject populations were acquiescent. Though oppressive, it avoided certain major errors which might have caused trouble. The Turks tended to keep to the towns, where they often pushed the Magyars into the suburbs. Inside the walls Moslemised Serbs and Bosnians, rather than the Turks themselves, replaced the native inhabitants and for their benefit mosques were built or, more commonly, old churches were converted into mosques. The secular testimonies of this Moslem dominance appeared at the same time, the baths and fountains and hostelries. Negotiations between Turkish officials and ordinary folk were made easier by a small class of Magyar scribes who had attended both at Christian and Moslem schools.[17] Outside the towns, the conquerors never tried to 'plant' the countryside. There could be no immigration of the kind noticeable in Bulgaria out of Anatolia in this and earlier periods. In Hungary the Turks simply took over from the old, and became the new, absentee landholders. They funnelled taxes and revenues from a given piece of ground into their own feudal system for the upkeep of troops, into their tax-farming system, and into their system of charitable and private endowments of various kinds. The treasury at Istanbul tried hard to keep copies of the main local schedules which listed the proper allocation of Hungarian resources. In a few areas, curiously enough, families long resident in Habsburg Hungary were able to preserve fragmentarily some of their original sources of revenue in spite of the Turks; but this was part of the double-taxation and mutual raiding common along the fringes of Christian and Turkish dominion, the normal fate of boundary lands which were 'contribution country'. Apart from this special type of exception, the class of substantial or hereditary Christian landowner had disappeared after the Turkish conquest, a fact which was one guarantee of the régime's stability. Others were a population gradually declining (in all probability), and a feeble economy. It was stability of a dismal kind, but adequate for its predominantly military function north of the area already protected by great and uncontrollable rivers, the Danube, Drava and Tisza, flowing amid miles of marshland in the region where their courses converge.

The Turks also treated religious problems with considerable shrewdness. They did not proselytise in Hungary, because they wanted subjects not

Moslems, nor did they conscript Christian boys for a military education in the schools of Istanbul, as occurred in the Balkans. On the other hand they limited strictly the right of Christians to protect, repair or build churches, though without persecution by *dragonnade* on the Habsburg or Bourbon model. Denying the Catholic hierarchy any chance of exercising public authority, they made it easier for Calvinism to survive in Hungary. The rival Christian faiths could quarrel under the eye of Moslem pashas claiming authority over both.

These arrangements also suited the Ottoman interest across the border, in Habsburg Hungary. Here the Magyars never learnt to combine for long under the Habsburg dynasts whom they nevertheless accepted as kings of Hungary. Whenever the royal authority appeared too weak to enforce order, or too harsh to be endured, there was always the strong probability that a party of patriots or rebels would look for Turkish support. A great conspiracy of the magnates Zrinyi, Nádasdy, and Wesselényi against Leopold in 1668–70, after a period of Habsburg military activity in warfare against the Turks (1660–64), and the rebellion which broke out in 1672 after the first rising had been crushed, were due to increased autocratic pressure by the Vienna government, and both illustrated the iron law of Hungarian politics in this century: that Magyar liberties under the Habsburgs depended on the presence of the Turks in the rest of Hungary. The constitutional weakness, a very old one, was intensified by the relatively modern antagonism of Catholics and Protestants. The Protestants, given the impartiality which the Turks mixed with oppression in matters of religion, were bound to look to them for support. Otherwise there would be no means of checking the Catholic counter-offensive to recover lost ground, which was perhaps more powerfully mounted in Habsburg Hungary after 1648 than anywhere else in Europe. The seminary for clergy at Trnava came into Jesuit hands in 1649; and the Jesuit academy in the chief Protestant city of eastern Hungary, Kassa (Košice), was accorded the status of a university in 1660. From these two major points, and a host of lesser ones, Catholic influence radiated fast. The bishops now formed a strong and zealous body of men, headed after 1665 by the implacable Archbishop of Esztergom, George Szelepcsényi. They enjoyed the Vienna government's firm support, because the Emperor Ferdinand II and his successors held explicitly that the Catholic creed was the surest test of political loyalty. Measures based on this premise were bound to push the Protestants into further acts of disloyalty.

As a result the Turkish authority in Buda, always confident of its power to hold Hungary with the standing Ottoman forces, viewed with pleasure and attention the predicament of the Christians across the frontier. Of course, the Moslem commanders were not dispatched to this distant exile for the sake of a quiet life, but their security was no greater than they would have wished. If the seventeenth-century courts of Vienna and Istanbul kept peace with one another between 1606 and 1663, and between 1665 and 1683, the border lands dividing the two empires were disturbed by continual forays. Raiders from both sides conducted their expeditions with varying success. The Turks expected a reasonable annual revenue from the capture of cattle, horses and prisoners, by looting or taxing the border villages. This contributed to the fortune of high provincial officials who were never left long at their posts by a suspicious central government, and government in turn increased its revenue by making them pay heavily for the privilege (sometimes unwelcome) of their appointment. But petty anarchy and violence never detracted from the essential strength of the Turkish position in the lands which marched from the middle reaches of the Sava and Drava northwards to Buda and Esztergom, and then gradually east and south to the Transylvanian frontier.

From here to the distant steppe of the Don basin, the Ottoman defences rested to a greater degree on political manoeuvre. The principalities of Transylvania, Wallachia, Moldavia, Polish claims in the lower Dniester and Dnieper valleys, the complicated rivalry of different Christian Cossack groups with one another and with Tartars in the same area (the outlying Tartars in the Dobrudja by the Danube delta or the more organised followers of the Khan in the Crimea) all had to be combined in one gigantic jigsaw, the pieces of which continually altered in shape and significance. The general strategy of the Turks was to restrain each by means of the other, with the minimum possible use of their own strength. This extraordinary system, comparable in its own way with the elaborate network of Bourbon diplomacy in northern and eastern Europe under Louis XIV had been devised gradually, first round the Black Sea, and then covering more and more ground towards the west.

In 1478 Mehmed II reduced the ruling Ghiraj dynasty of the Crimean Tartars to an honoured but subordinate status. The Black Sea was closed to western trading fleets. In the seventeenth century the revenues of the busy port of Caffa[18] in the Crimea, fell to the Ottomans who garrisoned it, by this means supervising and subsidising the Khans who held sway over the rest of the peninsula from their splendid palace at Bagchi Serai in the hills above Balaclava. Some members of the Ghiraj family were usually held in Constantinople as hostages for the Khan's good behaviour and would be sent to replace him if necessary. The subsidies partly paid for the great forays to the west – to Polish and Transylvanian territory or elsewhere – which the Sultan from time to time ordered the Tartars to undertake. The balance of their payment was found in the actual booty of an expedition, particularly the slaves who were disposed of at Caffa. These, with the profits of other raids carried out against or without Ottoman consent, and of the more ordinary commerce flowing south from the Russian lands, once again swelled the revenues of the Crimean ports. The total result in terms of high politics was to place at the Sultan's disposal a large if erratic force of nomadic cavalry which could usually be directed where it was wanted. The activity of the Tartars in Poland in 1657–8, in Transylvania in 1660–2, in Moravia and Hungary in 1664, in the Hungarian campaigns from 1683 onwards, was remarkable. They preferred to cross the steppe while snow still covered the ground, and in consequence reached the western lands no later than an army coming up from the Balkans. They pushed through the Carpathian passes, or traversed Moldavia and Wallachia to join the Turks farther south. It is arguable that they were far more destructive, and did far greater damage to a countryside than the more tightly ordered Ottoman troops. However difficult to control, they were effective auxiliaries. If not disciplined, they were highly trained.

The Sultan, meanwhile, kept his grip on the lands which lie along the eastern slope of the Carpathians. Without much difficulty, pliant candidates were placed on the thrones which controlled uneasily the Moldavian court at Iaşi, and the Wallachian court at Targovişte or Bucharest. In spite of their very mixed origins, Greek, Albanian, Polish, as well as Romanian, these princes or 'hospodars' were still closely linked with local and patriotic interests. They intermarried with descendants of the native dynasties. They were patrons of Romanian and Greek literature. But the Ottoman government nearly always maintained its suzerainty and squeezed a large revenue from the two principalities in the shape of douceurs, tribute and military supplies demanded from the hospodars. The dominant families transferred the burden to a peasantry gradually declining in status. The Turks also relied on their substantial garrisons along the Danube below the Iron Gates, which in emergency they could assist with much larger forces. Instead of taking the Belgrade road, an expedition for this purpose followed the other old Roman itinerary which climbed the most easterly pass through the Balkan range, and was at once ready for action.

Farther north the Turks either built new or, more commonly, used old fortifications: at Chotin and Akermann on the Dniester; at the mouths of the Dnieper; at the strait leading into the Sea of Azov and the mouth of the Don. Sometimes but not always, garrisons were left at these points. A navy on the Black Sea was an additional safeguard. Political management, occasionally braced by the deployment of great military force, held their position intact from Azov to Bucharest.

Transylvania remained the most important Turkish dependency, because its obedience or disobedience affected profoundly the security of the frontiers farther east and farther west. The country consisted of a central lowland surrounded by great afforested ramparts and these were pierced by a number of passes, so that invasion (or punitive raiding) was always possible, but at the same time difficult and costly. Although a part of the medieval kingdom of Hungary, by 1500 its viceroy enjoyed extensive and princely authority. When Hungary collapsed in the sixteenth century under Turkish pressure, the Transylvanian princes and estates struggled hard to keep their precarious freedom by never deferring completely to the dictation of Istanbul or to that of the new line of Hungarian kings, the Habsburgs; but they normally had to recognise the Sultan's suzerain power and to pay tribute to him.

Such was the situation in eastern Europe down to 1648, and twenty-five years later the political system of the Ottoman frontier still seemed in good working order. In 1683, the Sultan's grand army came up to reinforce the troops at the disposal of the pashas in Hungary. The princes of the Crimea, Transylvania, Moldavia and Wallachia obediently crossed the hills to join Kara Mustafa in the Danubian plain. The eastern sections of the frontier were docile while battle was joined with the Habsburg Emperor. But the fact was that there had also been successive upheavals and violent dislocations, which step by step transformed the situation.

IV

Indeed, one can watch the action of something like a magnetic pull from central Europe during these decades. It was to be exerted with the greatest force in 1683, when the Ottoman besiegers drew towards Vienna the German and Polish soldiers who relieved the city; it was only just not strong enough to bring in the French as well, and the Lithuanians, and the north German princes. But earlier there had already been a displacement of Turkish power itself from east to west. Crises in Transylvania, Poland and the Ukraine were followed by the crisis in Hungary, which first tempted Kara Mustafa to frame his plan for an attack on Austria. In the background France contributed to this pull towards the centre of the continent. Louis XIV's agents, in Istanbul and Warsaw and Transylvania, did their devious best to divert Ottoman forces from the area beyond the Carpathians, and to make them advance up the Danube instead.

The Polish colonising movement into the Ukraine was the most spectacular enterprise of the Poles in modern history. Gathering momentum in the second quarter of the century it progressed in an easterly direction towards the Dnieper, but the strains set up by this expansion proved intense. The antagonism of the Ukrainians to the Poles, of Orthodox to Catholics, of free settlers to the menace of serfdom imposed by the greater landlords, of nomads to colonists, caused the mammoth Cossack rebellion of 1648, with which was soon linked Russian and Swedish attacks on Poland. All this favoured the Turks, who welcomed the disarray of neighbour states. However George II Rákóczi Prince of Transylvania, tempted by these developments to try to rise above that modest station in life which the Ottoman court required from a subordinate ruler, intrigued in Moldavia and Wallachia, and intervened in Poland. In 1656 he joined an alliance of Sweden, Brandenburg and the Cossacks for partitioning that country. He threatened to become so much more powerful that it appeared a matter of obvious urgency for the Sultan's government to crush him; and, just then, the hard-headed Mehmed Köprülü took over the office of Grand Vezir. He was nothing if not thorough; under him, both Turks and Tartars made terrible incursions into the three Carpathian principalities. Rákóczi was deposed and in 1662, after a confused interregnum, a subservient nominee of the Sultan was brought in to govern Transylvania: Prince Michael Apafi who loved his Calvinist books and his bottle, and hated politics.[19]

At the same time, it became clear that the restoration of order in the Ukraine depended not only on the Poles but on the Czar of Muscovy. They bargained and reached a settlement at the famous truce of Andrusovo in 1667, which divided a vast tract of land on both sides of the Dnieper into Polish and Russian spheres of influence. But there had already been signs that the 'free' Cossacks would prefer the Sultan as a distant overlord to either the Czar or the King of Poland. Led by Peter Doroshenko, their Hetman, they formally offered to recognise Ottoman suzerainty in 1669. The Grand Vezir seized this opportunity. He could buttress his régime at home by continuous military activity in a remote area. He could use his dominance in the principalities, now firmly re-established, as a base for intervention and expansion farther north. The Polish and Ukrainian campaigns of Fazil Ahmed Köprülü and his successor, Kara Mustafa, covering an apparently limitless territory, soon began. In 1672, the Turks captured Kamenets, a stronghold in the Dniester valley, and a key to the security of southern Poland. In 1673 the Poles counter-attacked with some success but thereafter the full force of Ottoman arms was exerted, and in 1676 the Turks compelled the new Polish King, John III Sobieski,* to agree to a truce which gave them Kamenets and much else besides. Unfortunately, inevitably, the completeness of their victory had alarmed the Cossacks; Doroshenko the Hetman changed sides and appealed to Moscow. The Czar intervened, and at this moment Fazil Ahmed Köprülü died and Kara Mustafa succeeded him.

The records are too meagre, there can be no proper biography of this cardinal figure in European history.[20] We must surmise that he was born in northern Anatolia at some date between 1620 and 1635, that his father was a soldier named either Uradj or Hassan, and that he was educated in Mehmed Köprülü's household. He married into the Köprülü family. In 1659 he secured the important post of governor of Silistria, and from 1660 onwards held a number of influential appointments. Ten years later he acted as Fazil Ahmed's deputy at the Sultan's court when the Grand Vezir was absent, and in 1675 was betrothed to one of the Sultan's daughters. No one expressed surprise when he became the new Grand Vezir and gathered up the reins of power without any visible challenge. All agree that his swarthy complexion justified the nickname of Kara, or black; in other respects, reports about him are very contradictory. There is occasional praise by diplomats for his courtesy. More often they were bewildered, and cowed, by his arrogance when he granted them official audiences. Possibly the displays of anger were well-controlled; intimidation is a point of politics. There are many references to the size of Kara Mustafa's household, the splendour of his stables and horses, the number of his concubines, and the avarice which sustained them all; but one Englishman, resident at Istanbul in 1676, added that he had earned the

---

*Sobieski's election as King of Poland in 1674 was partly due to the prestige which his success as a military leader had given him the year before.

reputation of a 'Great Souldyer, and a Great Courtier and of a very Active Genious.'[21] Venetian and French ambassadors analysed his qualities at more length, but in substance failed to improve on that somewhat slight appraisal. The actions of this Ottoman politician, rather than the words of others about his character, prove to be his only trustworthy memorial. They were at least in part dictated by historical forces of more permanent significance than one man's intense personal ambition.

It was believed a few years after 1676 that Kara Mustafa had disapproved of the course of events in the north.[22] He did not understand, it is reported, why Fazil Ahmed Köprülü concentrated on warfare in the Dniester valley, or treated so coolly the Magyars in rebellion against Leopold who appealed to him for aid. But there is no solid evidence that Kara Mustafa, on his accession to power, hoped to attack the Habsburg lands in the near future. Certainly, he could not easily disengage from the Ukraine. The Poles had recognised the Turkish claim to keep garrisons along the Black Sea coast, and at one or two points on the lower Dnieper. This safeguarded communications by land with the Crimea, and no responsible Turkish statesman wanted to whittle down the advantage of the concession by failing to press for an equally satisfactory settlement with the Cossacks and Muscovites. Moreover, the Hetman's disobedience was a blow at the whole system of dependent princes which the Köprülüs had restored to good working order. So the Ukrainian war against the Czar and the Cossacks went wearily on. A new Turkish nominee for the post of Hetman was found. Dreadful devastation took place, which pushed innumerable families from the right to the left bank of the Dnieper. Kara Mustafa accepted enormous losses in manpower, wasting the Janissaries and other standing corps severely, in order to defeat the enemy. Above all he tried to capture the Cossack capital of Chigirin, 'that unsupportable place Chagreen'[23] as an English envoy to Moscow called it, and also their advanced base 200 miles farther down the river. In 1677 a massive Turkish army failed to accomplish anything. In 1678, under Kara Mustafa himself, they took Chigirin but were next year driven back again. The fighting degenerated over a wide area into a purposeless deadlock for the main protagonists. The reasons for putting an end to it gradually impressed them both. An ambassador from Moscow reached Istanbul in March 1680, and negotiations began.

In consequence, close observers felt that the time was coming nearer when the Ottoman politicians would need 'fresh woods and pastures new', if the system and initiative of the last two Grand Vezirs were to be maintained. The Poles foresaw that Lvov and even Cracow were vulnerable to a renewed Ottoman attack, although they had accepted Kara Mustafa's draconic terms for a treaty of peace in 1678.[24] The Venetians, far to the south, feared for the fate of what remained of their Adriatic empire. They showed themselves nervously ready to swallow every insult, and to comply with every demand for extravagant financial compensation, when small frontier incidents occurred in

Dalmatia. Luckily for Venice, luckily for Poland, the affairs of Hungary offered the Grand Vezir a much clearer opening.

Here the Viennese court had governed autocratically after 1670, discontent led to disorder, disorder to more repression which then touched off a rebellion. A stream of exiles – the 'Malcontents' – found their way east to Transylvania, and organised a number of raids back into Hungary from 1672 onwards.[25] Fazil Ahmed Köprülü refused to support these and instructed Apafi to hold aloof, but some of the rebels took refuge on Turkish territory in Hungary, where the local commanders allowed bands of their own soldiery to help in attacking neighbouring Habsburg districts. A pattern of guerrilla warfare was soon imposed on northern Hungary. Desultory but brutal fighting disturbed a part of each year. Desultory but inconclusive negotiations between Vienna and the rebels tended to take place each winter and spring.

An influential Magyar nobleman, Stephen Thököly, died in 1672; Habsburg troops had captured his stronghold of Árva in the extreme north-west corner of Hungary, and confiscated his property. His son, Imre, grew up in Transylvania where he secured by inheritance very extensive revenues. He was alert, attractive, and passably well-educated. He possessed the talents and personality of an instinctive leader. He never felt timidity or scruple, he had craft rather than judgment, but men followed him. In 1678 the Malcontents summarily chose the twenty-five-year-old Thököly as their commander and immediately, in the course of a few months, they won a series of spectacular engagements. The important points of Murány, Baňská Bystrica and Árva were taken. Booty, especially in the form of coined and uncoined precious metal from the Slovakian mining areas, was considerable. Thököly's prestige soared, and he soon enjoyed unchallenged control of the Magyar patriot force. During the next two years he held his own against the Habsburg garrisons in Hungary; he rattled and weakened them. He discredited the authority of Apafi's chief adviser in Transylvania.[26] Agents from Warsaw and even Paris bid high for his support. Kara Mustafa, inactive but watchful in Istanbul, slowly learnt to appreciate Thököly's nuisance value in the politics of the intricate Carpathian world, of which he may have felt that he knew too little. He had still to decide how best to use this new star in the firmament.

Early in 1681 Leopold at last summoned a properly constituted Hungarian Diet.[27] His ministers recognised, very late in the day, that their costly autocratic experiment in this region weakened Leopold's whole position in Europe at a time when they were determined to resist Louis XIV's expanding power. They had to admit the advantages of the old Magyar constitutional procedure. But long before the Diet opened in May, in the town of Sopron by the Neusiedler See, Kara Mustafa took definite counter-measures. He persuaded Thököly to repudiate it by instructing the rulers of Moldavia, Wallachia and Transylvania, as well as the Turkish command in Hungary, to bring substantial assistance to the rebels.[28] Thököly turned down Leopold's invitation to come to Sopron. Although discussions continued during the summer between

Habsburg statesmen and those Magyars who were willing to work for a settlement, Thököly still refused to appear. Forces gathered in the north-east, both Christian and Moslem fighting men, in order to help him against Leopold's troops in Upper Hungary. The Transylvanians under Prince Apafi at length arrived but the hostility of the local Turkish pashas towards them, and their own unwillingness to reinforce Thököly, were equally evident. Then Apafi withdrew, and the campaigning season came inconclusively to an end. It was still possible that the tranquil close of the Sopron Diet, which had solved one or two of the outstanding constitutional and religious problems of the day in Hungary, would draw off some of the Malcontents. Thököly stood where he was. The Ottoman government, on this occasion at least, had moved somewhat cautiously, promising more than it cared actually to give. Far away to the south, Kara Mustafa had to digest the affront of Admiral Du Quesne's demonstration of French naval power in the Aegean between July 1681 and March 1682.

During the winter Kuniz, the Habsburg envoy at Istanbul, tried to negotiate seriously for a renewal of the treaty between Emperor and Sultan which was due to expire in 1684. His political opponent, the French ambassador Guilleragues, soon swung into action. He resisted the Ottoman demand for satisfaction from Louis XIV for Du Quesne's exploits but incited the Grand Vezir to attack the Habsburg Emperor. On Louis' instructions, he suggested that the King of France would not refrain from helping the Poles if the Turks attacked up the Dniester, but on the other hand would refuse to help the Habsburgs in the event of war between Emperor and Sultan.[29] The language of these colloquies was shrouded, and their influence on the Ottoman minister is open to debate. The political condition of eastern Europe both drove and tempted the Turks to intervene on an increasing scale in Hungary, but the arguments of Louis' envoy at least did nothing to deter them. For that matter, neither did those of Kuniz. He gloomily reported to Vienna the Grand Vezir's unbending refusal to discuss a settlement. His letters persuaded Leopold to make a new move on the board, by instructing a second envoy to go to Istanbul. Unfortunately, although this decision was reached in August 1681, the ambassador extraordinary – Albert Caprara* – only left Vienna in February 1682, and reached Istanbul in April.

Such sloth was partly explained by Thököly's skilful tactics. He never allowed the Habsburg court, and the powerful party at Vienna which preferred to neglect the dangers in Hungary, to write him off as irreconcilable. Indeed, he had very strong motives for following a sinuous and complicated line of

---

*A professor of moral philosophy at Bologna University, who wrote a charming version of Aesop's Fables, Albert Caprara (1627?–1691) was more a man of letters, and an 'orator' who took formal messages of condolence or congratulation from court to court, than a serious politician. Albert is to be distinguished from his cousin Aeneas Caprara, the Habsburg general. This was a most curious and unsatisfactory appointment.[30]

action. First of all, it was obvious prudence to force the Ottoman government to raise its bid for his support. Then, while he wanted to reap a due reward for military victories over the Habsburgs, he also wanted to strengthen his territorial position by one of the commonest gambits open to princes and magnates. In north-east Hungary, without any doubt, the greatest single complex of lands and revenues still belonged to the combined inheritance of the Rákóczi and Báthory families. The Habsburg government relied much on the goodwill of that militant Catholic lady, Sophie Báthory, the widow of George II Rákóczi. The opposition relied on Helen Zrinyi, whose father was executed after the conspiracy in 1670, now the widow of Francis I Rákóczi (who had died in 1676). Therefore Thököly contemplated a match with Helen. Unfortunately, Sophie Báthory countered this by tying up much valuable property in her will and appointing Leopold the executor for Francis Rákóczi's young children, and their guardian. She died in 1680, and it became a part of Thököly's policy to secure Leopold's consent to his union with their mother, Helen. This became one of the agenda in diplomacy which continued during the winters of 1680–1 and 1681–2; for both parties it seemed a useful lever for putting pressure on the other. Vienna miscalculated: it could neither bully nor befriend its opponent. Leopold finally consented to the marriage, his representative was present at the festivities in the great castle of Munkács (Mukachevo) during June 1682. Immediately afterwards Thököly unmasked again, to become the Sultan's firm and formal ally.

In fact when Caprara reached the last stage of his long journey south, at Adrianople, he met the Magyar envoys returning from Istanbul. They had reached an agreement with Kara Mustafa, and therefore Thököly soon prepared for a fresh campaign. The Turks once more ordered up men and supplies from the principalities, and also from Bosnia and Serbia. The pashas and the Magyars began active collaboration in July. In August the great council of state was held at Istanbul, which foreshadowed fighting on a much grander scale in the following year; and the Diploma was drawn which proclaimed Imre Thököly the prince of 'middle' Hungary under the Sultan's protection.[31] It reached the theatre of war after the city and citadel of Kassa had fallen to the Malcontents, and a combined force of Magyars, Turks and Transylvanians had completed the destruction of Fülek (Fila'kovo) – forty miles north-east of Buda – by a devastating siege. Thököly received the insignia of authority under the Sultan from the governor of Buda.[32] The Magyars continued for a few weeks to push farther into the territory still held by Habsburg garrisons, causing particular alarm to the Poles on the other side of the Carpathians, and then the campaign came to an end[33] just when the Sultan and the Sultan's troops set out from Istanbul to Adrianople.

V

It is clear that the Grand Vezir now judged the situation ripe for major changes in Hungary and the adjoining lands. The Magyar rebellion had continued for many years, but only in 1682 did Kara Mustafa decide that he could exploit it fully. Moreover for him, as for other Turkish statesmen, Hungary itself was primarily a frontier province with a cluster of fortresses in water-logged country, which served to protect the inner lands of the Balkan empire. It was not a rich or fruitful territory, even if richer than the empty plains of the Ukraine in which they had fought against the Muscovites before 1681. The gains to be expected from a modest local advance, such as the capture of Györ or Komárom, and the squeezing of the nearby lordships of Magyar magnates, would be correspondingly meagre. On the other hand Vienna, a hundred miles beyond Györ, was a glittering prize. Those Turks who had been there, as members of an embassy which visited the city in 1665, seem to have brought home impressions completely in harmony with the old Moslem legend of the 'Golden Apple'; that apple of the heart's desire, said the legend, was the splendid Christian city of the infidel Emperor, to be captured at some golden moment in a future age.[34] Evliyá Chelibi accompanied this embassage, and what seemed to western travellers of the seventeenth century a rather dull city, and a dull court, appeared to him staggeringly rich and attractive. The ambassador himself was Kara Mehmed, one of Kara Mustapha's most trusted advisers and commanders in 1683. Useful information about the military defences of Vienna meanwhile came from renegades in the Sultan's service; an un-named ex-Capuchin friar, for one, claimed to be an engineer and know the city well.[35] The relative poverty of Hungary, the alleged wealth and weakness of the centre of Habsburg power, as well as the effect on Leopold's position of Louis XIV's strength in the west: these must all have been commonplaces of discussion in Istanbul. At the very least, in the summer of 1682 the expansion of the Ottoman empire into Habsburg Hungary was planned for 1683.[36] The army would march, there would be conferences with Caprara in order to discover whether he had been given authority to surrender territory or citadels, the army would in any case occupy still more territory and live on the spoils; and whatever transpired in the immediate future, an attack on Vienna was also to be regarded as an item in the Grand Vezir's secret catalogue of possible objectives.

Caprara was in fact instructed simply to try and renew the treaty of peace on its existing basis. Already in the course of his journey through Hungary he learnt enough to report home that his prospects were hopeless unless he offered territorial concessions, or disposed of sufficient funds to bribe the Istanbul politicians on a redoubtable scale.[37] Arrived at the Sultan's court, he wished to delay negotiations, trusting that new orders would reach him from Vienna. He heard nothing. At a meeting held on 23 June the Turks ran through a long list of alleged Habsburg infringements of the old treaty – such as the building of new Habsburg fortified points, and the taxing of Turkish subjects, in Hungary – and with scarcely veiled threats asked Caprara what price the Emperor was willing to pay for a fresh agreement. They argued that compensation by Leopold for his breaches of the existing treaty was the only acceptable basis for a new one. The envoy felt disturbed, but not yet desperate, and his report on this discussion reached Vienna in time to be considered by the statesmen who advised Leopold on 11 August.[38] On the other hand, his despatch analysing a second conference (of 6 July) could hardly have been gloomier, and it was an added misfortune that no courier could at first be found to forward it, so that the Habsburg government did not understand the true position until mid-September.[39] The Turks asked for a number of changes in north-west Hungary but constantly shifted their ground, substituting one explicit demand for another. They began by requesting Leopold to demolish the fortifications at Leopoldstadt,* and they wanted him to acknowledge their right to take larger contributions from territory along the frontier. Caprara retorted that the Sultan himself had broken the old treaty by recognising Thököly, to which the smooth and menacing answer was given that Thököly first appealed to the Sultan, who could not refuse him protection.

Then, finally, the Turks demanded Györ as the price of peace. But Györ was universally considered a cardinal point in the defence of the Habsburg position in Hungary and in Austria. Its loss and recapture by the Christians were famous incidents in the warfare between 1593 and 1606. It could not have been given up again, by a mere stroke of the pen, without a catastrophic sacrifice of military strength and political prestige. If the Turks were in earnest, this demand was really a declaration of war because no diplomatic bargain would justify, from the Habsburg standpoint, the surrender of the place. From the Turkish standpoint it was equally a rational military objective. Yet military considerations, in the strict sense, hardly determined the Grand Vezir's policy. The character and constitution of the Ottoman empire at this period did determine it. The demand for Györ was an explicit admission that the state of war, with all its opportunities for further expansion, was preferred to the maintenance of peace.

At Adrianople the demand for Györ was repeated. Yet the idea of an assault on Vienna appears to have attracted Kara Mustafa increasingly. Caprara wrote on 20 March[40] that Thököly's emissaries warmly pressed it, and he was informed that in Vienna other agents of Thököly (ostensibly negotiating with Leopold) were making drawings of the city; but his considered opinion was still that the plan of campaign had not been finally settled. At Belgrade, he gleefully told the Turks of an alliance recently completed between Leopold and the Republic of Poland. We cannot be certain, but the Grand Vezir may

---

*By the treaty of 1664, Leopold gave up to the Turks his fortress of Neuhäusel, twenty miles north of Komárom, together with a small area surrounding it. He soon began to build Leopoldstadt north-west of Neuhäusel, which remained a Turkish enclave in predominantly Habsburg country. See illustrations I and II and the end maps (pp. xiv–xvii).

have argued that this news strengthened the case, not for a more cautious strategy, but for keeping his enemies guessing about his intentions. A subtler diplomatic sense would have suggested that the Poles were less likely to prove good allies to the Austrians if he had made it clear, at a much earlier date, that they were not the target of his forthcoming attack on the Christian world. Nor are we better informed of the views of Kara Mustafa's opponents in the Sultan's entourage at this point. But the more insistent their criticisms, the more tempting was a military operation of the most spectacular kind, intended to place the Grand Vezir on, the highest possible pinnacles of prestige and power.

At Belgrade Caprara also handed in a letter from Herman of Baden, President of Leopold's War Council.[41] It said, quite simply, that the Emperor had made every effort to keep the peace; but he now recognised, with infinite regret, that a state of war existed between the two great empires, and in accordance with the law of nations the President asked the Grand Vezir to arrange for Caprara's departure from the Ottoman camp. This letter reached Belgrade on 11 May. Kara Mustafa at first delayed his reply. Then, at Osijek, he returned a reasoned and sober answer, 'courteous in tone';[42] Caprara, with this message, was able to leave for Buda on 12 June. Kuniz remained with the Ottoman army, a more or less privileged captive. By now the Grand Vezir certainly knew what he wanted to try and do. Thököly had arrived with a large following at Osijek on 10 June. He seems to have promised to put sizeable forces of his own into the field, and the Turkish accounts suggest that not only was the Vezir strongly urged by his Turkish servants (particularly by the director of his chancery) to attack Vienna, but that he himself informed Thököly of such a plan – which included a vague proposal to make the 'king' of Hungary a 'king' in Vienna. The two men in conversation undoubtedly spurred each other on to adopt the most aggressive tactics possible, and this at a moment when news reached them that the Habsburg army was besieging Neuhäusel north of the Danube. Next day, Kara Mustafa crossed over the Osijek bridges.

A week later, while the troops moved northwards, it became known that the siege of Neuhäusel had been raised.[43] No other item of news could have encouraged militant leaders more thoroughly. The army moved on again, and its commanders duly arrived at Székesfehérvár.

Here the Grand Vezir held his final council of war before the fighting began.[44] Among those present were certainly the Khan of the Tartars, Murad Ghiraj and members of his family, the Aga of the Janissaries, Prince Apafi of Transylvania, and a number of senior Ottoman provincial governors. It is possible that the aged and experienced Ibrahim, *beylerbeyi* of Buda, was deliberately not summoned to attend, even though he knew far more about conditions on this frontier than anybody else. Kara Mustafa announced that, although it was his intention to march towards Győr and Komárom, this alone could not result in a sufficient extension of the Sultan's power. He proposed to advance on Vienna itself. A section of the defences in front of the Habsburg Emperor's palace there, he claimed to know from first-hand accounts, was unable to stand an assault. The Tartar ruler demurred, arguing that the wiser course was to capture Győr and Komárom first, ravage the Austrian countryside, and winter in Hungary.[45] He suggested an attack on Vienna in the following spring. Apart from the Khan, and with the possible exceptions of Sari Hussein *beylerbeyi* of Syria, Ahmed of Timisoara, and Ibrahim of Buda (if he was present, which is not certain), no one ventured to disagree with the Grand Vezir. Undoubtedly Ibrahim thought the decision a profound mistake. He either said so at the conference or during a separate interview soon afterwards with the Grand Vezir, who brusquely called him a cowardly old grey-beard. He was ordered back to Buda.

Caprara long hesitated to believe that Vienna itself was in any danger, because he despised the whole Turkish military force. He emphasised its 'weakness, disorder, and almost ludicrous armament'. It could never resist, he wrote, the 'genti d'Allemagna'.[46] At Belgrade, he estimated that there were 20,000 good fighting men in the entire army; his secretary Benaglia put the figure considerably higher, at 39,000; the rest were a rabble.[47] Later on, the ambassador set out the opinion which he had formed before he left Osijek in these emphatic terms: 'I cannot believe that the Vezir proposes to go to Vienna, and that so ambitious a design can be based on such mediocre forces. It is possible that brutal resolutions of this kind may be inspired by sheer pride; but the judgment of God will fall upon them.'[48] The Grand Vezir himself took a different view of his resources. He was right. His audacious bid for a sensational victory only failed by a hairsbreadth, and his defeat was due to serious errors of his own making at a later stage of the campaign.

2

Leopold I and the City of Vienna

I

The target of this great assault was the Habsburg authority in central Europe, an authority vested formally in the hereditary prince who was also Holy Roman Emperor.

In 1680, Leopold I's powers of judgment should have been well matured; he was forty years old, and had ruled over Austria and Bohemia and Habsburg Hungary since his father died in 1657. Observers at his court agree that he was highly educated, dignified, and eager to understand the sequence of political events which occupied him in the course of business. If he liked best to take part in religious ceremonies, to hunt and read and direct the music-making of his household, he never neglected affairs of state; and he had strong general convictions, such as deep piety and a firm belief in the divinely sanctioned status of the Habsburg family. Unfortunately he only made up his mind on practical questions with timorous reluctance. Protestants, and the Venetian ambassadors at Vienna, blamed the Jesuits for an education which had moulded him too severely and repressed his native energy. They chose to assume that, as a boy, he showed signs of a more active spirit which his teachers took care to subdue. There can be no proof of this, although he was destined for high ecclesiastical dignities before his elder brother Ferdinand IV died, during his father's lifetime; and a number of Leopold's most sympathetic clerical advisers vehemently criticised him for his irresoluteness. Other men held, very plausibly, that it was a mistake to exaggerate this failing which the Emperor counterbalanced by an underlying obstinacy.[1]

His traits as a ruler were fixed by 1680. He had no doubt that the final responsibility was his, and no one ventured to browbeat him. The 'favourite' (the *valido* of the Spanish Habsburgs) had no place in Leopold's system of management. Instead, he considered it his duty to listen attentively to his ministers and courtiers, and to listen to as many ministers and courtiers as possible. Up to this point he was enlightened; beyond it, his gifts failed him. Infinitely susceptible to contradictory counsels, he was betrayed into excessive caution and only too often the results were inaction and delay. He foresaw but never anticipated. When it was his duty to choose men for high office, he listened once more to rival suggestions and dithered long before making up his mind. Thereafter he was unwaveringly loyal to the officeholder, and indulgent to a fault. These hesitations also involved a tame acquiescence in the traditional framework of court and government, the old hierarchy of offices, and the customary overlapping of responsibilities between them. He never dreamt of himself as a reforming statesman; he inherited the duties of an autocrat surrounded by privileged orders, and felt unhappily that God had chosen him to play a part for which he had no talent. Leopold was colourless, he was cautious, patient, weak, but sometimes unyielding.

He preferred to have men about him, in the superior offices of his own household, who came from the great Austrian, Moravian and Bohemian families with a tradition of service to the Habsburgs. John Maximilian Lamberg, an old friend, had been Chamberlain and then *Hofmeister* since 1661, and his death in December 1682 was a sorrowful landmark in Leopold's life. One of the Dietrichsteins succeeded Lamberg as Chamberlain, and Ferdinand Harrach (the great collector of fine pictures) became Master of the Stables in 1679. In the same year Albert Zinzendorf was appointed Marshal of the Court and, later, the *Hofmeister*. None of these men held emphatic political views, but they were extremely close to the ruler and their own connections linked them with other figures of distinct political importance. Montecuccoli, the great Italian soldier who served the Habsburg Emperors so faithfully and well, President of the War Council until 1680, had married into the Dietrichstein family. Zinzendorf supported, and was normally supported by, Sinelli the Capuchin preacher who commended himself to Leopold by a useful blend of piety and apparent shrewdness. This highly influential adviser was made Bishop of Vienna in 1680.

The character of the ruler was reflected in the composition of his household. On the other hand the disorderly cluster of the institutions of government owed even more to past Habsburg history, and it is not always clear which were the outer or the inner works of a very complex structure.[2] The Holy Roman Empire had created a chancery, treasury and tribunals. The different hereditary kingdoms and duchies of the Habsburgs had done the same. To a bewildering extent Imperial and Habsburg institutions now co-existed in Vienna, and Leopold would normally rely for guidance on the chancellors or presidents of most of the principal offices; but not all office-holders of this rank were counsellors in matters of high policy; and there were unofficial advisers like Sinelli. At this period, Hocher the Court (or Habsburg) Chancellor, Königsegg the Imperial Vice-chancellor, and Schwarzenberg the President of the Imperial

Council, were men of the very greatest importance. The Emperor constantly asked for their written opinions on matters of foreign policy. The senior Bohemian chancellor, Nostitz-Reineck kept more in the background. After 1680 the President and Vice-president of the Treasury, Christopher Abele and John Jörger, were both weighty men, the latter a classic instance of the loyal Catholic aristocrat whose forebears had been strong Protestants and rebels against Habsburg authority.[3] The Presidents of the War Council, first Montecuccoli and then Herman of Baden, shared in the determination of general policy. They handled Leopold's diplomatic correspondence with the courts of eastern Europe, and therefore in 1682 Baden was the statesman responsible for sending instructions to Caprara at Istanbul.

Hocher, the son of a professor of law at Freiburg University, had been the most powerful politician in Vienna for a number of years. Originally a jurist and administrator, he joined with Schwarzenberg, Sinelli and Lamberg in bringing Leopold into the coalition against France in 1673. The stage was set for a period of unyielding opposition to Louis XIV, and Hocher was perfectly attuned to the arguments for continuing it after the Austrian setback at Nymegen. At the same time he championed the authoritarian experiment in Hungary. It followed that he was not the man to recognise very quickly the need to revise or reverse this double programme of militancy in the west, and autocracy in the east. In 1682 his health deteriorated, and his failing powers were a grave misfortune for the government of which he remained so important a prop. Königsegg, whose family came from Swabia, was a younger man. He had many departmental differences with Hocher, but he tended to agree with his rival on diplomatic questions and his advice to Leopold ran along similar lines. Schwarzenberg, whose family ranked infinitely higher than Hocher's, and somewhat higher than Königsegg's, cannot be fitted so easily into this group. He joined the party of Hocher and Sinelli in 1673, but ten years later the French ambassador at the Hofburg believed that Schwarzenberg was the one politician in Vienna friendly to France, and who therefore spoke good sense: that is, he recommended Leopold to accept Louis XIV's terms for a settlement in Germany on account of the Ottoman danger.[4] He died on 26 May 1683, eight weeks after Nostitz-Reineck, twelve weeks after Hocher; the Turks reached Vienna eight weeks later still. Leopold allowed his servants to grow too old or too ill in office. It was another sign of his uncertain touch in using them.

One of the strongest interests in the Hofburg at this date was represented by the reigning Empress. Leopold married for a third time in 1676, choosing for his bride Eleanor-Magdalene of Pfalz-Neuburg. It was a decisive moment in the rise of an ambitious princely family. If Philip William of Pfalz-Neuburg's inheritance of Berg and Jülich in north-western Germany, together with Neuburg on the upper Danube, was modest, if he had spent a long and restless life on a variety of unsuccessful attempts to better himself, his daughter's alliance with the Emperor opened up reefs of the purest gold for this minor branch of the Wittelsbachs. Philip William exploited his diplomatic triumph to the uttermost, and the new Empress soon combined her supreme title with sufficient influence over Leopold. The results were spectacular. One sister became Queen of Spain, another Queen of Portugal. The eldest brother married a Habsburg princess, another was *Deutschmeister* or Master of the German Order, and others accumulated ecclesiastical benefices at Brixen, Trent, Breslau, Freysing and Augsburg. In 1685, with the Emperor's support Philip William himself succeeded to the Elector Palatine's title and inheritance. The rise of the Neuburgs involved the ascent to power of a new statesman in Vienna.

Theodore Stratmann, Philip William's vice-chancellor, had helped to negotiate Eleanor-Magdalene's marriage, then transferred to the Emperor's service, and rose to a post of the very highest importance in March 1683 when he became Court Chancellor on Hocher's death.[5] Stratmann was a fine and level-headed man of business, who handled affairs of state with considerable skill during the next ten years. It cannot be doubted that he served the Habsburgs well, nor that he continued to take sympathetic account of the Neuburg family interest in western Germany.

Another circle in the Hofburg was presided over by the dowager Empress Eleanor, Leopold's Italian stepmother, a gifted and animated leader of society for many years; and among those who turned to her for patronage, and appeared at her brilliant parties, was a refugee prince named Charles of Lorraine.

Charles,[6] born in 1643, had inherited a claim on the succession to the duchy of Lorraine but his uncle Duke Charles IV long refused to recognise it, while the French systematically set about converting their military occupation of most of the Lorraine lands into a sovereignty ratified by international treaty. So the young boy flitted uneasily from court to court, discredited by many matrimonial schemes and a few irregular romances which all broke down. He settled in Vienna after 1662, volunteered in time for the battle of St Gotthard, and competed unsuccessfully for election as King of Poland on two occasions; he hoped to marry the dowager empress's daughter (also called Eleanor) but this depended on winning a suitable title, in Poland or Lorraine or elsewhere. Then he made his mark, fighting superbly in the wars against Louis XIV, and reached the rank of Field-Marshal in 1676. His uncle had died by then and most states recognised him as the rightful Duke, Charles V of Lorraine. The Emperor allowed the marriage with Eleanor to take place in 1678, and soon afterwards Charles was appointed his viceroy in the Tirol. He failed to recover his duchy in the course of the diplomacy which put an end to the war in 1679, but his court at Innsbruck was well placed to keep an eye on future developments in the whole area west of the Rhine. His personal advisers were nearly all exiles from Lorraine and their primary impulse was to scheme for the day when the Duke could enter Nancy in triumph. In Vienna the dowager empress consistently championed her son-in-law's interest.

By this date Charles looked an insignificant man in poor health, not fully recovered from war-wounds; but his appearance masked his piety, reserves of stamina, and willingness to take difficult decisions. That exuberant prose-writer, John Sobieski, composed the best pen-portrait of this unassuming warrior. The one great Christian hero of the year 1683 wrote of the other: 'He has an acquiline nose, almost like a parrot's; he is scarred by the small-pox; and he stoops. He wears grey, unadorned (except for some new brocaded gold buttons), a hat without a feather, and boots which were polished two or three months ago, with cork heels. His wig (a rotten one) is fair in colour. His horse isn't bad, with an old saddle and trappings of worn and poor-quality leather. He is obviously little concerned with his appearance. But he has the bearing, not of a trader or an Italian, but of a person of quality . . . he deserves greater fame and fortune.'[7] This was written after Charles had spent a whole summer fighting the Turks, but the impression given seems to do justice to the prince. He had a reasonable claim to the highest military offices at Leopold's disposal. Indeed Montecuccoli died in the autumn of 1680, after combining for many years the two great posts of President of the War Council and the supreme command of Habsburg armies in the field. Leopold at once issued a patent reserving the second of these to Charles of Lorraine in the event of a future war.[8]

The man who was to be his colleague in 1683 and his fiercest enemy at court, Herman of Baden, also moved in the dowager empress's circle in the 1670s. A younger son of the noble but impoverished house of Baden in western Germany, he had spent his youth restlessly striving for advancement. He collected ecclesiastical prebends (and became a Canon of Cologne Cathedral), took some share in impracticable plans for colonisation overseas, but finally made his career as a soldier and politician. He too distinguished himself in the campaigns against France. He was brave, ambitious, fussy and not very articulate in discussion; but he stoutly upheld the alleged need to continue at all costs and in all seasons the policy of resistance to French aggrandisement in the Empire. This accorded well with the general bias of opinion at court. Leopold, therefore, after some delay, appointed him in 1681 to succeed Montecuccoli as President of the War Council. The defence of Habsburg interests, particularly the distribution of forces between the eastern and the western fronts, would depend on the judgment of the new president.

Opposed to the international policy of Hocher and Herman of Baden was a strictly Catholic interest, which aimed at far more than mere defence of the Church. The dynasty appeared rigorously Catholic. The conversion of all Protestants who came to the Habsburg court, and wished to make a career, went remorselessly forward during this period. The great Protestant families of two generations back, in Bohemia and Austria, were Catholic again. Leopold, obedient to a tradition which had been thoroughly worked into his education, strove always to take account of the Church in his general conduct of affairs. But at the same time his ecclesiastical advisers had to take account of his predicament as a ruler who was often compelled to disregard the purely clerical standpoint. He, and they, had to tack accordingly. Eager to defend and to strengthen the privileges of the clergy (and the ecclesiastical estates) they were occasionally forced to defer to the tough legal maxims and administrative practice of the Habsburg and Imperial chanceries, which wished to protect the interests of the state in questions of taxation, or of appointment to benefices. They likewise protested in vain whenever the Emperor's diplomacy involved concessions to Protestant minorities in Hungary or Silesia. But what caused much more heart-burning to rigid Catholics was the military alliance of 1673 between the Emperor and the heretic Dutch, for a war against the Most Christian Louis XIV. Sinelli, the most influential of Leopold's spiritual counsellors, had himself come to accept the necessity for this Protestant alliance. He certainly held that the Habsburg government was bound, first of all, to defend its interests against France. He could be satisfied that, in Hungary at least, the Catholic monopoly was growing more complete, but he had to neglect the larger issue of Ottoman dominance beyond the eastern frontier.

The accession of Innocent XI as Pope in 1676 made this sort of compromise much more difficult.[9] Innocent sharpened all the dilemmas. His ambition to pacify the west in order to launch an attack on the Sultan never slackened from the day of his election. He was the supreme exponent, in the seventeenth century, of that school of thought in Rome which paid particular attention to the Ottoman lands, supporting the missions (above all, Franciscan) in that area, pondering the memoranda of those who painted a facile picture of the radical flaws of Ottoman government, and concluding that this government was not only vicious and menacing, but weak. A holy alliance of the Christian princes against the Sultan, therefore, appeared the grand necessity of the time. Innocent believed in the absolute priority of the eastern question over the problems of the west. He judged the Nymegen peace-treaties simply as a means to this end, and in his view an obstinate Habsburg refusal to consider sympathetically Louis XIV's further territorial demands after 1679 was an unworthy refusal to attend to the crucial issue in Hungary, Poland and the Balkans. He urged at Vienna a policy of appeasement towards Louis, and the result was a bitter struggle at court, with the papal nuncio Buonvisi firmly opposed by those who felt that the defence of Leopold's stake in Germany and Flanders was overwhelmingly important.

In fact, for a number of years Buonvisi negotiated without any success.[10] Innocent aimed at the speedy completion of an offensive alliance between the Poles and the Habsburgs and (if possible) the Czar of Muscovy, directed against the Sultan. This was premature, and not least because the Viennese court remained determined not to weaken its position in western Europe by provoking the Turks. The Ottoman campaigns in the Ukraine appeared to suit Leopold's interest perfectly. Buonvisi argued, in 1678, that troops should be withdrawn from the west to take up their quarters in Hungary. The government agreed, after Nymegen, that some forces should be kept in being and not dismissed, but proposed to use them for the defence of the Empire against further French aggression. Buonvisi went so far as to counsel a change of policy in Hungary, including the offer of some very modest concession to the Protestants; he had the greater menace of the Turks in view. But Leopold, advised by Hocher, refused to consider a more flexible policy until 1681. When he did so, his government was primarily disturbed by the imminent collapse of its position in Germany under Louis XIV's pressure. The ministers were justifiably unable to concentrate on the alleged danger from Islam. Unjustifiably, they neglected it. The nuncio was powerless until the Turks began to intervene on a larger scale in Hungary. Then the government, Sinelli, and most of the interests with a voice at court, slowly swung round in order to face a threat which they had underestimated for too long. The nuncio, and also his colleague Pallavicini in Warsaw, were able to contribute effectively to the making of that alliance which had been part of Innocent XI's purpose since 1676.

While Buonvisi tried always to focus the attention of the Austrian court on the eastern question (in its seventeenth-century form) the masterful ambassador from Madrid looked just as steadily to the west. Charles Emmanuel d'Este Marquis of Borgomanero, arriving at Vienna in May 1681, benefited from the labours of his immediate predecessors in the same post, who all worked to re-knit the combined front of the two Habsburg lines, after the catastrophic split between them which had contributed to the ending of the Thirty Years War, Austrian defeat in the Westphalian treaties of 1648, and the isolation of Spain later on. An accomplished diplomat, he pointed insistently to the dangers threatening the Habsburg position in Italy and Flanders, and rallied to the so-called 'Spanish' party in Vienna all the interests which Louis XIV had alienated in the Empire, even though they constantly tended to fall apart again into smaller, bickering fractions. For him the fate of rich territories stretching from Antwerp to Genoa was the paramount question of the future. His obvious ally among diplomats in Vienna was the Dutch envoy, his outstanding friend among the Viennese statesmen was Herman of Baden. If one factor stood out quite distinctly in the medley of Leopold's court, it was the political antagonism of Buonvisi and Borgomanero, those two impressive Italian noblemen.

At this date, around 1680, a sense of acute crisis troubled not only the Emperor's advisers but all the peoples of central Europe. There were the premonitory rumblings from Istanbul, added to news of a deadlock in Hungary. Louis XIV was at the height of his tremendous powers. Much worse, in the thought of ordinary men, was the fearful progress of a greater enemy, bubonic plague. It carried off thousands in the Danubian lands in 1679–80, especially in the whole area of the Wiener Wald, drove Leopold out of Vienna, ravaged Saxony, and provoked the authorities in Venice to the strictest enforcement of their meticulous quarantine regulations. Its effects, however serious, were exaggerated and popular fears redoubled. Widespread agrarian riots broke out in Bohemia, followed by severe repression. A comet appeared in one year and then returned, shining even more brightly in the next. The preachers promptly took their cue, lashed out at every manifestation of human iniquity, and brought the divine wrath heavily home to the people.[11]

Father Marco d'Aviano, an Italian mission preacher calling to repentance, did not stint his zeal at this gloomy moment.[12] For some time previously his reputation had attracted attention north of the Alps. Charles of Lorraine's court at Innsbruck wished to invite him, but Pope Innocent at first refused permission. Then the Wittelsbach court in Munich, Philip William at Neuburg, and finally Leopold, joined the chorus. In 1680, Innocent gave way. The long and consistently astonishing episode of Marco's influence in Germany and Austria began. In September he reached Linz, where the panic-stricken Habsburg government had taken refuge. Leopold was deeply impressed by the personality of his visitor; then Marco set out for Neuburg, Bamberg and Würzburg, before returning to Italy. Everywhere he left behind him an extraordinary name for sanctity and miracle-working, both in the courts and among the crowds. Philip William, for one, linked bodily health with the health of the soul: he had been sick, he gave the credit for his convalescence to the Capuchin. At Innsbruck they were interested in Marco partly because of Lorraine's frailty; the Habsburg family chose to regard a turn for the better in his condition as one of the saintly works of Marco. In 1681 the friar attempted a mission to France, but Louis had him unceremoniously expelled from the country, which simply added to his prestige east of the Rhine. In 1682 he came to Vienna and was blessed for Lorraine's recovery from a second bout of illness. But more important, in the highest court circles the attitude of Pope Innocent XI towards Islam was then, and henceforward, to be strongly defended by this remarkable man, whose correspondence with the Emperor for a period of nearly twenty years (until 1699) is one of the most curious memorials of the age.[13] It testifies as much to the piety of the layman as of the priest; and the priest assured the Emperor, insistently, by letter or in the course of occasional confidential interviews, that the overcoming of the Turk was necessary, possible, and the vocation of God's servant Leopold. Buonvisi had found an ally.

II

The scene of a Habsburg ruler's daily life in Vienna had altered comparatively little in the last fifty years. His palace, the Hofburg, occupied a large area within the wall and ramparts of the southern side of the city. If Leopold stepped out of the main doorway he saw the courtyard so beautifully depicted by a Dutch painter in 1652.* Opposite was the 'new' Burg (which is almost

---

*See illustrations V and VI.

unchanged to this day), with a massive front and a steep roof, surmounted by a cupola with a broad clock-face. To his left ran a more modern range of apartments, the so-called Leopold Wing. On his right some of the principal government offices were housed, including the Imperial Chancery and the Treasury, and probably the Emperor's library. These buildings had been extensively remodelled between 1560 and 1570; they were then barely touched until the eighteenth century. The Burg itself enclosed a more ancient quadrangle. Over three of the four corners, towers of an antiquated style still remained, but the other had fallen down without being replaced.[14] Near the south-east angle stood the medieval chapel, the Hofkapelle, recently redecorated by Leopold's father Ferdinand III. Probably under the south-western tower was the large hall where the Emperor, in his capacity of Archduke of Lower Austria, had received the allegiance of the Lower Austrian Estates at the beginning of his reign. The dowager Empress Eleanor lived for some time in rooms on the north front, and when she looked out of her windows she could see a formal garden of fair size which was flanked on the left by a bowling alley and a bath-house, and on the right by a ballroom. At the end of the garden ran the palace wall, and behind this stood (and stands) another building, of great importance to the court, the Stallburg or stables.

East of the Burg was an open space where horses and horsemen exercised, with a covered riding-school at one end which adjoined the main wall of the city. The view eastwards was closed by the church and library of an Augustinian foundation which the Habsburg family had patronised for many centuries. A gallery connected the convent and the palace, making it a simple matter for Leopold to go to listen to the famous preacher Abraham a Sancta Clara (a member of the order), who spared neither the humble nor the proud in hitting at the sins of the world with his redoubtable vernacular eloquence.

Such was the general aspect of the Emperor's domain in Vienna. It looked unimpressive to Italian or French visitors because money, and perhaps also the desire, for spectacular architectural expansion had been lacking here in the earlier part of the century, although the court grew bigger and needed more room. The one major improvement of recent years was certainly the Leopold Wing,[15] (the Trakt), designed to join the older to the 'new' Burg by a building which ran immediately behind the ramparts along the line of the city wall. That part of the original palace which the Trakt now extended was also refaced, and as a result the whole south frontage of the Hofburg for the first time looked reasonably imposing.* This was the target offered to the Turkish gunners in 1683, long rows of windows and a vast expanse of high-pitched roof. Leopold also put up a new theatre, a timber structure, on the rampart behind the riding-school; in 1681 he began to build a new school, planning to house

---

*The Leopold Wing is the prominent building placed between numbers 12 and 15 in illustration VI. The Herrengasse is number 25.

his books in its upper story. This school, but no new library, was completed in the lifetime of Leopold – the greatest bibliophile among European rulers in the seventeenth century. In due course Charles VI's glorious Hofbibliothek and Riding School together replaced it.

North-westwards from the Burg ran the Herrengasse, from which nobility and officials had almost entirely expelled the ordinary burghers of the city. The Landhaus[16] was on this street, the headquarters of the Estates of Lower Austria, with separate chambers for Lords, Knights and townsmen (the clergy assembled elsewhere), a great hall for common sessions, their chapel – once the focus of Protestantism in Vienna but Catholic again after 1620 – and a magnificent 'Deputies' Room' which had been decorated for the estates in the days of their glory a century earlier; the *Verordneten,* or deputies, forming a permanent committee which defended the estates' interests in the interval between sessions, and supervised their administrative organisation. For if Leopold's grandfather Ferdinand II had deprived the estates of political independence, he broke their fall by giving the members, as individuals, a chance to reacquire power in the service of the Habsburg dynasty. Some of them became councillors in the 'government' of Lower Austria, which was presided over by the Archduke's Lieutenant (or *Statthalter).* At the same time the estates were able to keep their grip on many of the taxes, to assess and collect them. This meant that in 1680 there was no clear division between Leopold's authority and that of the estates of the duchy. The two were interdependent.[17] They governed together but in uneasy partnership, even when the menace of a Turkish invasion threatened them both.

Appropriately, behind the Landhaus stood another house, soon to be transformed into the first great Viennese baroque palace.[18] It belonged to Conrad Balthazar Starhemberg, perhaps the richest of Lower Austrian noblemen, secure in Habsburg favour but by no means dependent on this for the accumulation of his gigantic assets. He was the *Statthalter* from 1663 until 1687; and his son Rüdiger, another soldier who distinguished himself in the campaigns against the French, was to be the strong-willed commander of the garrison which defended Vienna in 1683. Rüdiger took up residence here in 1680.

III

The court and government of Leopold I, concentrated in this small area of the city, embody the Habsburg dynastic interest which impinged on the entire political system of Europe. The municipality in the shadow of the Hofburg was much less important until Kara Mustafa thrust fame upon it.

Vienna had been partially prepared by the intermittent labours of a century and a half to stand a second siege.[19] After the first great Ottoman attempt to capture it in 1529 by Sultan Suleiman, even more after 1541 when he occupied Hungary, there was justifiable nervousness about the future. Ruler and citizens both realised that the older military works ought to be rebuilt and modernised;

and they knew well enough that Italian engineers had recently improved the whole science of fortification. But they were reluctant to find money for this, knowing that the Ottoman forces might be directed to many alternative targets. It looked more sensible to concentrate on strengthening the citadels in western Hungary. If there was no certainty of an attack, there was no absolute emergency. Only very gradually, therefore, were the defences of the city remodelled.

The military architecture of this period was designed to keep the besieger at a distance as long as possible. The ground in front of the main defences would be cleared of buildings, and even levelled – this was the 'glacis';* along the *outer* rim or 'counterscarp' of the moat a well-protected walk, the 'covered way', was constructed – usually of timber spars and palisades – from which detachments of the garrison could command with their fire the open ground in front of them; and the covered way had to be laid out so that they could command it from a number of angles. Next, and perhaps most important, the main wall overhanging the *inner* rim of the moat was reinforced at intervals by new bastions, which became increasingly elaborate in their design. Attackers on the glacis, those who reached the counterscarp, those even who got as far as the main wall, were all exposed to fire from artillery and marksmen on the bastions. Wherever possible, stone-work was buttressed by earth-work in order to lessen the impact of a hostile bombardment. In addition more fortifications were built in the moat itself: these, the 'ravelins', either masked the stretches of wall between the bastions, or the city-gates which pierced the wall. They also provided a second line of defence if the enemy seized the counterscarp. Finally, it was necessary to devise efficient communications, with 'sallyports' in the walls and bastions, and bridges or causeways across the moat to the covered way and ravelins, so that troops of the garrison could move easily from sector to sector.

The Viennese authorities had to adapt this theory of a sound defence to the special features of local topography, and it is not difficult to visualise these. The Danube valley narrows as it cuts between the hills of the Wiener Wald on the south and the other heights north of the river, and then widens again. Here the river divided into a number of channels, including the most southerly arm which is nowadays called the Canal. It was therefore easy to ford, and this had been the reason why Vienna came into existence in the remote past. A traveller coming south from Bohemia in the seventeenth century, crossed the Danube by various bridges, continued on his way through the wooded Prater island formed by two more arms of the river, entered the suburb of Leopoldstadt, and

---

*This was the term commonly used in the seventeenth century, but here it should not be taken to imply that there was a slope up towards the counterscarp outside the walls of Vienna. For the military architecture of the city, see also the drawings on p. 101 below, and illustration VII.

†This crossing of the canal ('Danubius Fluvius') is shown in the 1649 drawing of illustration VII.

finally crossed the Canal by another bridge.† He then found himself at the north-east corner of the city. From this point the old wall of Vienna practically skirted the Canal westwards, and then turned south-west and south as far as the Schotten-gate, adjoining the church of Our Lady of Schotten. Within this segment of ground the most important military feature was the Arsenal. Boats entered through a water-gate into a small inner dock here. They could bring in supplies and also, when necessary, take refuge or dart out to the attack. From the Schotten-gate the wall – with a moat in front of it turned south-east and east past the Hofburg (with its Burg-gate) as far as the Kärntner-gate.* From here it ran due north to reach the Canal again. At some distance from this last section of the defence-works a small river, the Wien, followed a parallel course before flowing into the Canal and provided an additional obstacle on that side – facing east, towards Hungary – from which the Turks under Suleiman had made their principal assault on the city.†

In 1544, Italian engineers began to construct the Dominican (or Burghers') bastion on an improved modern pattern, at the cost of the municipality. This model was copied in the work on at least six other bastions during Emperor Ferdinand I's reign, and most of these were placed in front of the old wall; new stretches of wall were built to connect them. Apparently more attention was paid to the eastern defences, Suleiman's target, than to the line from the Hofburg around to the Schotten-gate. But after 1561 there is little to report for a long time, and the costs of maintenance were judged a sufficient financial burden. All the ravelins probably date from the seventeenth century, and in fact the other important periods in the history of Vienna's military architecture before 1683 were the years 1634–46, and 1656–72. In addition to the ravelins, some of the bastions neglected earlier were redesigned and rebuilt. If the surviving plans or views of different dates are compared, it can be seen that the old bastion guarding the Hofburg was, by 1670, simply an inner defence, in front of which projected a much larger bastion of a later design (VII). This was connected with the neighbouring Kärntner and Löbel bastions by new walls, and these were masked by ravelins in the moat. The moat itself was channelled farther out, and enlarged. Substantial changes are also visible along the Canal frontage. Two new bastions there were aptly named the Big and the Little Gonzaga, after Hannibal Gonzaga, President of the War Council at the time of construction (VII).

In spite of such improvements, it is not easy to say when the defences were at their best. Progress in one area was often counter-balanced by dilapidation elsewhere. An expert's memorandum, together with other testimony, painted a gloomy picture in 1674.[20] The masonry generally was then in a bad state of repair. Access from the walls and bastions to the moat was in most cases

---

*Viz. the road south-west to Carinthia (Kärnten) and Italy, via the Semmering pass, left Vienna by this gate.

†The road to Hungary, the Landstrasse, crossed the Wien shortly after leaving the city by the Stuben-gate, adjoining the Dominican Bastion (illustration VII).

faulty, from a military point of view. The water-level in the Canal was far too low, with a number of unfortunate consequences. The Canal itself no longer provided a real defence, because it could be forded too easily. Not enough water flowed into the moat, except for a short distance at each end; but on the other hand it had seeped into many of the fortifications, and weakened them. The lack of any proper works on the north bank of the Danube, to protect the bridgehead, was also judged very serious; a powerful bastion was needed there, partly because the northern defences along the shallow Canal seemed so inadequate. The counterscarp everywhere was in a ruinous condition, and the timber supports of the covered way had rotted. The glacis was no longer open ground because too many buildings had been put up there. The existence of suburbs beyond the glacis, and straggling into it, constituted a final deviation from the strict rules of a scientific military defence.

The critics were right. Clamped within the walls but expanding in numbers, the citizens of Vienna had tried to build upwards. They added an extra storey to some 400 out of 1,100 houses in little more than a century. But inevitably the suburbs also grew, spreading out into the countryside – and in towards the city. By 1680 there were large settlements in Leopoldstadt on the Prater island, by the right bank of the Wien on the east, round the hamlets of Wieden and St Ulrich south and south-west, and on the western side.* Particularly here the new building approached very close to the fortifications. The government had over and over again ordered the demolition of dwellings within a given distance of the walls, but to little effect. If a maximum estimate of Vienna's total population brings it to nearly 100,000 people, a sizeable proportion must have lived in these suburbs, which would in due course give accommodation and protection to a besieging army.

There was also no real garrison. The City Guard,[21] a regiment paid by the Emperor, had been decimated by the plague in 1679. They were ill-trained, and ill-housed in cramped quarters inside or on top of the walls and bastions. Most of them scraped an existence by following a variety of civilian trades, to the annoyance of the civilians with whom they competed. There were in addition eight burgher companies, recruited from the eight wards of the city. They made a brave show on ceremonial occasions, and could act as a police in emergencies, but did not regard themselves as soldiers. If the well-stocked municipal armoury supplied them with weapons, their military exercises were leisured enough to suit even those elderly burghers who were the senior officers.

The report of 1674 was once believed to give a fair account of the condition of defences when Kara Mustafa arrived in 1683; it made his final defeat sound all the more striking. In fact we know that there were considerable improvements from 1680 onwards.[22] Extra money was allocated to the repair of the walls, bastions and ravelins in that year, and in 1681. Even so, no radical reconstruction took place; and in 1683 old and somewhat inadequate fortifacations still visibly enclosed the city in which the burghers and other

---

* For a panorama of the suburbs of Vienna, see illustration IX.

inhabitants had to go about their daily business.

IV

The municipal privileges of Vienna were based on charters granted by the Babenberg and Habsburg dukes of Austria. These built up the complicated edifice of the 'Wiener Stadtrecht' in the thirteenth and fourteenth centuries. The duke gave certain privileges to the citizens, but from time to time claimed to decide who should be admitted as burghers. He accepted the institution of a municipal council, presided over by an elected burgomaster, but not before he had also created the office of recorder, or *Stadtrichter*, whom he always appointed. He granted the right to hold markets and fairs, and the various rights bound up with a medieval 'staple'; but he did not lose the power of exempting special groups or individuals – his own coiners or the Flemish traders, for example – from the control of the very institutions which he had allowed to develop. On the other hand, the Vienna burghers then chose their councillors and burgomaster, exercised their own jurisdiction in the city and its immediate neighbourhood, and could discriminate lawfully against merchant-strangers and interlopers. Perennial and sometimes fierce disputes with the ruler always continued; but to a much greater extent than in the days of Leopold I the townsmen were independent. They built their most splendid monument, the Cathedral of St Stephen, in the fourteenth and early fifteenth centuries while they enjoyed this relative freedom.

Favourable economic conditions explain the growth, wealth and vigour of the city.[23] Central Europe wanted the precious metals (and, a little earlier, the salt) mined in Hungary; and the Magyars, with their metal, could pay for the products of the west. The Venetians, if they wished to tap the market of Bohemia and Poland, had to take the obvious route over the Semmering pass and across the Danube into Moravia. Trade came to the cross-roads of Vienna and the burghers, brandishing their privileges of pre-emption, became the universal middlemen. Their own exports increased, especially of wine from their vineyards, but were of slender importance by comparison with the easy profits of the staple. This halcyon period ended in the fifteenth century. Everything then turned against Viennese business activity. The development of mines in the Tirol and Bohemia broke the near-monopoly of Hungary as a source of supply. A staple at Passau blocked the staple at Vienna. The Austrian currency collapsed, trade found new routes from Venice and Germany into eastern Europe, and for some years the King of Hungary occupied Vienna. All this meant that the capitalists of Ulm, Nuremberg, Regensburg and even of Passau easily outstripped the Viennese. Habsburg rulers came to depend on German loans for the financing of their government. They made slight use of Vienna, either as a source of revenue and credit or as an administrative centre. They were irritated by democratic elements in the town, which were often dominant in a period of economic instability and weakness. This party came into prominence for the last time immediately after the Emperor Maximilian I's death in 1519; Ferdinand I brusquely restored order, revised the framework of municipal government in Austria,[24] and put an end to the radical tradition in Viennese municipal politics until the nineteenth century.

In Leopold's reign, then, the city was administered by 100 burghers, divided into an Outer or common council of seventy-six, an Inner council of twelve, and a Tribunal of twelve for legal business.[25] The seventy-six elected the twenty-four senior councillors, but the twenty-four elected the seventy-six. Only propertied burghers who were not mere tradesmen could sit on the two smaller bodies, and the latter naturally took care to choose for the common council substantial men like themselves, or the 'better' masters from the trades. Elections were for life; and all vacancies were filled up at an annual ceremony on 21 December, St Thomas's Day, when the 100 councillors assembled to vote under the watchful eye of a Habsburg commissioner. His approval was required before any election could be ratified. They also chose their new burgomaster if the office was vacant; and a good glass of wine completed the transaction of business. The burgomaster normally presided over both the Inner and Outer councils and kept the keys of the eight city gates, but by this period he had become as thoroughly submissive to the ruler as the recorder, who presided in the Tribunal. Other important functionaries were the registrar (or Syndic) – much the most highly paid – the senior and junior treasurers and the Master of the City Hospital. A personnel of inspectors, clerks and tax-collectors assisted them. Rates, control of the markets, weights and measures, public health, the relationship of the guilds with one another and with the councils, and all the miscellaneous problems of local government in a heavily populated area, gave them plenty to do.

A tiny group monopolised high office and we can watch its members, turn and turn about; we shall meet them again. Between 1678 and 1683 John Liebenberg was first the recorder, then burgomaster. Between 1680 and 1684 Simon Schuster was successively treasurer, recorder, burgomaster. Daniel Fotky was treasurer, then burgomaster. From 1691 until 1707 two other worthies alternated as burgomaster and recorder, administering each office for two separate terms of years. They no doubt formed a clique within a somewhat larger circle of solid but less active councillors. But even these men must never be confused with the families which merely kept their place on the Outer council; nor the latter with the poorer sort of master craftsmen in the guilds; nor the masters with the artisans and labourers. For the city had its own steeply graded hierarchy, whose upper levels were in turn completely overshadowed by the grander hierarchy of the Estates and the Hofburg.

V

At this single point on the map of Europe, therefore, in the decades before 1683, a municipality and a court and a government were locked together within the city walls. A poor carter would come down the high road from Bohemia,* pass the Danube, pay the dues on his goods at the Rotenturm-gate, and enter the town. Ahead of him was the street which led to the Cathedral. If he followed it, at some distance on his left stood the University, controlled by its Jesuit rectors. Farther ahead, towards the Kärntner-gate, was the great City Hospital, maintained by endowments and various municipal taxes raised for its benefit; close to this appeared the Augustinian church and then the Hofburg. Away to the right were a number of market-places, particularly the Hoher Markt, where many of the guilds had their headquarters; and behind this was the town hall. The carter was a humble man. Above him ranked all the higher orders, with their place in society and their standard of living carefully (but ineffectively) regulated by the latest sumptuary ordinance of 1671:[26] at the bottom, artisans and school-teachers; then masters in the crafts, and liveried servants; then lawyers, auditors, other professional men and some musicians; then the burgomaster, doctors of medicine and law, and the Master of the Court Chapel; and above all these the noblemen.

Laws of singular complexity divided noble families by rank. Those of ancient lineage, with titles and properties enrolled for generations in the registers of the Austrian or Bohemian Estates, were often reluctant to accord full recognition to others only recently ennobled (or promoted to a higher rank) by the ruler's patent. But if the question of precedence deeply concerned individuals, the spectacular trait of this period was the sheer number of the privileged orders who pressed towards the centre of government at Vienna. As the preacher Abraham a Sancta Clara remarked of the year 1679, just before the dreadful months of plague began: 'the NOBILITY, in crowds which I could not count, and extravagant to a degree, dutifully attended the court.'[27] These noblemen gradually bought up large amounts of house-property, so that the burghers' share of real estate within the walls declined, and the richest began to build for themselves in the outskirts of the city. What they built did not as yet compare in stateliness with the churches and convents inside and outside the walls, which had been put up in the course of the great Catholic offensive since 1600 by the Capuchins, Franciscans, Jesuits, Calced and Discalced Carmelites, Barnabites, Servites, Ursulines and others. In conjunction, however, church and nobility – with their servants, their expenditure, their privileges – seemed to share in the Hofburg's dominance of Vienna. Whereas the municipal pretensions, and prestige, of the medieval city had been thoroughly trimmed by the late seventeenth century.

The townsmen knew their place. Only the absolute compulsion of the siege would force them momentarily to the forefront of world affairs. This crisis was imposed on them by the miscalculations of grandees in the palace.

---

*The 'Taborstrasse' in Leopoldstadt gets its name from Tabor, 100 miles NW of Vienna, on the road to Prague.

3

The Defence of Habsburg Interests in Europe

I

The Empire, Burgundy, France, Italy and Spain had been the dominant concerns of the Austrian Habsburgs of many generations, who all turned intermittently and unwillingly to deal with Danubian or Balkan problems. Accordingly, at this date the menace of Kara Mustafa's ambitions was underestimated; but later, with Vienna actually besieged, the Habsburg politicians were right in thinking that the repulse of the Ottoman army depended on the alignment of forces in western Europe (and in Poland) and on their diplomacy at these Christian courts.

The terms of the treaties of Nymegen were a triumph for Louis XIV. He took from Leopold Freiburg and the district of Breisgau east of the Rhine, while handing back to the Empire the demolished fortress of Philippsburg, some fifty miles farther north. All his claims on Alsace remained intact, he kept his hold on Lorraine and Franche Comté. Immediately afterwards he detached Frederick William of Brandenburg from the great alliance which had opposed him, and he retained old friends, Saxony and Bavaria. The ecclesiastical Electors of Trier, Mainz and Cologne, with the Elector Palatine, continued to take their cue from him. Nor was Louis helped only by the nervous calculations of these Rhineland princes. In broad stretches east of the river the population naturally desired to get rid of all the troops quartered on them during the war. Leopold had to withdraw regiments from Württemberg and Franconia.[1] When the Bishop of Münster offered to recruit for the Emperor, the Estates of the Wetterau and other districts north of the river Main formed a Union* to defend themselves, because the Bishop threatened to maintain on their territory the forces which he raised.[2] The dislike of smaller and unarmed states for the 'armed' principalities of the Empire was indeed one important

---

*It was inspired by George Frederick, Count Waldeck, the militant ruler of three tiny principalities in that area, and from 1672 until 1690 the trusted adviser of William of Orange.

Germany in 1679

consequence of the recent war.[3] It made more difficult the task of setting on a sound basis the organisation of military forces strong enough to check the French monarchy.

It was soon clear that the German courts would have to reckon with an increase in Louis' power over and above the gains scheduled in the peace treaties. First of all, his troops were slow to leave areas on the left bank of the Rhine where they had been stationed in the last stages of the war.[4] Then his tribunals at Metz, Besançon and Breisach began to issue judgments giving to the appellant (the King of France) whatever he claimed as his rights and sovereignties in the Empire. They automatically accepted his interpretation of the Westphalian and Nymegen treaties, and of all documents relevant to the old connection between fiefholders now subject to Louis and their feudal dependencies in the Empire. The latter were 'reunited' to France. The consolidation of French authority in the upper Moselle valley, and between the south bank of the Moselle and the west bank of the Rhine, swiftly entered a new and decisive phase in 1679 and 1680. Important new citadels were built at Saarlouis, Mont-Royal far down the Moselle, and at Fort Louis on the Rhine, facing Hagenau.[5] With the French already occupying Freiburg, across the river, no one could know where this advance by erosion would stop. When Strasbourg was occupied by force of arms, in September 1681, an Imperial City which the claim by 'reunion' could not remotely cover, the event simply confirmed much rumour and prophecy in the previous two years.

Louis XIV also threatened, less tangibly, Leopold's constitutional authority in the Empire. Leopold at last had an heir, Joseph, who was born in 1678; but Louis' secret agreements with some of the German Electors included a clause binding them to vote for him, or for a candidate named by him, in a future election to the title of King of the Romans – and the King of the Romans automatically succeeded the reigning Emperor. It was argued at the time, it has been argued since, that the French ministers never seriously intended to use such promises as more than a useful bargaining point.[6] But rumour about this aspect of their diplomacy was a reasonable cause for alarm at Vienna, and all Louis' manoeuvres farther afield in Poland, Hungary, Transylvania or at Istanbul could be interpreted as means to a greater end: the Imperial crown itself.

There was equal uncertainty about the future of the Spanish empire. Franche Comté had fallen to France in 1678, apparently for ever. Austrian statesmen began to worry about Milan. In Flanders, the terms of peace by no means settled the territorial question. They left the King of Spain 'free' to choose between 'alternative' sacrifices of various towns and strips of countryside, the details of which were to be agreed after further negotiation: an easy and calculated opening for Louis, in the next round of discussions, to make further demands. Leopold, who never lost sight of his reversionary claims in this part of the world, could not disregard these difficulties in Flanders. If he did, momentarily distracted by the crises elsewhere, the Spanish interest at his court was quick to correct him. It was supported by the Dutch envoy, and by all those statesmen who had learnt from bitter experience during the past decade how closely the affairs of the old 'Burgundian Circle' were still linked to the Empire. In any case reliance on Spanish subsidies, with little justification, still featured with curious prominence in diplomacy at this period. Their importance was overestimated whenever alliances against France were discussed, at Vienna or elsewhere.

The Habsburg court therefore felt bound to try and recover from a defeat which threatened even more serious consequences. The decision to join the Dutch a few years earlier had been a very difficult one, causing the downfall of the most important politician in Vienna, Zdenko Lobkowitz, who opposed it. Those who first determined on resistance to France, like Hocher, Schwarzenberg, Königsegg, still surrounded Leopold. If they retreated in 1678 and 1679, neither they nor Leopold were prepared to surrender. But this resolute bias against Louis XIV involved them in problems of the utmost complexity.

One decision, not to disband all the troops in Habsburg pay, was at least simple enough in theory. They were brought back into the hereditary lands, and with them came the men originally raised by the Dukes of Lorraine during their own struggle against the French.[7] Some of the best regiments to survive partial disbandment were stationed in south Germany, and kept watch over Louis' advanced position at Freiburg. Even so, it remained difficult to pay and quarter them indefinitely; and the area farther north was still unguarded. Another decision, to try to reknit the alliance with the Dutch, also looked straightforward but the Dutch government was hardly in a mood to respond.[8] Encouraged by the French ambassador at The Hague, the peace party in Holland checked its opponents William of Orange and Waldeck. The Habsburg envoy here made no headway between January 1680, and the autumn of 1681.

The worst complications were in the Empire itself, dependent on the intricacy of the Imperial constitution, and the labyrinth of interests connecting princely families, cities and governments. The statesmen in Vienna had to pay close attention to a very large number of these separate courts: to the Electors of Brandenburg, Saxony and Bavaria at Berlin, Dresden and Munich; to the four Rhenish Electors, and to the more important princes of lesser rank like the three Brunswick rulers of Hanover, Celle and Wolfenbüttel, or to the ambitious Bishop of Würzburg and Bamberg, who all disposed of significant bodies of troops. They had to instruct the Emperor's representatives at the Regensburg Diet itself, where envoys from the Estates of the whole Empire – in spite of many absentees – sat in permanent session, and the formal decisions of this great body politic were taken. They had to keep an eye on such centres as Ulm and Wiesbaden and Wasserburg, as well as on the more prominent capitals already mentioned, wherever members of different Circles, the *Reichskreise,* were accustomed to confer. A few of these loose historic groupings of states within the Empire, at least in Franconia and Swabia, had functioned with increasing vitality since 1648;[9] they were concerned first of all with such things as currency, police and Imperial taxation, but could not evade the problems of defence and the quartering of troops, which were bound up with taxation. Nor could the Emperor's statesmen safely neglect the larger Imperial Cities, like Frankfurt and Hamburg, which normally looked to him for support. And everywhere the Hofburg's envoys criss-crossed with other envoys from the German states, or from Holland and Sweden and Denmark. Everywhere they encountered Louis XIV's allies and emissaries, who were competently directed, on the watch to emphasise that Habsburg influence had always in the past threatened the liberties of the 'Empire of the German Nation'.

A long series of efforts to do business with Frederick William of Brandenburg ended in failure; and unfortunately he controlled the largest single force in Germany. From February 1680 until August 1682, except for one short interval, John Philip Lamberg, son of the *Hofmeister* Lamberg, struggled unavailingly in Berlin. Rébenac, the French ambassador, held the field and a sequence of agreements (in 1679, 1681, 1682, and again in 1683), linked Brandenburg firmly enough to France.[10] Frederick William's attitude towards the great question of the day was never really in doubt. What Vienna opposed, he favoured. He argued that a public acceptance by the Emperor and the Empire of recent French gains in western Germany was the one practical policy at a time of dangerous uncertainty everywhere. He helped to frustrate Leopold, when the Hofburg wanted to make the Regensburg Diet protest officially against the occupation of Strasbourg.[11] He believed that his own treaty with Louis, in January 1682, barred further French inroads into the Empire. He sent Krockow to Vienna in August 1682, and Schwerin in the early part of 1683, to argue the case. He, and they, laid great stress on the problems of the Magyars and Turks in Hungary: in 1682 his envoy said that one reason for making peace in the Empire was the military weakness and incompetence of the Turks by contrast with the far greater weight and efficiency of Louis XIV's army. In 1683, the second envoy preferred to plead that a firm peace in the Empire was indispensable if the Turks were to be resisted with any success. If the Emperor and the Empire accepted the French demands to date, Frederick William was willing to co-operate in reorganising the defence of Germany, and to negotiate a separate treaty with Leopold. On both occasions Hocher and his colleagues firmly rejected the argument.[12]

Another envoy, from another of the great families of Habsburg noblemen, had been doing his best in a different quarter. Ferdinand Lobkowitz first visited Munich officially in November 1679.[13] It was one of the most important centres of French influence in Germany. Throughout the previous war the lamentable effects of the Elector Ferdinand Maria's friendship with France, and of his hostile neutrality in the course of the campaigns, were plain for every Habsburg soldier or politician to see. Bavarian territory blocked the routes from Austria and Bohemia to south-western Germany, making it much easier for the French to operate in the upper Rhineland. It deprived the allies of resources from the whole Bavarian Circle. Early in 1679 Nostitz-Reineck, the Bohemian chancellor, first attempted to improve relations between the two courts;[14] but the death of Ferdinand Maria a few months later offered a better chance of reviving a sense of common interests which had been repudiated for so long at Munich, and Lobkowitz was instructed accordingly. The Regent Max Philip was sympathetic on a number of minor points, but he could not alter the alignments of Bavarian diplomacy in any decisive way. Soon Max Emmanuel, thrusting and youthful, got rid of his uncle the Regent; it was regarded as a blow to the Austrian interest. The new Elector had no intention of shackling himself to the political traditions handed down from Ferdinand Maria's time, but was too shrewd and also too uninterested deliberately to reverse them. For the moment he refused to take anything very seriously except the pleasures of his court, and he let the old policy ride. He agreed to the marriage of his sister Christina to the Dauphin, which took place in 1680, and always responded guardedly to the patient Lobkowitz. The Francophile Bavarian chancellor, Caspar Schmidt, remained in office and the French ambassador at Munich held his ground.

The Habsburg ministers fared little better in Dresden. In September 1679 John George II approved a treaty with Louis XIV, which appeared to meet every French demand in return for a generous subsidy. His principal advisers, the Wolframsdorfs, uncle and nephew, were the Saxon counterparts to Schmidt at Munich, but the Crown Prince had already come far closer to joining the interests at court opposed to his father's government and to French influence than Max Emmanuel ever did before 1683.[15] It was therefore possible for Leopold's vigorous envoy, the Abbot of Banz, to stir up protests against John George's latest agreement with France. Yet the Austrian initiative soon faded. The Dresden court preferred momentarily to contemplate an alliance between the more important German states, designed to steer a middle course between the systems of Vienna and Paris, rather than a firmer attachment to the Habsburg interest.[16] No radical changes were likely as long as the old Elector lived. He died in September 1680. Undoubtedly the accession of John George III was a boon to Leopold, but some time passed before he was willing or able to make his weight felt in the Empire.

Lamberg, Nostitz, Lobkowitz and Banz had toiled away; Herman of Baden also put in a brief appearance at Dresden and Berlin. The Hofburg strove to strengthen its position at the three major courts of Brandenburg, Saxony and Bavaria, hoping to use their considerable resources to check the growing ascendancy of France. No real progress was made. French reunions and encroachments continued. French diplomacy never flagged. The rulers of central Germany had not yet been convinced that their vital interests were affected by events in the Rhineland. Yet the Hofburg held to its course, it refused to listen to offers from Poland and pleas from the Pope for an aggressive alliance against the Turks, and prepared instead to try new tactics in Germany.

In January 1681, Leopold's commissioners at Regensburg offered a proposal to the Diet for raising 40,000 (subsequently 60,000) men from the Circles. They justified it by referring to the Turkish danger, and to the common duty of all to guarantee security within the frontiers of Germany – by which they meant the duty of the Diet to organise resistance to French designs. By the end of May there was an agreement in principle, and during the next twelve months a series of decisions in detail settled what was due from individual Circles. These were then left to divide out their quota between member-states, which could contribute with either men or money. However, the whole cumbrous scheme was not much more than a warning to Louis XIV, who had responded by sending his troops into Strasbourg on 21 September.

The immediate consequences of this great stroke are very difficult to evaluate. There were too many courts, too many conflicting interests in Germany, for the natural sentiments of alarm and indignation to bring them into harmony. The differences of opinion were accentuated because Louis now began to make offers for a permanent settlement to a conference held at Frankfurt, and then to the Diet, provided that the Empire recognised French sovereignty in Strasbourg and the places 'reunited' to France before Strasbourg fell. In any case, in the autumn of 1681 two points were soon clear. No organised military force was ready to oppose Louis XIV; and the campaigning season was nearly over. The future turned on the preparations, both diplomatic and military, to be made for the following year. The conference at Frankfurt continued its intermittent sessions, where Leopold's envoy now took the lead in obstructing any serious discussion of the French offers. In Regensburg the Habsburg government still tried hard to tap the resources of the Circles.

Serious rearmament at last began elsewhere. In the disarray at Dresden which clouded the last few months of John George II's life, this ruler contemplated asking the next meeting of his Estates for supplies to raise a new army, to be regarded as permanent (a 'perpetuierliches Werk') until the peace of the Empire was assured;[17] two years previously he had dismissed most of his troops. Both his government and people were distracted by the plague in 1680,[18] and the Estates did not assemble until November 1681. They soon discovered that the new ruler, John George III, indeed aspired to be 'the Saxon Mars'. He proposed a detailed and definite military programme. He wanted one million thaler a year for a field army of 10,000 men, and payments in kind to stock the necessary magazines. He wanted the citizens to honour their immemorial obligation to provide, and exercise, a militia. Much debate followed, because the powers of prince and nobility were still evenly balanced in Saxony, but in March 1682 both parties settled for a grant of 700,000 thaler, to be raised by taxation in each of the next six years. Recruiting began at once, and the new regiments began to take shape towards the end of the year.

Max Emmanuel in Bavaria followed suit. He expressed alarm at the fall of Strasbourg, and annoyance at the uneven flow of French subsidies. Lobkowitz was sent from Vienna to try his chances in a second mission. Although the Elector refused to commit himself to an alliance with Leopold, his martial instincts developed quickly. He realised that he had it in his power to keep abreast with all the other great princes of the Empire. He wanted an army for himself. The rearmament of Bavaria began. The year 1682 is the convenient date which initiates the continuous history of a permanent, standing army in both Saxony and Bavaria.

Ernest Augustus, of the Brunswick family, had succeeded to the principality of Hanover in 1679. A man of vigorous ambition, he already ruled Osnabrück and claimed the reversion to Celle. His earlier essays in diplomacy were interrupted by a leisurely and lavish tour in Italy between November 1680 and April 1681, but no one was more alarmed by the fall of Strasbourg and he began to negotiate directly with the Habsburg court, sending his adviser Falkenhayn (a Silesian Catholic) to Vienna early in 1682 to continue the discussion.[19] For Leopold, this seemed a point gained in the uphill struggle to find allies in the Empire.

Very naturally, Vienna also paid close attention to developments at The Hague.[20] French aggressiveness here and the shifting alignment of powers in the Baltic – Denmark moved into the system of Louis' alliances, and Sweden moved out – had brought William of Orange and Charles XI of Sweden together. They agreed in principle to defend the territorial settlement of Europe laid down by the great treaties of 1648 and 1678–9, and to invite other states to join their 'Association'. The Austrian envoy was at once instructed from Vienna to agree unconditionally. It appeared a useful step forward, although politicians were well aware that an agreement of this kind was a sham, unless detailed clauses about troops and subsidies to enforce it were added later. Meanwhile, Waldeck had strengthened his own Union in Germany,[21] and linked it with the Franconian Circle by a compact of 31 January 1682. He championed a new plan for defending the Empire with Bavaria and Austria holding the south, the Franconians and the Union and Saxony placing 16,000 men between Philippsburg and Koblenz, and the northern Circles guarding the lower Rhineland. Something of this kind was certainly needed to strengthen the Association, if its members were to defend the Empire at all. Leopold's ministers agreed, and when William suggested that the Diet at Regensburg should be invited to join the 'Association', they stipulated that the Emperor and individual German states or groups of states must first settle between them the details of a workmanlike military partnership. Equally Spain asked the Dutch for material guarantees of support in Flanders before they too entered the alliance. This sounded good sense, but it meant further delay when the matter was urgent. Everyone feared the worst for the summer months of 1682. Men asked themselves whether Louis would treat the Imperial city of Cologne as he had treated the Imperial city of Strasbourg. Many also asked, as they measured his power, if they ought not to make the best possible bargain with him, even on unsatisfactory terms.

The more pessimistic view was not shared by the dominant factions in Vienna. They preferred a policy of appeasement in other parts of Europe, but not in the west. They decided on Caprara's mission to Istanbul in August, 1681, and patched up a reconciliation with most of the dissident Magyars in November (see p. 21). They issued patents for the raising of new regiments. They welcomed the negotiations with Hanover and sent Lobkowitz once more to Munich.

Renewed contact with the major German states in 1682 produced nothing tangible. Vienna did not gain an inch at Munich, Hanover, Berlin or Dresden although the stakes rose higher every month, in that each of these powers was increasing the size of its military force; while Louis noisily threatened action. Instead the intricate diplomacy which had inspired men like Waldeck reached its curious climax, in a document finally signed in Leopold's hunting lodge at Laxenburg* in June 1682 by the Habsburg ministers Hocher, Königsegg, Schwarzenberg and Herman of Baden, by a representative of the Franconian principalities, and by Waldeck on behalf of his Union. It has been described as the programme of a war-party. The Spanish ambassador in Vienna was of course its eager champion. The preamble stated that this compact anticipated a final settlement of ways and means to be devised for imperial defence by the Diet at Regensburg. Meanwhile, the signatories and their allies bound themselves to organise three armies in order to secure the Rhineland. Leopold promised some 20,000 for the south, and 3,000 from Bohemia as a reinforcement to the army of confederates holding the central stretch between Philippsburg and Koblenz. In the north reliance was somewhat piously placed on the local Circles, and on states like Hanover. Negotiations with the Elector of Bavaria and a number of other princes were promised as soon as possible. The whole scheme aimed to defend the Empire in a period of emergency, the campaigning season of 1682. Some of Leopold's troops began to move west immediately after the treaty was signed. There was a calculation here that, in spite of the rebel Thököly's refusal to accept the pacification of Sopron, the position in Hungary could be held; and that the Turks would not attempt anything serious before the treaty with them expired in 1684. One, if not two, years were available for mounting an efficient defence in Germany. If a stand was to be made against Louis XIV, this was the time.

A number of factors still obscured the issue. Louis temptingly offered first to return Freiburg if his main demands were accepted, then to give up certain claims in Flanders if Spain gave him Luxembourg. The Spaniards refused, and thereupon asked for help from the Dutch; the Dutch finally promised to send an expeditionary force of 8,000 to Flanders if Louis would not come to

---

*Ten miles south of Vienna. The Habsburgs enjoyed extensive hunting rights over much of the plain immediately east of the Wiener Wald.

terms. But William of Orange realised at the same time how inflammable the situation had recently grown in north Germany. Charles XI of Sweden stood to lose his valuable possessions, the prizes of the Thirty Years War, which stretched from Pomerania to the lands of the old archbishoprics of Bremen and Verden; while his enemies – Denmark and Brandenburg and Münster, cleverly egged on by France – hoped to win them. The future of such areas as Holstein and East Friesland* was equally in the balance, depending on the feverish rivalry of their stronger neighbours. The Hanoverians, aggressive but vulnerable, were arming furiously. All this made the Dutch very unwilling to expose themselves in the Rhineland, where the ecclesiastical Electors remained obsequious to French pressure. News of Thököly's successes in Hungary caused further alarm during August and September, suggesting that Leopold could no longer dare to resist Louis' demands for a new settlement in the Empire. Fortunately, Louis in fact still hoped to get what he wanted by substituting, for open conflict, menaces one stage removed from a direct French attack. And the Sultan, as everyone realised, had his part to play in this context.

Louis XIV's earlier attempts, in 1679 and 1680, to persuade Kara Mustafa to intervene as a principal in the Magyar rebellion had not been successful. His talented envoy at the Porte, Guilleragues, was unable to prevent the two governments drifting still farther apart in the course of 1681, when the occupation of Strasbourg (and of Casale in northern Italy) by French troops coincided with Admiral Du Quesne's accidental bombardment of Chios. Guilleragues and the Grand Vezir also quarrelled bitterly over the treatment to be accorded to the ambassador at formal audiences, a dispute taken very seriously by the Turks and by the French. In 1682 Louis shifted his ground and adopted more subtle tactics. As in the past, the ambassador was to impress on the Sultan and his ministers the grandeur and power of the French King, but he was ordered to settle peaceably the problem of ceremonial, and to transmit to them Louis' expression of regret for the misadventure at Chios. Above all, while steering clear of any commitment by the French to attack Leopold he was to point out, insistently, that the dispute between Leopold and Louis XIV in the Empire offered the Grand Vezir a marvellous opportunity for aggressive action.[22] The King of France, instructed by many passages from Guilleragues' reports, never rated the Ottoman armament highly; but he did consider it menacing enough to force Leopold to come to terms – with the King of France.

Then, having tightened one screw, he tried to tighten another. In April 1682 he withdrew his forces from Luxembourg, which his troops had been blockading for many months, and gave wide publicity to his alleged motive for the generous gesture: the peril, for central Europe, of an Ottoman invasion.[23] But he informed Guilleragues that his real intention – which could be

---

*The county of East Friesland lay between the Dutch province of Groningen and the duchy of Oldenburg, but the King of Denmark was the Duke of Oldenburg.

explained to the Grand Vezir – was to be in a position to threaten the Emperor with his whole force. Meanwhile the French ambassador still feared that the Turks proposed to attack Poland, not Austria; and he therefore pointed out to them, as we have seen, that Louis might judge it necessary to help John Sobieski, whereas French aid for Leopold was out of the question.[24] This was important, because the Turks remembered well enough that the French had sent one powerful expeditionary force to assist Austria in 1664, and another to Crete in 1669. In fact Louis did his diplomatic best to push the Ottoman army into Hungary, and the threat to Austria from the eastern front grew stronger with every month that passed in the second half of 1682. To strengthen it still further, Louis announced in September that his offers to negotiate a settlement in the Empire would lapse on the last day of November.[25]

By then Leopold knew that an immense Ottoman army was being assembled in the Balkans. But he did not move. He did not contemplate any surrender to Louis XIV. The campaigning season for 1682 was over, and he believed that he still had time in which to seek allies and to raise armies.

II

After the close of the long wars between the Sultan and the Czar of Muscovy in 1681, no one expected the Ottoman government to refrain indefinitely from military enterprises on the grand scale; and, at the best, no one could be positive that the treaty of peace between Sultan and Emperor would be renewed on reasonable terms unless the Habsburg defences were strong and impressive enough to deter Kara Mustafa. In addition, if it was a delicate problem to settle the size of the forces to be allocated to the two potential theatres of war, in the Rhineland and in Hungary (with Croatia), it was easier to agree that a larger total force was needed by the Habsburg government as soon as possible for use in either theatre of war. Leopold's diplomats, in spite of their untiring activity in a number of courts, had no solid victories to report to him between 1679 and the summer of 1682. His administrators, whose main business was with money, men, and the repair of fortresses, were more effective.

To Christopher Abele, President of the Treasury from 1681 to 1683, must apparently go most of the credit for the increase in 'extraordinary' taxation laid on the provincial estates of all the Habsburg dominions in the years 1681, 1682 and 1683.[26] In 1677, during the war with France, they had agreed to vote 1,800,000 florins.* Six years later they voted 3,700,000 florins. It was an epoch in the history of Habsburg taxation.

The 'extraordinaries' in the financial system were the complicated product of much past history. The *Hofkammer* or Treasury, after consultation with the

---

*The florin of the Austrian financial estimates was less valuable than the thaler of the Saxon estimates (p. 49 above). The rate of exchange was commonly 1½ or 1¾ : 1.

War Council, estimated what was needed each year, and divided the amount into those fractions of the total which each duchy or kingdom was supposed to pay in accordance with a schedule more than a century old:[27] two-thirds from the lands of the Bohemian crown (Bohemia, Moravia, Silesia), one-sixth from the duchies of Inner Austria (mainly Styria, Carinthia, Carniola) and one-sixth from Upper and Lower Austria.* The various chanceries then brought the 'postulates', or demands, before the different assemblies of estates during the winter.[28] The estates, usually (but not in all provinces) constituted by the bishops and other privileged ecclesiastical foundations, the magnates, the lesser nobility, and certain municipalities, preserved the right to discuss the sovereign's demands for extraordinary taxes, to negotiate before consenting, and to collect them. They actually spent many of the taxes on the sovereign's behalf. The whole process of discussion before the final vote or 'conclusum' customarily dragged on for months, often until the following autumn. It was all very solemn, and a fantastic waste of energy and time. In any case the peasants paid by far the largest share of the tax, partly because in most areas the units of assessment were calculated from the number of peasant-holdings in each lordship. To a considerable extent the estates had therefore simply agreed to increase the charges which they themselves laid on their tenants and subjects. After the tax was collected, their officials made deductions for expenses, and for interest on previous loans or advances from the estates to the ruler, before surrendering the balance to the government. Months passed before the various Habsburg exchequers gathered in a major part of the sums voted; the minor part never came in at all.

George Sinzendorf, President of the Treasury in Vienna from 1656 to 1680, personally adroit but scandalously corrupt, a politician whom Leopold should never have tolerated for so long in high office, accepted all these anomalies with remarkable complacency. In particular, the estates were tending more and more to include part of the taxes which they had voted in one year, but not paid, in the amounts which they voted for the following year, so that the Emperor lost accordingly. In 1680 Sinzendorf was at last dismissed, and there is a distinct change in the tone of all these transactions not long after Abele took charge of them.

During the winter of 1680–1 Leopold decided to add 20,000 men to his standing army, bringing the total up to over 50,000 Abele reckoned the extra cost at 2,000,000 florins[29] a year, of which the major part could only come from taxes raised by the estates. In consequence, the 'postulates' which Abele moved the chanceries to lay before the various assemblies were enormously increased, and he proposed a whole range of new taxes. We have detailed evidence about the discussions which then took place in Vienna, where the

---

*Strictly speaking, 'Upper' Austria is 'Austria-above-the-Enns' with Linz as capital, and 'Lower' Austria is 'Austria-below-the-Enns' with Vienna as capital. The river Enns is the boundary between them south of the Danube.

Lower Austrian Estates met in the Landhaus. These Estates paid 200,000 florins in 1677. Abele now asked for 1,100,000 florins, and insisted on payment before the end of 1681. A tremendous wrangle followed. The Estates were well aware that the opening demand of the central government, in accordance with its usual tactics, was far higher than they need accept. They also realised that a sharp increase would now hit the privileged orders most, because the maximum burden on the peasantry was limited by their poverty – if it was exceeded, the peasants simply could not pay the tax, nor could they pay rents and dues to their lords. The upshot of the debate may be guessed. It was a three-fold rise, a vote of 600,000 florins, which was increased slightly in the next two years to 650,000. The negotiations, and the results, seem to have followed a parallel course at Linz, Innsbruck, Klagenfurt, Graz, Ljubljana, Prague, Breslau and Olomouc. They account for the estimated total grant of 4,200,000 florins from this source of revenue in 1683.

The real difficulty continued to be the long interval between votes of supply and the actual transfer of funds to the government. In the autumn of 1682, when Abele argued that a Turkish war in the following year was absolutely certain,[30] and expenditure was running at a high rate, these delays became dangerous. He had already hinted that he might be compelled to ask for a direct tax on the privileged classes, enforced in a time of emergency by the ruler's authority without the consent of the Estates. He now arranged for the issue of Leopold's decree to this effect in December; the Estates were summoned in January.[31] Negotiations during the first few months of 1683 were as unfriendly as they had ever been in the past. The government pleaded the great crisis of the hour. The Estates pleaded, not only their privileges, but a real inability to pay. The result seems to have been that the flow of revenue was kept up to the level of the preceding year, but not substantially increased. The régime of privilege in the system of taxation, together with the losses in wealth and population caused by epidemic in 1679–80, were as responsible as anything else for the weakness of the defence in 1683.

Even so, the new revenues had one important consequence. The administration was able to raise new regiments. In 1679, ten out of twenty-one foot-regiments, ten out of twenty-one cavalry, two out of four dragoon-regiments, and most of the Croat mounted troops, were dismissed after the treaty with Louis XIV.[32] By April 1681, Leopold had made his decision to maintain an additional 20,000 men under arms, and gradually the recruits were found. During 1682, commissions were given to a number of officers and noblemen empowering them to raise these new regiments, nine of foot-soldiers, five cavalry, and three of dragoons. On paper the full quota of an infantry regiment was reckoned at 2,050 men, while cavalry and dragoon units contained 800 apiece; in theory, therefore, another 25,000 had been mobilised. There were many reasons, even at the time, for discounting so high a figure. In 1679 a deliberate attempt had been made to economise and still to retain as many soldiers as possible, by attaching certain men and officers, taken from the regiments which were dissolved, to the regiments which were kept in being. Between 1679 and 1682, for example, a whole category of so-called 'aggregierte Reiter' were loosely joined to the units still on full pay. When the moment for expansion came, a very large number of companies or troops from the standing regiments became the nucleus of the new formations; while a number of the new colonels had been colonels or lieutenant-colonels before 1679. In any case, desertion and sickness and 'dead pays' of one type or another diminished the complement in every company, so that the total increase in 1682 must have been under 20,000. Then, while the Ottoman power was being assembled in Adrianople further additions were agreed at the court of Vienna.[33] In January 1683 Leslie, Daun, Württemberg, Croy and Rosen – conspicuous military leaders in the next twelve months – received their patents to raise infantry regiments. The young Louis Jules de Carignan-Soissons, cousin to the Duke of Savoy,[34] was given a new regiment of dragoons; although in this case it is noticeable that no less than five out of eight of the companies were taken from older regiments.[35] Dupigny, an officer of many years standing, became colonel of another regiment of cavalry; in March, the d'Herbeville dragoons were commissioned. If the funds were still short, the size of Leopold's army was almost doubled within two years, just before the crisis broke. The repulse of the Turks in 1683 would have been unthinkable without this increase.

In discussions with the Estates of Lower Austria, in 1681 and 1682, the Habsburg government emphasised that their properties were particularly vulnerable to the Turks. Only the Danubian fortresses and a narrow strip of Hungary lay between them and the Turks. This was the argument which most obviously justified a demand for copious taxes in this part of Leopold's dominion, and in any case there seems no doubt that both Abele and Jörger (his admirable colleague in the Treasury) were well aware of the real danger threatening from the east. The diplomatic labyrinth of the Holy Roman Empire was not their business. In March 1681 the new President of the War Council, Herman of Baden, took over the title and duties of commanding officer at Győr. During the summer he brought into Leopold's employ one of the most celebrated military engineers of the age, George Rimpler, a Saxon who had seen service against the Turks at Candia and against the French in the Rhineland. Baden proposed to use Rimpler's skill to modernise the Habsburg citadels along the Danube.[36] Likewise the appointment in February 1680 of the Statthalter of Lower Austria's son Rüdiger Starhemberg, as commandant in Vienna and colonel of the City Guard there, had already given authority to an energetic soldier with enough influence to make his weight felt; he was soon getting a little more money spent on the fortifications of Vienna, and recruiting more men for the garrison. Yet most Habsburg officials continued to think first of Louis XIV and his aggressions in the Empire. Some of the new regiments were placed in the western Habsburg lands, while the large forces in Bohemia were ready to move into Germany through the western tip of the country at Cheb. It was still hoped to pacify Hungary by means of the Diet summoned to Sopron in 1681, and the rearmament in that area was entirely unhurried and inadequate. Herman of Baden himself was a thorough exponent of the case for concentrating the maximum force against France. The course of events, therefore, gradually began to reorientate opinion at court and in the army, but the government was very slow to modify its general strategy.

After Caprara had reported the total failure of his discussions at Istanbul in August 1682, it at last reacted more promptly. Whatever the lingering hope that Thököly might be bought off during the customary truce of the winter season, the immediate stiffening of the defences in the cast was now essential from a military point of view; and any future bargain with either Thököly or Kara Mustafa clearly depended on their opinion of these defences.

As usual, therefore, appointments were made and special committees set up. On 11 January 1683 a committee of high ranking officers was instructed to take charge of the problem of the defence of Hungary. It included experienced commanders like Aeneas Caprara, Starhemberg (temporarily withdrawn from his post in Vienna), and Lewis of Baden,* and also experts on supply like Caplirs (who was vice-president of the War Council), and Breuner, chief of the commissariat. Their prime preoccupation was with the fortresses along the Danube – Komárom, Györ, Pressburg – and also with Leopoldstadt, which stood about 30 miles north of the main stream. A good deal of money had been now allocated to the works in these places, above all at Györ, regarded by the Ottoman and Habsburg commands alike as the point on which the defence of the Danubian gateway into Christian Europe most obviously depended.[37] When Herman of Baden came on a tour of inspection in this area during the early spring of 1683,[38] it was to the works here that he and his advisers gave their closest attention. Naturally among those present was George Rimpler. Orders were also given which aimed to secure a sufficient number of armed boats for use on the waterways between Györ and Komárom.

Indeed, much turned on the efficient use of the river system. At Pressburg the Danube itself divided, and the principal channels below the city enclosed a large tract of country called the Schütt. The southern arm received a number of tributaries, particularly the Leitha and the Rába (with the Rabnitz); Györ itself, an island site, stood where the Rába and Rabnitz together joined the Danube. Any enemy coming up from the cast and south would have to capture or seal off the fortress, and get across these smaller rivers before he could advance westwards. He would have to cross the Danube itself in order to attack Habsburg forces camped in the Schütt. But the Schütt ended where the principal arms of the river met again at Komárom, another Habsburg stronghold; and at this point the Danube met two more important tributaries flowing down from the north, the Váh, and the Neutra. An enemy coming up

---

*The famous 'Türken-Louis' (1655–1707) was Herman of Baden's nephew. Best known to English readers as the unimpressive colleague of Marlborough and Eugene of Savoy in the Blenheim campaign twenty-one years later, he was a splendid and fiery commander in his prime.

the left bank of the river from the east had to get across this second network of streams before he could approach Pressburg or threaten Moravia.* But the Turks possessed one forward base in this area, Neuhäusel on the Neutra; not very far north-west of it was the Habsburg garrison at Leopoldstadt.

It was generally held that the natural defences, at least on the southern side of the Danube, were very strong. If the enemy ever got across the Rába (and its right-bank tributary, the Marcal) at any point more than twenty miles upstream from Györ, he was likely to find himself trapped in the immense wilderness of marshes which in those days stretched for miles westwards, until they merged into the waters of the Neusiedler See. The course of the Rabnitz was one long swamp. It practically surrounded a firmer tract of ground known as the 'island of Rába'; to the north-east communications with Györ through the marsh were reckoned difficult, and impossible for large bodies of troops without further bridge-building; to the south, the 'island' was delimited by the River Rába, here following a semi-circular course. The 'isola Rab' no longer appears on modern maps, because drainage during the last century has altered parts of the landscape; although, with their help, it is still easy enough for us to visualise its waterlogged character in 1683. Leopold's military advisers knew as much as this, but no more. They examined plans of the citadels like Györ or Komárom, sketched by their engineers, but their military science did not include the mapping of the surrounding countryside, so that they only hazily took into account distances, contours, and the position of fords and marshes – all factors more readily appreciated by their children and grandchildren. It remained for a solitary Italian volunteer in the Györ garrison to begin to remedy this deficiency at the end of 1682, by sallying out to survey and sketch the course of the Rába above Györ. He was the young Luigi Ferdinando Marsigli,[39] one of the great geographers of the next generation.

The government also put too much confidence in the territorial magnates of this region. The wealthiest of them, Paul Esterházy, was undeviatingly loyal, and for the best of reasons. Before 1670 his lands were already extensive on both sides of the Neusiedler See. Since then Leopold had granted him rich neighbouring properties confiscated from Nádasdy, a leader of the great Magyar conspiracy of that year; and the daughter of another conspirator, Zrinyi, had married Thököly.[40] Esterházy certainly stood to lose by the triumph of 'King' Thököly, and spared no expense to raise forces for the defence. By contrast the Draskovich family, which owned lands and subjects along the middle course of the Rába, and Christopher Batthyány, whose domain bordered the Turkish frontier still farther south, were differently placed. True, they were Leopold's subjects and they co-operated with the War Council early in 1683, asking for money and technical advisers to help them in fortifying the line of the river. But they would also be the first to suffer if Kara Mustafa advanced, and therefore tried to insure against possible

---

*See maps, pp. 14–17, and p. 24.

disaster by keeping secretly in touch with Thököly; and this weakened their determination to resist either him or his frightening ally.[41] They were by no means so committed to the Habsburg cause as Esterházy.

When Herman of Baden came to survey the general situation in Hungary, he appears to have left out of his military calculations the whole territory of Upper Hungary lying to the cast, and even the mining towns in the Carpathians. His papers[42] showed him that there were still Habsburg garrisons in these areas, with 1,700 men far away in Szatmár (Satu-Mare), and perhaps 3,000 more dotted about in smaller groups, but they could offer no real hindrance to Thököly's forces. The Turkish danger made it impossible to spare troops to reinforce them; and it had always been Herman's personal policy to advocate the appeasement of Thököly at any price. The effective frontier between Leopold's power and that of his opponents, therefore, ran from north to south and south-east, from the Jablunka pass (which led over from Hungary to Silesia), then down the Váh valley until it reached the Danube at Komárom, then to Györ, and from here south-westwards up the River Rába, and into Croatia as far as Varasdin; then from Varasdin to the fortress of Karlstadt and the Adriatic coast. The greater part of this immense frontier, with forces and fortified points on each side sufficient to check the other's more dangerous threats, had stood since the Ottoman conquest of Hungary in 1541. But if the frontier was always one of the great permanent preoccupations of the War Council, in 1682 Herman of Baden and his colleagues – perhaps with their gaze too often fixed on Germany – failed to grasp early or clearly enough that the arrival of Kara Mustafa's grand army was bound to upset the existing balance of forces in Hungary; and that this would be the case even if the principal Habsburg citadels in the crucial area below Pressburg were strengthened, and the whole line was stiffened with extra troops. To man the frontier zones Baden at first reckoned on a corps of 10,000 under General Schultz, to cover the Váh from Leopoldstadt northwards. From Leopoldstadt, past Komárom and Györ up the Rába to Körmend, the Magyars under Esterházy and Batthyány were to be posted with perhaps another 10,000; 1,600 horses and 3,000 foot would hold the next part of the line as far as the River Mur. From there to the Adriatic, the defence depended on forces at the disposal of the Ban of Croatia and the government of Inner Austria.

This was totally inadequate. Gradually, both Emperor and War Council came round to the view that the chain of existing fortresses needed the support of an independent army in the field.[43] Once the Turks had committed themselves (it was argued) to a particular line of advance or point of attack, it would be possible to use this army to good effect. Then the argument was pushed a step further forward: if the regiments were ready for the field well before Kara Mustafa reached Hungary, they could take the initiative, and thereby disrupt his plans by compelling him to turn aside in order to retrieve or avenge what had been lost by the Turks early in the season. There can be no reasonable doubt that a determination to put a field-army into Hungary at the first opportunity was one reason for the issue of commissions to raise eight new regiments in January 1683. They would replace, in the Rhineland and elsewhere, troops now to be sent to a rendezvous in Hungary.

The discrepancy between an Austrian force of 30,000, and an invader whose numbers were never calculated at less than 100,000 remained very great. Some Viennese politicians certainly still hoped, against the evidence, for a change of sides by Thököly. Failing that, the majority of Habsburg advisers had to pray for a campaign in which the aggressive power of their field-army, and the defensive power of one or more of their fortresses in Hungary, would combine to check the enemy. The interaction of relieving armies, besieging armies, and besieged garrisons, was a favourite and obvious theme in the military science of that period. In the end these Habsburg advisers were right; but it was the very last of the fortresses which they considered in danger, Vienna itself, which held out, while the relieving army needed the heaviest reinforcement from Leopold's allies.

Few middle-aged men in Vienna could forget the sense of panic and crisis in the city twenty years earlier, before the battle of St Gotthard. Now something had to be done, not only because of the real risks of the situation, but to calm public fears. Highly placed officials began to realise what was afoot in the Ottoman empire. From the beginning of October 1682 orders and instructions streamed out from the various offices of the court and municipality.[44] Parts of the moat were cleaned. Several hundred workers were employed on the main works, and they reinforced the wall adjoining the Hofburg, as well as the defences of the Rotenturm-gate, which faced the Canal. By the end of the year there was an undoubted improvement along the whole line from the Burg-gate in the south as far as the New-gate at the north-west corner of the city. Contracts for munitions were discussed; and Starhemberg had already prepared a detailed memorandum of certain essential requirements, which included 250,000 pieces of timber of different specifications (above all, 200,000 palisades for the moat), 400,000 sand-bags, and 300,000 fascines.* It was decided that the magazines in Vienna must be on such a scale that they could comfortably supply both the garrison and the army in Hungary. There were prolonged debates, at last, on a scheme for building a proper bastion across the Danube at the north end of the bridges, one of the most vulnerable points in the whole landscape round the city. It was also considered that an attempt would have to be made again to divert more water from the main streams into the Canal. At meetings of the War Council in December the agenda on Vienna fairly overflowed.[45]

Paper resolutions are one thing, but it is of course difficult to discover how much was actually achieved during the last three months of 1682. Many delays occurred owing to the haphazard arrival of supplies.

---

*Cylindrical bundles of sticks, bound together, for making parapets and raising batteries.

Timber, for instance, proved a singularly difficult problem. Abele had applied to the Habsburg Forest authority (the *Waldamt*) in the Wiener Wald, which declared that it could not possibly supply more than a fraction of the amount asked for, advising that the balance should be taken from private owners of woodland.[46] We do not know what happened next, how much was bought from whom, or whether the treasury officials set aside too little money for this item; but in February 1683 the government solemnly appealed to the Estates of Lower and Upper Austria for help. Lower Austria grumbled hard, as usual, before placing an order with three timber merchants to deliver wood for 80,000 palisades by the middle of June. Some supply must have reached the city before this. The government also found that there were not enough labourers at work on the defences, and it had asked the Estates to arrange for the compulsory attendance of 3,000 men for eight weeks. The municipality of Vienna at once declined to produce its own share of this quota, 300, but agreed to find accommodation for the rest.[47] In March the Estates, city and government came to terms; 2,700 countrymen were brought in slowly and fitfully, according to the distances they had to come, and were set to work. Half an infantry regiment, the Alt-Starhemberg, arrived from winter quarters in Moravia to help them; but they left for Hungary at the end of April. Half another regiment, the Kaiserstein, took their place. Even then, the maximum numbers employed in this way can never have been more than 4,700.

Less was accomplished on the other side of the Danube. When both time and supplies were running short, it appears to have been a most difficult technical question to decide how best to protect the bridges over the river, or the islands between them. Rimpler looked at the site in October and early in 1683 Peter Rulant, another expert, was summoned from the Rhineland to give an opinion. He came, saw, and recommended that blockships should be built. This meant getting special types of timber from places far up the Danube and the Inn. Unluckily, as news-letters from Vienna to London tell us,[48] the winter was very severe and the ice melted late, so that transports coming down the river were held up and Rulant's ships were never built. Starhemberg also tried hard to have the inlet cleared which led from the Canal into the Arsenal. When the spring came and the ice had gone, a picked detachment of workers was ordered to contrive, by dredging, the diversion of more water into the Canal – and so into the Arsenal's dock, and into parts of the moat round the walls. They had little success.

Another awkward problem was demolition. Now, more than ever before, the experts were perturbed by the ease with which a besieging army would certainly find shelter close to the counterscarp. In January a commission representing both military and municipal authorities inspected the glacis, and drew up the itemised lists so dear to bodies of this kind. It scheduled all the walls and buildings which ought to be destroyed at once. Vested interests soon gathered hotly in protest. An imperial resolution, signed on 22 April, sought to enforce the commission's will; but as late as May and June little had been done – to the despair of soldiers arriving hot-foot from Hungary in July.

Of the high-ranking officers, Starhemberg left Vienna in April in order to take command of the artillery in the field. He was replaced by Colonel Daun, who apparently lacked the fire and pertinacity of his predecessor. The change came at a moment when in any case the energies of the government burnt rather low, because the success of its diplomacy abroad (especially a new alliance with Poland), seemed to guarantee effective assistance from other quarters; a mistaken optimism was now satisfied by the slow tempo of improvement in the defences of Hungary and Austria. But the name of Ferdinand, Marquis Obizzi, must be honorably mentioned. This officer had earlier been Starhemberg's deputy as commander of the City Guard. In December he also took charge of the Arsenal where the stores, foundry and workshops were really the heart of Vienna's defence; but they had to supply an army as well as a city. In a number of respects, to equip one meant depriving the other. On 21 April Leopold reviewed in the Burgplatz sixty-four cannon and their crews under Starhemberg's command – then off they moved towards Hungary, and Obizzi naturally deplored their going. The casting of more and heavier pieces for use on the walls was begun at this time, but (according to critics) never in sufficient quantity. Obizzi also fretted over the supply problems of shipping. He needed fireships, warships, pontoon-boats. More ordinary types of craft were requisitioned in towns up and down the shores of the Danube, and commissioned from the wharfs at Linz and Gmunden.

Ball and bullet were ordered mainly from Steyr; iron ore, at least, was plentiful in the Austrian duchies, and not too far distant from Vienna. Merchants in Breslau had to supply 300 handmills for the manufacture of powder in Vienna. Time pressed, much larger quantities were required, and the flow of munitions preoccupied Abele himself. Evidence on the whole business is scanty,[49] but the most important contractors were Böhm (of whom absolutely nothing certain can be said), and John Mittermayer, Administrator of the Habsburg mercury and copper mines in Istria and Hungary. He was a brother of the Master of the Vienna Mint. One document refers to a total expenditure of 521,800 florins on munitions in 1682 and the first six months of 1683. A second describes Böhm's contract as an agreement to supply 6,000 hundredweights of powder, and Mittermayer's as one for 4,000 hundredweights; and the third states that only ten per cent of Böhm's consignment was delivered by August 1683. A meeting of senior officials was held on 9 March to question Mittermayer. Those present learnt from him some of his difficulties in trying to scour the market. Cash in advance was often demanded; Hamburg and Amsterdam were remote but essential sources of supply; while the greater their distance from the Danube, the higher the cost. By June reasonable quantities of powder, bullet and ball were assured, but without freeing the administration from continual anxiety. There was a distinct possibility that either the army in the field, or the Hungarian citadels, or Vienna (if besieged), ran the risk of running short. Fortunately, as things turned out, Vienna itself was the main base for supplies.

A keen observer gave this account of the city on 22 April:

> Here we think of nothing except military affairs. Last Monday the Dieppental battalion, 500 strong, was inspected by the imperial commissaries. Nine hundred horses and 169 wagons for the artillery, and 19 large anchors for warships, also arrived; while the same day, the foot marched out along the Tabor road to the suburbs, and went down the Danube next morning. On Tuesday 3 craft from Steyr came in, with 2,000 canon-ball, and many thousands of smaller shot. Half the Scherffenberg regiment (with 1,020 men) also arrived, and marched through the city . . . Today, half the Mansfeld regiment (again 1,020 men) were stationed outside the Burg-gate at 9 o'clock, when the Emperor went out of town to hunt; he took the opportunity to inspect them. They were well clad in grey, with blue facings . . . Count Windischgrätz, last Thursday, arranged to have his son and daughter signify their submission to the Roman faith in the Jesuit Church.[50]

III

These preparations on home ground were accompanied by further sustained efforts to strengthen Leopold's position, by diplomacy in foreign courts.

One set of negotiations was a total failure. An envoy named Waldendorf was instructed, on 17 November 1682 to go to the Rhineland and confer with the three ecclesiastical Electors and with the Elector Palatine.[51] The proposal which he took with him suggested a meeting between these Electors and the Emperor at the Regensburg Diet in the early spring in order to discuss the joint defence of the Empire against the Turk. The irruption of the Grand Vezir with the Sultan's grand army from Hungary into Silesia, Poland or Moravia, and from there into the 'viscera' of the Empire, was held out as an immediate threat in the coming year. But Waldendorf, after visiting Mainz, Ehrenbreitstein, Cologne and Heidelberg in December and January, found that not one of these rulers felt disposed to fall in with Vienna's wishes. They were all far too frightened of Louis XIV and all said that, if they appeared in Regensburg to confer with Leopold, French troops would at once move east into the lands of the Empire. The gravity of the Turkish danger absolutely required an agreement between Vienna and Paris, they argued, before any other steps could be taken. They pointed out that Louis had now left open until the last day of February 1683 his offer to negotiate a settlement with Leopold and the states of the Empire.

Meanwhile another envoy, Martinitz, had been sent into Italy to press Innocent XI and the Italian rulers for financial and diplomatic assistance.[52] For many months his reports made gloomy reading. Rome persisted in the view that the great crisis in eastern Europe required a policy of harmony and appeasement between the western states.[53] Lamberg, also, continued his efforts in Dresden and Berlin, but was unable to deflect the policies of these Protestant princes.[54] John George continued polite but negative. The Habsburg government paid the Elector's expenses when he spent the Easter holiday at Teplice, the Bohemian spa, but John George continued to look northwards over his shoulder to Berlin, determined to keep on good terms with a powerful neighbour who obstinately preached the doctrine that peace in the Empire must be preserved by making the necessary concessions to France, and who clearly hoped to aggrandise himself in north Germany, to the possible detriment of Saxony as well as of other states.

It was all the less likely that Lamberg would gain a hearing in Berlin. Frederick William refused to discuss an alliance with the Emperor unless Louis XIV's claims in Germany were first accepted. Hocher and Königsegg, commenting on this, again reminded Leopold of Louis' lack of scruple, his perpetual aggressions, and their unyielding attitude to France remained the core of Habsburg policy. All the same they managed to complete other agreements of the greatest importance, and first they came to terms with Max Emmanuel of Bavaria.

The Elector's new army had been taking shape in the summer of 1682, and during the period of its first autumn manoeuvres – in which he shared – serious bargaining with the Hofburg began. Max Emmanuel demanded large subsidies, and territorial pledges for their punctual payment; he had his eye on Habsburg lordships along the upper Danube and the Inn. He wanted an assignment of the greatest possible number of Habsburg troops to defend the Empire against France, and some sort of guarantee that other German states would follow him in joining Leopold. Until the beginning of December Leopold prevaricated, but his position in Hungary was now so insecure, the French ultimatum to the negotiators at Frankfurt so likely to expire without a further renewal, that he felt compelled to act. A new ambassador, Kaunitz, assisted by his dazzling wife, came to Munich and agreement was reached in the treaty of 23 January 1683.

The two princes joined in stating the broad principle that the Empire must be defended: therefore conversations with Louis XIV's envoys should be continued, in order to reach a settlement on the basis of previous treaties. Aggression was to be resisted by force of arms. Leopold would assign 15,000 men to defend his hereditary lands against the Turks, and at least 15,000 for the defence of the Empire; this second figure whittled down the original Bavarian demand for 25,000.[55] The Elector agreed to place 8,000 men in the field, but they were only obliged to assist Leopold against the Turks if there was no emergency in the west; Leopold's first request had been for 10,000 Bavarian soldiers. Max Emmanuel's government, in return, secured subsidies of 250,000 thaler a year in time of peace, and 450,000 thaler in war. These amounts were slightly less than Max Emmanuel asked for, but Leopold reluctantly gave him pledges to surrender territory if the subsidies were not paid; and the agreement, valid for five years, was not to bind Max Emmanuel if Leopold's other allies left him. A further clause anticipated that Bavaria and neighbouring Circles in the Empire would discuss the common problem of military defence. By the end of March Max Emmanuel, and the Bavarian Circle, did indeed come to terms with the Franconians. The Swabians demurred.[56]

For the Hofburg, this was undoubtedly a step forward. If the Elector still enjoyed great freedom of manoeuvre, he had quit the policy of outright friendship with Louis XIV. His army, in certain circumstances, was available for use against France or against the Turks. French diplomacy had lost one of its safest footholds, a change illustrated by Kaunitz' second triumph, the dismissal from office of Caspar Schmidt, the chancellor who had been friendly to France for many years. Next, Max Emmanuel himself accepted an invitation to Vienna. Much flattering entertainment, arranged for him by Leopold and by noblemen like Kaunitz and Liechtenstein as he passed through Austria to Vienna, and through Moravia and Bohemia on his way home again in the spring of 1683, certainly helped to make sure of his friendship for the time being. He was present at Kittsee (near Pressburg) on 6 May when the grand ceremonial review of Leopold's field-army took place. On that occasion he no doubt flattered himself that he had his own army, and his own military ambitions. It also accorded with his interests of state to employ the one, and satisfy the other, in warfare against the Turks. Provided that Louis XIV made no move of a transparently aggressive kind in the Empire, the use of Bavaria's new armament in this way would leave intact as much of the old friendship between Bavaria and France as the Elector judged desirable.

On 14 January Leopold's ministers also completed their treaty with Ernest Augustus of Hanover.[57] Falkenhayn shuttled backwards and forwards, he did his best, but only when he arrived again in Vienna, at the end of November 1682 was it at last possible to make progress. Ernest Augustus had become very alarmed by the whole situation in Germany. He enlarged his army rapidly during the winter, which made him the more anxious to raise additional funds. He failed to squeeze anything out of the Dutch, so he now offered to place 10,000 men in the Rhineland under his own command in return for a promise of 700,000 thaler; this sum was to be taken, with imperial authority, from the 'unarmed' lands of the Empire, plus 50,000 thaler paid direct by Leopold to cover a part of the initial expenditure. Leopold at first offered less than half this total. Then, with a few modifications, he accepted the bargain. At least on paper another sizeable force had been conjured out of the German labyrinth for imperial defence.

It was only on paper. What had really persuaded Ernest Augustus to sign the treaty soon threatened to divert him from the Rhineland: the crisis in the north.[58] Here the alliance of Brandenburg, Denmark and Münster against Sweden, the Duke of Gottorp-Holstein and the house of Brunswick, appeared to grow stronger with every month that passed. Ernest Augustus and his cousins armed to meet and defeat it. They wanted allies. They wanted subsidies. They knew that France, at this stage, busily encouraged Brandenburg and the

Danes; and there were rumours of a projected French attack on Westphalia through Cologne. It was this which had led Ernest Augustus to offer his 10,000 men to the Emperor, and to this extent he felt deeply concerned for the defence of western Germany. But the longer the French assault was delayed, the more completely he became absorbed by the prospect of warfare along or across the Elbe valley. The surprising restraint shown in the next few months by two greater powers, Louis XIV and Charles XI, gradually damped down these northern fires, but not before they had left Leopold little to hope for from diplomacy in that quarter. When Vienna was besieged and he begged urgently for help, Ernest Augustus' reply was strictly determined by the necessities of his position. He sent to Passau apologies, and to the relieving army no more than a company under his son George – who became, in due time, King George I of England.

Much strenuous discussion at The Hague accomplished even less. By April 1683 the Austrian envoy had seen a conference of the interested powers talk itself to a standstill, but he had failed to get from any of them a promise to defend the Empire against a French attack. The ministers in Vienna were disappointed, but still they resolutely refused to treat with Louis XIV, or to consider accepting his demands in order to free more troops for the coming struggle with the Grand Vezir. Their stubbornness on this point measures precisely the extent to which they believed that western Europe, and western politics, were their prime concern.

East of the Empire, Habsburg diplomacy secured one conspicuous and fundamental triumph, in Poland. In another area, in Hungary, it met with a crushing defeat.

IV

In the intricate pattern of diplomatic and military preparations for the coming tussle of arms, nothing is stranger than the obscure story of the approaches made by the Vienna court to Thököly during this winter.[59] In November 1682 Leopold had concluded the usual seasonal truce with the Magyar leader after discussion with two envoys sent to Vienna for the purpose, Szirmay and Janocki. Thököly then summoned a Diet of all the Hungarian counties to meet him at Košice in January. The Palatine,[60] Esterházy, protested that this assembly was utterly unconstitutional; but when it met, and through it Thököly began trying to subject much of the country to a firm administration under his control by the rigorous collection of taxes, the Habsburg court nevertheless empowered an envoy to be present at the Diet, and to negotiate with Thököly and the assembled deputies. Herman of Baden, in a memorandum of 7 January, had been emphatic that a treaty with France was out of the question, and that therefore it was essential to bargain and compromise in the east. He believed, quite wrongly, that Leopold could win over Thököly. He also believed, and his opinion was grotesque in all the circumstances, that Thököly could then be persuaded to win over the Turks to the idea of a peace with Leopold. The envoy in Košice, Hoffman, was ordered to follow out this line of policy. Only one point in his instructions made good sense: he was to woo all those deputies at Košice who appeared sympathetic to the Habsburg interest. Undoubtedly not every Magyar in Thököly's camp had accepted his autocracy, or the Ottoman overlordship. But Hoffman utterly failed to influence the views of the delegation sent by Thököly to the Sultan. It duly reached Belgrade and soon informed Kara Mustafa of Leopold's secret diplomacy. It was these men who pressed for an immediate assault on Vienna. One of them, Szirmay – recently returned from the Habsburg court – apparently handed over sketches or plans of the fortifications of the city to the Turks, who studied them eagerly.

Caprara realised what had happened and was able to report to Leopold. Even so, the conversations with Thököly were continued. Colonel Saponara, commandant of the Habsburg garrison at Patak, replaced Hoffman. He listened while Thököly, as the price of friendship, affected to demand lordships in Hungary from Leopold, the title of Prince of the Empire, and the Golden Fleece. Vienna took these points seriously, and was ultimately willing to grant them all provided that Saponara haggled 'per Gradus', in order to give away the minimum needed to satisfy Thököly. But the weeks passed, and the time for the active military partnership of the Magyar 'King' and Ottoman Sultan was at hand. Thököly, on 21 June, abruptly announced the immediate cessation of the truce, although the original agreement required that a month's notice should be given. Even then, Saponara was told to continue discussions. Leopold went so far as to advise him that the Habsburg troops would not break the truce for another month. The policy of appeasement, on this occasion, had deceived nobody except the policy makers of Vienna. Its most sinister consequence must have been to slacken – over a period of months – the vigour with which the military defences of Hungary were prepared for battle.

In Poland matters turned out differently. The very uncertainties of the position in northern Hungary were important here, and Vienna played its hand more skilfully, but Kara Mustafa was really the prime architect of the treaty between Poles and Habsburgs. Obviously aggressive, he preferred not to publish his plans; therefore both powers were equally alarmed, and were forced into partnership. Even so, the negotiations proved very difficult, taxing the ingenuity of politicians who had to reckon with the peculiar structure of an unstable Polish constitution.

Events in Hungary, during the summer and autumn of 1682, had focused the attention of the Poles on their Carpathian border, from the Stryy pass in the south-east to the Jablunka pass in the south-west. Thököly captured Kassa with Turkish support, he entered the towns of the Polish-held region of Zips (Spiz) farther west, and his lieutenant Petrozzi raided as far as Silesia.

As Sobieski realised, Cracow and the whole surrounding country were now vulnerable.[61] If a large Ottoman army appeared in the following year, 1683, to support or supervise Thököly in Hungary, it might be directed by its commander towards Györ and Vienna, or fanned out into Moravia, or moved up the Váh valley towards the Jablunka pass. It was possible that he would attempt to combine these plans. In any case an attack northwards from Kassa, or a fresh Turkish advance from Podolia towards Lvov, were two other Polish nightmares advancing swiftly from the background to the middle distance. This accumulation of threats to Poland helps to account for the personal agreement secretly negotiated during the autumn of 1682 between Leopold and John Sobieski. The King had gone to his estate at Jawarów, in Ruthenia. Some of his most important statesmen were joined there by the Austrian envoy Zierowski.[62]

Caprara's reports from Istanbul had at last forced Leopold to modify his old policy towards Poland. He gave up his objection to the plan of an offensive alliance, once judged likely to provoke the Turks unnecessarily, and he prepared to buy the promise of a Polish military diversion in 1683 directed against the Turkish positions around Kamenets, which was to be supplemented by a promise of help if Vienna were attacked. John Sobieski secured financial help to ease the task of putting a Polish army in the field; and he gave up, at least for the time being, his old demands for the marriage of a Habsburg princess to his son Jacob. Having made these calculations, the two rulers and their advisers came to terms.[63] Neither made any difficulty over a promise to put his troops in the field against the Turks in 1683, or over a further promise not to make peace without the other's consent. The Poles wished to recover their previous losses in Podolia; and, for this, a combat in Hungary was needed in order to pin down the Turks west and south of the Carpathians. Vienna still hoped to strengthen its defences in the Danube valley, and to conciliate Thököly, but it was necessary to increase the chances of success by a Polish diversion pinning down as many Turkish forces as possible north and east of the Carpathians. Vienna, therefore, agreed to put 60,000 into Hungary and to subsidise Sobieski, who agreed to raise a Polish army of 40,000. This arrangement squared with the most favourable view possible of the immediate future: a danger of great but not intolerable magnitude compelled the two powers to act simultaneously, but in widely separated theatres of war. On the other hand they also arranged, if the worst imaginable possibility occurred and the Turks laid siege to either Vienna or Cracow, that the threatened government could call on the direct aid of its ally. This was an emergency stipulation, mutually acceptable.

It remained for the two courts to coax and coerce the Polish Diet; no treaty pledging the Republic was valid without the Diet's confirmation.

The deputies duly assembled at Warsaw early in the new year, and appointed a committee of thirty-eight members to bargain with Leopold's ambassador extraordinary, Waldstein, who laid his master's proposals before them.[64] Their basis was to be a common undertaking to make war on the Turks, for the glory of God and the recovery of lost territory; the details were those previously agreed between Leopold and the King of Poland. The Poles accepted readily the general project of an alliance, but prepared to question all the practical measures which embodied it. Members of the unwieldy committee indulged to the full the national vice of interminable oratory, which barely concealed the venom of current opposition to Sobieski, or the importance of bribery as distinct from argument. Zierowski, the resident Habsburg envoy, and Waldstein, both tried to limit Leopold's financial commitments, because he was too poor to pay for what they knew he had to buy. Their ally, the nuncio Pallavicini, shuttled backwards and forwards between the protagonists. He had orders from Innocent XI to use the revenues of the Church, and the privilege of the Church exempting it from ordinary taxation, for the purpose of making agreement possible. All three were engaged in battle against the French ambassador, de Vitry, and his principal Polish confederate, the Treasurer Morsztyn. The opposition in the Diet began to ventilate their objections, some merely obstructive, some points of genuine difficulty. There was the query, prompted by an envoy's arrival from Moscow, whether other powers should be included in the treaty. This pretext for delay was met by drafting a clause inviting them to join the alliance, but with the consent of the original signatories. There was the problem of drafting the pledge by which Leopold should accept the agreement, complicated by his dual status as Holy Roman Emperor and hereditary ruler of the Habsburg duchies. The Poles demanded a form of oath which the Austrians judged dishonourable, and this required careful handling and an ingenious compromise. Above all, the whole treaty might be worked out in detail and accepted by the Poles; but then, if a single deputy 'disrupted' the Diet by imposing his veto on any of the proceedings, there was a risk that the entire legislation of the session (with the treaty) would be rendered null and void. The negotiations in fact ended in agreement on 31 March, and the Diet closed quietly on 18 April, but the period between these two dates was one long agony for friends of the Habsburg alliance.

Undoubtedly, they had to rely mainly on a patriotic and commonsense Polish estimate of the Ottoman peril but the King also behaved with great skill.[65] Prompted by the nuncio, he stopped angling for a bargain with the Swedes to molest Brandenburg, and this moderated the energy with which Frederick William's ambassador usually interfered in the proceedings of a Polish Diet. The deputies from western Poland, often susceptible to Brandenburg's influence, were a fraction less obstreperous than they might have been. Sobieski also put the whole force of his personality into the struggle against Morsztyn.[66] Intercepted letters were used to confound and discredit this polished, wily intriguer. After a thundering denunciation by the King himself, he was robbed of the power to do major damage at a critical moment; and instead, he crept away into a comfortable French exile.

This in-fighting serves to show how important, and how difficult to settle, were the financial transactions connected with the treaty. At the end of 1682 Leopold, disregarding the objections of his Treasury, had clearly made up his mind to buy from Poland what this obvious ally could be induced to sell. Quite apart from the military alliance under discussion he wished to hire Polish soldiers for his own army in Hungary. Having received Sobieski's consent, he authorised a separate negotiation with Jerome Lubomirski, one member of this great clan which dominated a broad area and a numerous population in south-western Poland. He undertook to finance Lubomirski for the hire of 2,800 men, at an estimated initial cost of 150,000 florins. Secondly, in order to have the treaty accepted by the Diet it became essential to subsidise the Polish politicians. Zierowski had been given 20,000 florins for this sort of expense in 1682,[67] but he and Waldstein had to spend nearly 70,000 florins during the first half of 1683 in order to outbid the French by a narrow margin. Thirdly, the treaty itself contained some awkward clauses when the Poles had finished with them. Leopold surrendered his claim for the repayment of earlier grants made by the Habsburgs to Poland. He surrendered a mortgage on the great salt mine of Wielicza, south of Cracow, which had been exploited by his own revenue-officers in Tarnowskie (Silesia) for a number of years. Above all, the principal subsidy promised to Poland amounted to 360,000 florins. This, with the 70,000 florins for the ambassadors' political expenses and 150,000 florins owed to Lubomirski, brought the total commitments of the Habsburg government in Poland to 580,000 florins. Additional items soon cropped up. In the winter of 1682–3, for example, dealers had been instructed to buy Polish corn to build up the magazines for use in Hungary. Zierowski's secretary, Jacob Wenzel, found himself appointed a commissary responsible for funds needed to maintain the Polish troops raised for Leopold's army as long as they were still in Poland.[68] However the figures were juggled, there could be no doubt that the Habsburg government needed large sums of ready money, for transfer to Poland with the least possible delay.

The obvious intermediary for business of this kind was the Silesian provincial administration. The most progressive part of the whole economy under Habsburg rule had its centre at Breslau, where the Silesian assembly of princes and nobles voted substantial taxes, the merchants handled large capital sums, and the Silesian treasury of the Habsburgs functioned; while Breslau was relatively close to Cracow. For these reasons, Leopold's cumbrous efforts to supply Poland can best be understood from the correspondence between Vienna and Breslau, eked out by hints from Zierowski's reports.

The effect of the earliest instructions from the Treasury had been modest. The Silesians were paying the salary, and an authorised supplement to the salary, of Leopold's resident envoy in Warsaw. Then they began to contribute to his, and Waldstein's, ever-increasing budget for extraordinary secret expenditure. Then an order reached the senior Habsburg official at Breslau, asking him to collect funds for Lubomirski's recruitment of troops. Then, most important of all, arrived general instructions concerning the principal subsidy.[69] It showed that the government hoped to divide the cost between Bohemia and Silesia, with Silesia finding the larger share: it reckoned to take 200,000 florins from the Silesian taxes, and 120,000 from Bohemia. On the other hand the Pope had authorised the sale of valuable properties attached to the Archbishopric of Prague, worth about 40,000 florins, for the government's benefit.[70] The total therefore came to the required 360,000 florins, one part to be transmitted from Prague to Breslau, and the whole from Breslau to Warsaw.

These were instructions. The Poles needed money. After a few days the Treasury in Vienna discovered that it had overestimated the amounts readily available in Prague, but promised to make good the deficit there by a transfer of its own to Breslau, hoping to balance the item against later remittances from other sources of revenue in Bohemia. Nor could the Archbishop's estates be sold overnight, although a little later a member of the Kolowrat family paid 48,000 florins for them. On 21 May Breslau held sufficient funds to pay one quarter of the Polish subsidy; the merchant house of Schmettau undertook to transmit them to Warsaw immediately, and to advance a further 50,000 florins within fourteen days. Pallavicini, the nuncio, reported that the first 100,000 florins reached Warsaw on 27 May.[71]

This was too slow. The Poles protested to Zierowski, Zierowski to Vienna, Vienna to Breslau. Breslau replied with a polite account of the difficulties. Zierowski began taking up copper money in Warsaw at ruinous rates of interest, borrowing from merchants with whom Schmettau refused to do business. Then Vienna itself, and the papal nuncios at both courts, and Breslau, all made further contributions. Money arrived from Prague. The greater part of the subsidy appears to have reached Sobieski during June. Officials in Vienna assumed, already on the 9th, that the complete sum had been paid over.[72] Their own records show that they were mistaken, and they were also evading the disagreeable fact that funds allocated to cover other urgent items of expenditure were being robbed; but their somewhat creaky organisation did finally honour the main financial clause in Leopold's treaty with Poland.

If the provincial authority at Breslau played its part in these transactions, so did the Church. A few years earlier Innocent XI had begun to raise money in support of his policy of urging the Christian states to take the initiative against the Sultan. Substantial amounts were held by the nuncio at Warsaw. Innocent was disappointed by Poland's failure to follow this policy in the period after 1679; by the end of 1682 he naturally concluded that Leopold, not Sobieski, would need all the assistance he could give in the coming year. He therefore ordered Pallavicini to transfer money to Buonvisi in Vienna, not very long before the completion of the agreement between the two rulers, although Pallavicini warned the Papal Secretary of State that funds would soon be required in Poland. After the treaty was signed, the money began to flow back. Buonvisi transmitted it from Vienna, and other consignments came from Rome to Warsaw by way of Amsterdam and Danzig.[73]

On paper, the kingdom of Poland maintained an army of 12,000 after the pacification of 1676, and the duchy of Lithuania 6,000. Again on paper it was now decided to raise a further 24,000 in Poland, and to double the Lithuanian contingent. The new treaty obligation to put 40,000 men into the attack on the Turks was comfortably met by this grand total of 48,000. The plan placed before the Diet also sketched in points of detail.[74] Troops were to be mustered by 1 July. Pay was guaranteed for twenty-one months, although it was hoped to dismiss most of the troops after the campaign ended. The soldiers must give cash for what they wanted, apart from accommodation and forage; they must keep to the authorised routes on their marches. The cost of winter-quarters would fall on the clergy and the Crown-lands, not on the nobility. In accepting such a scheme, and in recommending it to the provincial assemblies, the Diet had done its constitutional duty and honoured the agreement with Leopold. The government, too, was optimistic. Sobieski, recovering from a bout of illness, hoped that his forces would be ready by the end of June. A council of war even allowed the Emperor's request for 4,000 men, to be sent to reinforce General Schultz in northern Hungary, while the main Polish army prepared to fight in Podolia and the Ukraine.

All together, the alignment of forces in many parts of Europe was now related, with ever-increasing distinctness, to the public theatres of war in Hungary and the Empire. Rulers, often with great difficulty, had tried to calculate how to adjust policy as a crisis of unusual magnitude came nearer. The Turks moved into Hungary. The Crimean Khan, the Princes of Wallachia, Moldavia and Transylvania, and the new 'King' Thököly made ready to join them. There was no overt repetition of that indiscipline in the Ottoman empire which had exasperated the first Köprülü between 1656 and 1661. The Habsburg court, less well placed, profoundly convinced that another round of warfare in the west was inevitable, profoundly disturbed by the mounting pile of evidence in proof of the certainty of an attack from the east, had at least secured two firm promises of help if Austria itself were threatened, from Bavaria and Poland.[75] Other powers, the Saxons, the Brandenburgers, the Dutch, and above all Louis XIV, still awaited further developments before they committed themselves to any decisive course of action. Neither they, nor anyone else, realised fully that Leopold's capital city was in danger.

4

The Threat to Vienna

I

In February 1683 Quartermaster-General Haslingen drew up a complete list of Leopold's troops and of the areas in which they were stationed. He counted seventy companies in Bohemia, forty-five in Moravia, and forty-eight in Silesia – with a complement, in theory, of 7,600 foot and 10,000 cuirassiers and dragoons.[1] There were seventy-five companies in western Hungary and thirty-eight in Upper Hungary, although a comparison with another of his memoranda seems to show that he was here counting some regiments and companies twice over; nor could he, or anyone else, rely on the estimates of men serving in the various types of Hungarian militia. In the Inner Austrian lands (Styria, Carinthia and Carniola) Haslingen enumerated forty-three companies – 5,600 foot and 1,200 horse; in Upper and Lower Austria forty companies – 4,000 foot and 1,600 horse; and in the empire eighty companies of foot and one of horse – 16,400 men. His figures for the number of companies were correct (except, no doubt, for Hungary); but on the premise that the full complement in foot and mounted companies was 200 and 80 men respectively, the grand totals of 44,800 infantry and 17,600 cavalry were no more than the roughest of guides to the size of the whole Habsburg force. They much exceeded the actual number of effective soldiers. However, the quartermaster could soon hope to add to it the bands of irregulars to be raised by Magyar magnates, three mounted regiments which Prince Lubomirski was commissioned to bring from Poland, and also the new regiments of the patentees nominated by Leopold during the winter.

The immediate problem, for the War Council, was to decide how many men could be safely moved east from the empire, in spite of Louis XIV's aggressive policy, in order to reinforce the contingents sent south from the Bohemian lands, building up by this concentration the strongest possible force in Hungary to oppose the Turks. The decision involved some of the best regiments at Leopold's disposal; it had also to take into account the treaty

73

recently agreed with Max Emmanuel of Bavaria, which obliged the Emperor to leave 15,000 men always available for the defence of the Empire. In fact, about 7,500 infantry from the old regiments were finally ordered to march from the western front to a rendezvous at Kittsee, near Pressburg, to join there the great majority of the regiments recently quartered in Bohemia and the various Austrian duchies.[2] In due course, 5,000 men from the new regiments were also available for the campaign in Hungary.

It was soon realised that one miscalculation had already been made. The troops, especially those in the Empire, took much longer than expected to make the long journey to the eastern front, and the date for the rendezvous at Kittsee had to be altered from 21 April to 6 May.[3] Sixteen days were thus lost, and the chance of taking the initiative before the Turks could arrive dwindled fast.

Another difficult point was the appointment of a commander in the field. Leopold, unlike his father, unlike such militant contemporary rulers as Max Emmanuel and William of Orange or John Sobieski, never imagined himself a victorious commanding general. He had always to choose a deputy, after taking into account the ticklish animosities of the military and political grandees of his court. In the last war against France, Montecuccoli, by combining the presidency of the War Council with the supreme command in the field, had caused them the greatest offence. Enemies and critics of Baden, the new President, were determined to deny him the same monopoly of power and they relied on the pledge, previously given by Leopold, to appoint Charles of Lorraine commander-in-chief if war broke out again.[4] This could not bind the Emperor. Circumstances alter cases, Charles had often been ill in recent years, while Herman of Baden certainly disliked and perhaps under-estimated him. In 1683, in spite of counter-intrigues, Lorraine's party at the court persevered and finally triumphed, so that he was instructed to be in Vienna by 10 April in order to discuss the strategy of the coming campaign.

He duly arrived from Innsbruck and a council of war was held on 21 April. It took a great many decisions in detail, but the guiding proposal was to place the field army in the centre of the frontier through Hungary, around Komárom. The council wanted to leave General Schultz with a strong independent force farther north, on the River Váh; and to ensure that the lower part of the Mur valley far to the south (which guards the approaches to Graz) was firmly held by troops from Styria and Croatia. The gaps between were assigned mainly to the Magyars, under Esterházy along the lower Váh, and under Batthyány along the line of the Rába. Lorraine's command of the field-army was publicly announced on 21 April.[5]

By the beginning of May troops were arriving at the rendezvous, a flat plain round the village of Kittsee, near the southern shore of the Danube where the last spurs of the Leitha hills die away opposite Pressburg.* While Lorraine

---

* Military movements, starting from Kittsee, can be followed from place to place on the maps (pp. xiv–xvii).

himself rode east to inspect the position at Győr, his officers remained behind to supervise the assembling of regiments which were coming in from the north and west. It was rainy, windy weather which damaged a pontoon-bridge leading across to the town. The officers felt perturbed by the shortness of forage, they grumbled hard at the lateness of the spring, but enjoyed plenty of leisure to discuss uncertain news filtering through about the entry of the Ottoman army into Hungary, or alleged difficulties in the Habsburg negotiation with Poland. In Vienna the Emperor prepared to come to Pressburg. So did courtiers, foreign ambassadors, fine ladies and sightseers. Splendid ceremonial tents were made ready for the review. Then Lorraine returned from his tour of inspection, apparently satisfied by what he saw at Győr and elsewhere along the border. The Magyars appeared, led by the Palatine Paul Esterházy. They were only 500 or 600 at first, not the 6,000 promised, but a few days later their number increased to 2,000. About 32,000 men – 21,000 foot and 10,800 horse and dragoons – were finally and elaborately assembled for a grand parade on 6 May when the Emperor crossed over from Pressburg to spend nine slow and crowded hours on the triple ceremony of a solemn Mass, an inspection of the troops, and a state banquet.[6]

It was a brave show that day; but the summer campaign of the Habsburg army proved a dismal failure, due largely to the paralysis of the command. Lorraine, as the general in the field, was required to consult with his council of officers, and the Emperor in Vienna, and the War Council which was dominated by Herman of Baden. The personal rivalry of Baden and Lorraine remained intense, and they differed over the whole strategy to be followed in the period (of uncertain duration) before the Turkish army reached the Austrian frontier. Exasperated by the general unwillingness of many high-ranking officers to accept his proposals with any cordiality, Lorraine fell ill with worry and exhaustion. The theatre of war was a complete novelty to him – apart from one campaign in Hungary twenty years earlier – and his touch was very uncertain, as if he did not realise the distances involved or even the ordinary difficulties of transport in this waterlogged area. His main idea was clear-cut: an aggressive march eastwards, followed by the capture of an important point held by the Turks, stood a chance of compelling the Turkish grand army to spend the rest of the summer and autumn in trying to recover what they had just lost. A powerful attack of this kind, at an early date, appeared to him the one possible method of defending the Austrian lands; there is no hint that he ever gave the defence of Hungary a thought, except as an aid to the protection of more westerly areas. The target which he suggested, at the conference held in Kittsee on 7 May – with Baden and nine senior officers present – was Esztergom on the south bank of the Danube, or alternatively Neuhäusel which lies well to the north of the river. Both were important Ottoman citadels. The argument in favour of an aggressive start was duly marshalled. It would raise the Emperor's reputation if a force were put into the field before the Turks were ready, and thereby strengthen his bargaining power in the Empire and in Poland; it would increase Turkish dissatisfaction with the Grand Vezir; and 'fix' the enemy, compelling him to concentrate on the recapture of a lost position in the coming campaign.[7] Baden apparently demurred. Most of the officers agreed to the course proposed by Lorraine, although they preferred the idea of an attack on Neuhäusel – which was separated from the approaching Ottoman army by the Danube – to an attack on Esztergom. It was finally decided to move the troops eastwards to Györ and to Komárom, the outermost Habsburg fortress, and then to reconnoitre in the direction of Esztergom, subject always to the Emperor's approval.[8]

During the next fortnight the army, split into sections in order to ease a shortage of forage everywhere, marched and rode slowly across the enormous plain. By 19 May the infantry reached the outskirts of Györ, and on the next day continued on the route to Komárom. Camps were set along the right bank of the river. Lorraine himself reconnoitred Esztergom while waiting for munitions and artillery. He held firmly to his project of an attack, even though he felt disconcerted by his officers' grumbling, by the indecisive instructions received from Vienna, and contradictory reports about the speed and direction of the Turkish advance. In spite of the council of officers, who met on 26 May and loudly opposed the move on Esztergom, Lorraine held firm and shortly afterwards ordered the troops to march.[9] They had already left the camp on 31 May when Lorraine returned from a further reconnaissance and countermanded the order. His reason for this was apparently a disturbing message from Styria, that the Grand Vezir had already crossed the bridge at Osijek, so that a further advance by the Habsburg forces looked exposed to an early attack in open country against overwhelming odds. Lorraine was in despair when he got back to his base. Then, temporarily, the position seemed to alter. Less alarming intelligence reached him about the pace of the Turkish advance, and he received a letter from Leopold encouraging him to persevere with an attack on some Turkish stronghold before the main body of the enemy arrived on the scene. But Lorraine dithered, and his faithful secretary Le Bègue began to think that a return to the duchy of Lorraine on terms imposed by Louis XIV would be a better fate than the infuriating perplexities of supreme command in Hungary. On 2 (or possibly 3) June the general proposed, for the last time, an assault on Esztergom. The officers protested and he began to reconsider the alternative of an assault on Neuhäusel; this the officers, somewhat grudgingly, approved.

Throughout the last three weeks, at almost every camp, Lorraine had received reports from Vienna which emphasised his isolation in the distant world of court politics. He attempted to brief his supporters in the capital by letter,[10] but far too many interests there were eager for his discredit by his failure as a general. Lorraine took it as an intolerable insult that Herman of Baden, returning from a tour of inspection to Györ in the middle of May, had not even stopped to confer with him.[11] He resented and probably exaggerated the hostility of some of Leopold's advisers, like the Bishop of Vienna and Zinzendorf. In any case their criticism had its justification. Laymen might be pardoned for thinking that the organisation of a defensive position along the Rivers Váh and Rába was the paramount concern. Certain of the professional soldiers, Baden or Rimpler, supported them. As things turned out, these experts completely underestimated the mass and weight of the Turkish attack but Lorraine made the greater mistake of wasting time and resources for six precious weeks. He had accomplished nothing at Esztergom; then he made the troublesome crossing of the Danube at Komárom and advanced towards Neuhäusel. All went well at first, although it was realised that more heavy artillery would be needed here. The outworks were quickly taken, and troops lodged in the island immediately opposite the inner defences of the Turks; and yet once again, by 8 June Lorraine was in despair. He was embarrassed by a letter from the Emperor which advised him to remain on the defensive, without positively forbidding an assault on a Turkish strongpoint like Neuhäusel. This he countered by a reply which asked for more explicit instructions. Then, during the night of the 7th, everything went wrong. The guns which the troops had with them were not sited in accordance with Lorraine's orders, and he inclined to think that the error was a piece of deliberate obstruction by the officers concerned.[12] Other, heavier weapons, on their way up from Komárom got stuck in the mud, and it soon became clear that they could not be brought into action against the enemy for several days. Finally, reports suggested that Tartars and some Turkish forces were assembling in great numbers near Buda to advance towards Neuhäusel. Confused and angry discussions went on all the next day at headquarters. In the morning Lorraine was still determined to go on with the attack. General Leslie arrived and joined the council of war. He supported the other officers, until Lorraine gave way and decided to return to Komárom without waiting for further orders from Leopold. His second attempt to take the initiative, before the grand army of the enemy arrived near the scene of action, had failed utterly.

On the next day the retreat began.[13] A camp was set on the left bank of the Neutra opposite Komárom, from which it was easy enough to raid into country beyond the frontier for essential supplies. For ten days the army rested, motionless in this central position, while Lorraine expected Kara Mustafa to show his hand by committing himself to a definite line of advance. News from stray deserters and other miscellaneous arrivals at the camp disclosed that the odds were in favour of a Turkish move towards Györ, with a slight chance that very large Turkish forces might still be sent to fight north of the Danube. On 18 May he received in audience envoys from Thököly, who were travelling towards Vienna to give Leopold formal notice that their master was ending the truce between them. Their word was not of the slightest value, but when they announced that Györ was the first Turkish objective Lorraine at last felt disposed to agree. Certainly, on the following day there are real signs that he was preparing to break camp and move his troops. On the 19th some detachments crossed the Neutra. On the 21st he sent the dragoon regiments of Castell and d'Herbeville to reinforce Schultz up in the north, and the Dieppenthal dragoons to Gúta (another small fortified post which he himself inspected). Starhemberg and Leslie set out on their way to Györ. Turkish raiders had already appeared near the now deserted camp across the Neutra, and the guns of Komárom fired warningly over the water at them.

During the next few hours a strong gale blew up suddenly and broke the pontoon bridge over the Danube. Fortunately a quick repair was possible and soon the troops of the field-army (preceded by Lorraine himself) got back to Györ.

It had become urgently necessary to settle on a plan for the proper defence of this neighbourhood.[14] Once again, Lorraine and his friends championed a forward position. A letter written some days earlier by Le Bègue, while he was still in the Schütt, shows that they wished to place their army in the angle between the right bank of the Rába and the Danube, in front of the fortifications of Györ. They held that the defences of the town were far too weak to hold out against heavy Turkish artillery. They believed that the alternative, sponsored by both Herman of Baden and by Leslie, of keeping a great majority of the forces in a sheltered position in the Schütt, would expose Györ to the risk of immediate capture. It would dangerously uncover the left bank of the Rába and possibly Austria itself. Once on the spot Lorraine personally surveyed the ground. He did his best to hasten the palisading of the counterscarp in front of the town, still far from complete, and soon 7,000 men were at work on it. He also started to fortify the heights at some distance from the town, across the Rába, in order to prevent the enemy from beginning their siege operations uncomfortably close to the main defences, which would have shortened the time needed by the Turks to prepare a final assault. The Lorrainers lamented that so little had been done at an earlier stage; but the engineer Rimpler disagreed and felt more confident, perhaps partly because he himself was responsible for much of the spadework carried out in and around Györ since 1681; and indeed, the Turks never took the place in 1683. Moreover Rimpler and other officers could not approve the plan to place the field-army in front of the works, and after detailed discussion the command decided on a new scheme of defence. It visualised a slight enlargement of the garrison in Györ and its outposts, while the greater part of the army was stationed along the left bank of the Rába. This decision was carried out amid scenes of hectic activity between 25 and 29 June. A redoubt and other works were built, to guard the fords immediately in front of the troops. Some cavalry and dragoons moved southwards, and others northwards over the Danube (into the Schütt), to ward off any movement by skirmishers in either direction. All the time different messengers were bringing in news of the Turks' approach, while on the 28th Lorraine himself led a cavalry raid into the countryside in front of them, in order to strip it of any supplies which the enemy could use. Soon, smoke rising over the horizon revealed the first incursions of the enemy. On the 30th, pickets of guards protecting labourers in the outworks had their first brush with advance bodies of Turks; and on the next day, 1 July, with perhaps 12,500 foot and 9,500 horse prepared for action behind the Rába, Lorraine and his officers watched vast numbers approaching them from the east.

The Italian Marsigli, who earlier drew attention to the importance of the defences above Györ, had been sent on a special mission to this area. His letters made gloomy reading ten days before the Turks appeared. The Magyars, he wrote, were utterly scornful of the Habsburg army which behaved so feebly at Esztergom and Neuhäusel. On 21 June some Tartars, already reported to be in the neighbourhood, caused panic at one small bridgehead where the Magyars on the spot refused to destroy the bridge. Marsigli himself and his troop of 200 dragoons did succeed in breaking down two other bridges over the Rába, but he warned Lorraine that there were 'three fords' to be watched between the marshes – his own sector – and Györ.[15] Unfortunately, while the Magyar leaders assembled their men on the 'island' and Lorraine prepared to fight in and around the citadel, neither party attended to these easy crossings of the river. The discord between Batthyány and Draskovich on one side, and the Habsburg authorities (who had never examined this stretch of the frontier with thoroughness) on the other, produced a fatal fracture in the whole system of the defence; and as Marsigli was later to insist, in the great book which he wrote on Ottoman military institutions, the Tartars were absolute masters of the art of fording rivers with their horses, baggage and even with prisoners.*

That night of 1 July, the Turkish camps were set on the right bank of the Rába and in front of the town, over a large area of ground which extended several miles upstream. Many other forces took up a position along the Danube and on the higher ground a little farther off. At two o'clock on the next morning Lorraine was woken, and tried to take stock of the position. As it grew light he could see the dense, irregular formation of the Turkish encampments, with large hosts of fighting men apparently getting ready for action. He roused up his own troops and put them in order of battle close to the river; batteries opened fire, attempting to drive the foremost Turks back from the edge of the water. Christian observers were guessing confusedly at the numbers of Moslems and Christian auxiliaries opposed to them: there were 80,000 there were 100,000 there were 150,000! At all events here was the enemy, looking as formidable as the most pessimistic reports had ever anticipated, with individual troops or groups testing the fordability of the Rába and riding upstream out of sight, well beyond the right wing of the Habsburg army. This crowded and confused spectacle slowly began to disclose a more regular pattern. Many Turkish or Tartar tents were struck and more men moved away to the south. The area round Györ itself was strangely still. During the afternoon these Turkish and Tartar horsemen got safely across the

---

*See illlustration VIII.

river, some making use of the fords, others swimming. The thin screen of Austrians from Styrum's regiment and the Magyar or Croat forces guarding this section of the front were completely outnumbered, and the accusation of treachery levelled against Batthyány the Hungarian commander makes little sense. Neither he nor Styrum could have stopped the foe. His own men quickly preferred to surrender while Styrum's fell back in disorder. And not much later smoke was visible a long way to the west.

Strangely enough Lorraine gave ground at once.[16] He never seems to have considered that, for the time being at least, he could disregard a host of irregulars riding rapidly west to fire the countryside provided that the great mass of the opposing army was still in front of Györ. Indeed, he also broke up his own force into smaller pieces. Another thirteen companies were sent to stiffen the garrison, accompanied by a few aristocratic volunteers, Leslie led the main body of infantry over the Danube into the Schütt, and Lorraine himself prepared to withdraw the cavalry. Baggage and artillery moved over the Rabnitz westwards almost immediately, and the cavalry followed as evening fell. The retreat continued overnight and during the next day. There were Tartars ahead of the Habsburg regiments, and Tartars at their heels. At one moment the rearguard was mauled, so that Lorraine himself had to turn back and go to the rescue. The enemy moved quickly, with small groups of horsemen dotted over a wide area. The Habsburg troops were divided into a van, a main body, and a rear, riding west in a tighter, more compact formation. Both protagonists were taking the same route, up the Danube as far as Ungarisch-Altenburg (although the Tartars obviously circled round the town itself), where Lorraine spent the night of the 2nd. Both then ascended the winding course of the Leitha. While the Tartars or Turks roamed over the whole stretch of country between the right bank of the river and the Neusiedler See, the Habsburg commanders kept between the Leitha and Danube, and headed for Kittsee and Pressburg again. They camped for two more nights in the plain at Deutsch-Jahrndorf, waiting and hoping for the situation to clear. At first the reports from Györ suggested that Kara Mustafa was settling down to besiege the place, while Lorraine hoped to recover the district round the Neusiedler See by sending off 800 horse under Colonel Heisler in that direction. Unfortunately, news then came through that large numbers of Turkish infantry were crossing the Rába, and at the same time Lorraine heard from Leslie, who announced that he intended to withdraw westwards with all the infantry under his command unless he was given distinct orders to the contrary by 4 July. Such a step appeared to mean leaving Györ to its fate, and the message was only received at headquarters on 4 July. Too late, Lorraine replied that Leslie must stay on the Schütt. Happily Leslie took no notice and began to retreat.

Lorraine rode ahead to Kittsee for a conference with the vice-president of the War Council, Caplirs, and on the 6th most of the cavalry camped round Berg. Here the plain ends, the ground rises abruptly some thousand feet.

Pressburg and the Danube lie a little way off on one side, and on the other the Leitha winds out of the Leitha hills into the plain. Lorraine was back in the landscape made familiar to many of his soldiers and officers by the rendezvous five weeks earlier; with this difference, remarked by everyone, that dust and smoke now thickened the air over the plain, dust kicked up by the moving horsemen, smoke from the fired barns and houses. Between the Leitha hills and the sharp outcrop at Berg smoother country continues in the direction of Vienna. It was a relatively narrow passage through which any sizeable invading force would have to pass, and Lorraine hoped to control it.

At the same time there was talk of building new bridges just below Pressburg. When it became clear that Leslie had definitely begun to draw back across the Schütt, the command planned to bring his infantry over these bridges across the Danube again, in this way re-assembling the entire field-army for the defence of the area between the Leitha and Danube. It seemed possible, and it was certainly essential, to hold up the advanced units of the enemy at Berg. If his main armament moved forward, it too would have to be resisted at this point but Lorraine hoped that Kara Mustafa himself – engaged on the siege of Györ – would not push beyond the Leitha: at Ungarisch-Altenburg Habsburg detachments still guarded the bridge and the fords across it, together with large magazines of food and munitions. Much farther off, Györ was momentarily isolated. Across the Leitha and towards the Neusiedler See, an area of lesser strategic importance, the situation meanwhile looked completely out of control. Neither Leopold's government nor his armies had any power to check the frightful course of devastation there, in the countryside once quietly ruled over by Esterházy and his peers.

II

At nine o'clock, on the morning of 7 July the whole position changed with appalling suddenness.[17] Lorraine was riding a mile or two from his headquarters when he heard that the Turks had entered Ungarisch-Altenburg in great force. The surprise was so complete that the defenders were unable to destroy the bridge and it looked as if the Grand Vezir had thrown into the campaign another 25,000 or 30,000 disciplined men, of whom the van was coming up fast, in order to attack the much smaller Habsburg concentration of cavalry and dragoons round Berg. These would be overwhelmed, allowing the enemy to strike deeply into Austria in the direction of Vienna itself. But while Lorraine and his staff discussed the new crisis, they saw large clouds of dust rising behind them far off to the west from farther up the Leitha, which suggested ominously that other Turks had already got upstream, having by-passed Leopold's troops. It was a double disaster; and Count Auersperg set out at once to inform the court that all hopes of pinning down the main mass of the Turks in the neighbourhood of either Györ or Berg had abruptly and finally disappeared on that morning of 7 July.

The Habsburg cause fared even worse in the afternoon. Fischamend, a crossing over the small Danube tributary of the Fischa, and half-way between Berg and Vienna, was the point to which Lorraine next directed his forces; they were divided into the regiments under his own command, a rearguard under Rabatta and Taafe,* and a van led by Mercy and Gondola. Ahead of the van went escorts with carts and carriages of equipment, while still farther in front were other transports containing the baggage of certain senior officers who apparently preferred to run the risk of sending their own goods forward, unprotected, as quickly as possible. Unfortunately for them, the Tartars suddenly fell on this part of the long and straggling train. Mercy and Gondola at once hurried up, drove them off and went on to Fischamend, fearing that other enemy bands would reach the fords there first. Lorraine, several miles behind and by now on relatively high ground farther east, was scanning the view and debating how to recover control of the country between his own troops and his van, when he learnt that another Turkish force (from the direction of Ungarisch-Altenburg) was assailing his rearguard. He turned back with all the men and horses he could muster, realising that he had not a minute to spare.

It is impossible to say exactly where the encounter took place, sometimes known as 'the affair of Petronell'. It was probably close to the famous Roman site of Carnuntum in the estate of Count Traun,† on undulating and thickly wooded ground not far from the Danube. The Habsburg cavalry of the rearguard, particularly Montecuccoli's regiment and Savoy's dragoons, was thrown into complete disarray. Lorraine, bringing up more squadrons of horse, at first utterly failed to rekindle the urge to stop and fight back. His pleas and his gestures – he even went for the men by thumping them with the butt of his pistol – effected nothing. 'What, gentlemen,' he is said to have exclaimed, 'you betray the honour of the imperial arms, you're afraid?' The left wing resisted the enemy onrush more steadily, at last a strong counter-attack was mounted and the Turks disappeared again. They were far fewer than their opponents realised, in this sudden and confused mêlée of horse and rider. Perhaps thirty-five lay dead on the field and the total loss of the Habsburg troops was 100 men; but before the engagement had ended one or more officers had left for Vienna, convinced that a very large enemy force was moving irresistibly forward.

The rest of the day passed off quietly and Lorraine spent the night at Schwechat, six miles from Vienna. At least Leopold's cavalry, if not his infantry, had been brought back safely for the defence of the capital city of the

---

*Francis Taafe (1639–1704), later the 3rd Earl of Carlingford in Ireland, was the inseparable servant and counsellor of Lorraine and his family for forty years. He was appointed Colonel of Lorraine's own regiment of cuirassiers in 1677.
† See illustration II.

whole dominion. But a major attack was now inevitable, and cavalry could not man a fortress.

On the next day Lorraine heard that the Turks had left not more than 12,000 troops at their camp in front of Győr. The rest were marching forward. He learnt that nearly all the Magyars in western Hungary had recognised Thököly's sovereignty. Thököly himself was at Trnava with his followers, which implied a distinct threat to Pressburg and to Vienna from the area north of the Danube. Fortunately Leslie and his infantry were already well on their way back through the Schütt to Pressburg, and Schultz had independently decided to withdraw his men westwards as quickly as possible even before he received orders to do so. In spite of these two items of good news, for Lorraine it had been twenty-four hours of repeated crises, and he was still unaware of their impact in Vienna itself.

One feature of this confusing week was the nervous response of the military command to the appearance of small hostile bands of horsemen, and to the fire and smoke perplexing its view of events in that wide plain. The civilian population reacted more sluggishly. True, many peasants were by now on the move, carrying their goods towards the walled towns or into the shelter of any buildings surrounded by walls, like the manor-houses of lords and monasteries, while the harvest stood ready in the fields but they were afraid to go out and reap it. Yet contrary rumours, that all was well, often stopped bolder folk from fearing the worst and they carried on with business as usual. We know something of wavering public opinion in the area from a journal kept by the choirmaster of Heiligenkreuz, the great and ancient Cistercian house in the Wiener Wald. [18] On 3 July a priest came into the monastery from the monks' parish of Podersdorf, by the shore of the Neusiedler See. He reported that the enemy was at hand, and was laughed at for his pains. His listeners believed that the Turks were in fact at Neuhäusel, a long way over on the other side of the Danube, and that the thick clouds of smoke on the eastern horizon resulted from the ordinary indiscipline of Leopold's own troops in Hungary. The opinion of these scoffers was partly based on the confident messages of a bailiff in charge of the monastic lands (particularly the quarries) near Bruck-on-the-Leitha; but a little later the Turks captured this man, they surrounded Bruck, and the stone-cutters with their families fled to Vienna. Meanwhile tension mounted in Heiligenkreuz. On 4, 5 and 6 July more and more refugees, with their belongings, crowded into the three great courtyards of the abbey. Onlookers were amazed by the mountain of chests, which held silverware and other valuables, in the inner court. Prosperous burghers hastened up the narrow valley from Baden and Mödling.* On 7 July a soothing, ill-informed message reached the chapter from the Spanish embassy in Vienna. Then on the 8th the blow fell, with authentic news of what had happened near Petronell and of panic in Vienna.

---

*For Heligenkreuz, Baden and Mödling, see the map p. 112.

The choirmaster hurriedly prepared to take his young choristers over the hills westwards.

As June had worn on, bringing no message of a Habsburg triumph against Esztergom or Neuhäusel, and gloomy reports of the Turkish advance through Hungary, popular fears increased in Vienna itself. An unceasing round of public religious ceremonies intensified them. By decree, the members of every trade and profession were required to attend for one hour a week at the service in St Stephen's: the Emperor himself took his turn at nine o'clock on Sundays, the Danube fishermen on Thursdays at eight, and the violin-makers on Saturdays at three. By decree also, the old usage was revived of the 'Türkenglocken'. Bells started to ring every morning through the city and the whole land of Austria, summoning all to kneel and pray for deliverance from the invader.[19] Some of the popular preachers thundered that God chose the Moslem terror to punish, when punishment was needed; but Abraham a Sancta Clara himself preferred the great refrain which was the title of his booklet just then going through the press: 'Up! Up! You Christians!' calling simply for courage and action against a brutal but cowardly enemy.[20] The entire week from 27 June to 3 July was organised by the ecclesiastical authorities as one immense petition for divine intervention. Yet if most men were devout, a few abused the clerical interest. If there were politicians who disliked the Pope, the nuncio and their allies for insisting on the Turkish peril and consequently on the need to give ground in western Europe, there were citizens who blamed the crisis on the church for persecuting uselessly in Hungary. One night they smashed the windows of the Bishop of Vienna's palace in the Rotenturmstrasse; though, ironically, the bishop was no friend of the nuncio.

Throughout 5 and 6 July officials at court worked long and hard. The conference of ministers, War Council, Treasury, and Government of Lower Austria, were all in session. First Philip Thurn was sent post-haste to Warsaw to ask for Sobieski's full support, now that the Turks appeared to be threatening Austria directly. Next, they tried to control the growing movement of refugees from the countryside into the city. They had strong guards set at the gates, to bar the entry of rabble elements which conceivably included traitors; the presence of Thököly's agents in disguise was suspected, and also Frenchmen. Supplies were discussed, and the official responsible for the purchase of corn happily stated that stocks were high. At a meeting in the Bishop's palace the clergy offered a loan to the government, but the tightness of funds still bedevilled administration as much as ever. The War Council and Treasury blandly decided to reduce their earlier estimate of military expenditure for the coming year from three million to two and a half million florins, a sleight of hand which could hardly have helped them to find the money they needed at once.

Stratmann, the new chancellor – Hocher had just died – went off to report to the Emperor on all these pressing items of business.

One point which worried the Habsburg advisers was the security of the

Crown of St Stephen of Hungary.[21] This highly important symbol of the royal authority in that country was always in safe-keeping in the castle of Pressburg; two of the most senior office-holders in Hungary were 'Guardians of the Crown'. The political consequences, if Thököly laid hands on it, would be serious indeed. At length Leopold decided to remove the insignia of Hungarian royalty from Pressburg to Vienna. A strong escort of cavalry rode off and brought the crown to the Hofburg on 5 July. On the same day Leopold also determined to authorise preparations for the departure of his children and their staff from Vienna, while by the 7th the valuables of his Treasury – jewels, crowns (including the Crown of Hungary), sceptres, crosses and the like – were packed away on transports, ready to leave the city. There was no specific decision about the Emperor's own departure. On the other hand, while refugees were pouring in from the east, many of the burghers and officials with their families had already left the city.

On 6 July Leopold went hunting near Mödling. He gave no sign that he contemplated flight to the safer and more distant part of his dominion, and one argument which kept the court in Vienna was certainly the Empress's advanced pregnancy. Physicians did not consider it wise for her to travel. But women of her household had letters from their husbands, officers serving under Lorraine on his retreat from Györ, who begged them to flee as quickly as possible. Buonvisi's account of a conversation with the Empress suggests that she herself was eager to go. The Emperor still demurred. He can hardly have failed to realise the consequences of the court's departure on the morale of his subjects.

From two o'clock onwards in the afternoon of 7 July, one messenger after another reached the Hofburg and transformed the situation.[22] The first, Auersperg, reported the attack on Ungarisch-Altenburg, which was enough to make most courtiers press the Emperor to leave at once. In Leopold's ante-chamber Auersperg and the counsellors were soon joined by General Caprara and Colonel Montecuccoli, telling of the Turks' sudden appearance in great strength much closer to the city, probably because they themselves had left the scene of the fighting between Petronell and Fischamend before Lorraine restored order, and anticipated his total defeat. Then Caprara's servant, in charge of his baggage, arrived to give an account of that sudden assault on the baggage-train, at a point even closer to Vienna. The counsellors conferred and their long debate went on, while at the city-gates townsmen and incoming strangers – some of them wounded – repeated rumours based on such things as smoke seen, or shots heard, on that day and on the day before. All these persons, Auersperg, Montecuccoli, Caprara, Caprara's servant, and the men who simply talked to other men, helped to spread the panic which seized the Emperor, his ministers, his courtiers, everyone in the palace, everyone in the Burgplatz outside and in the now crowded streets which led from here to the rest of the city. 'The Turk is at the gates!' was the cry; and though we know that each report of the day's fighting had been inaccurate, the worst fears of most people then were confirmed by the cumulative effect of so many messages and rumours. All who could prepared to quit the city immediately. The Emperor, his nerves overbearing his sense of dignity, listening to the pleas of his ministers and family, decided to sanction his own retreat from what looked like the point of maximum danger, Vienna itself.

He held a final conference at six o'clock in his private apartment. The decision to go at once was formally announced and it remained to choose the route to follow. The direct road to Linz over the Wiener Wald was proposed and rejected; the Turks would threaten it too quickly. Flight northwards to Prague, or south-west into the hilly country by Heiligenkreuz and so round to Linz, was considered. The counsellors at length advised the Emperor to cross the Danube, and then to move upstream along the farther bank towards Upper Austria.

The bustle and confusion in the Burg and the Burgplatz were by this time tremendous. The doors of the palace were left wide open, and every kind of wagon and cart or coach was being crammed with every kind of necessity and valuable which could be moved. The less fortunate, who owned or who could find no horses, made ready to walk. In the town the government tried to get each householder to send a man to work on the fortifications. It tried to requisition all the boats on the river, with their boatmen, and to send them down the Danube in order to meet the infantry regiments marching westwards from the Schütt. The conscripted labourers who had been working in Vienna downed their tools, and fled. Coming the other way population from the outskirts packed into the city as never before, if only to pass the night in the security of the streets. Then, at about eight o'clock in the evening the Emperor left the Hofburg. A not very orderly procession made its way out of the Burg-gate, round the city wall to the Canal, through Leopoldstadt, and over the Danube. Later still the dowager Empress Eleanor, whose staff had hardly recovered from the toil and annoyance of bringing her possessions into the city from the 'Favorita', her palace in Leopoldstadt, set out with a great transport to the west by way of Klosterneuburg on the south side of the river.

Sleep and Vienna were strangers that night. Men and women sorted out their goods, put one part in cellars (the cellars of the city figure conspicuously in the legends of the siege) and one part in packages for their flight to the west. They hammered and corded. Yet several hours after Leopold's departure, a despatch arrived from Lorraine which gave a more consoling picture of the whole position: the Habsburg cavalry was now in good order again, approaching Vienna fast, with the main Turkish force at least some days' march behind it. (This news caught up with Leopold in the course of the night.) Encouraged, at three o'clock in the morning Herman of Baden called a meeting to announce the Emperor's instruction for the government of Vienna in the immediate future. Present were the burgomaster Liebenberg, the syndic, and other municipal councillors; also Daun the acting military commander, and Colonel Serenyi, an old and very senior officer who was in the city more by chance than because of any proper posting. Baden gave notice that Starhemberg had been given the supreme command.[23] Administration was placed in the hands of a *Collegium* – a select committee of two soldiers (Caplirs, the experienced vice-president of the Habsburg War Council, and Starhemberg) and three civilians (the Marshal of the Estates of Lower Austria, an official of the Government of Lower Austria, and Belchamps of the Treasury). Caplirs was to preside over it. Baden also declared that a section of the War Council would be left behind in the city to handle ordinary military business; and Caplirs would direct it. The municipality was to cooperate with Starhemberg, the *Collegium* and War Council in all matters. Supplies were sufficient to stand a siege. In response, the burgomaster solemnly promised to do his best. But neither Starhemberg nor Caplirs had as yet reached Vienna, and in these dark minutes of the early morning no one could visualise clearly how these arrangements would work in practice.

In fact, confirmed and elaborated by a message from Leopold some days later,[24] they effectively met the emergency of the next three months. They gave the military the necessary powers, but permitted some civilians to share in the discussion of urgent problems. Even so the municipality of Vienna was not directly represented in the two highest committees responsible for the public safety. Caplirs had to harmonise the different and sometimes conflicting interests civil and military. On the one hand he directed the personnel of the War Council and collaborated with Starhemberg. On the other, he dealt with the burghers, who inevitably tended to find themselves overwhelmed by the emergency, and their rights disregarded. The whole administrative structure, apparently, depended on the coordinating ability of Caplirs in spite of his age and inveterate pessimism. Partly owing to the shortage of good evidence, historians have differed over his merits during the crisis. He certainly returned to Vienna very unwillingly on 10 July, no doubt sighing for his new palace and picture gallery hundreds of miles away in the peaceful woods of northern Bohemia, the most recent rewards of a long and successful career.[25] But he soon set to work; if Starhemberg was much the more militant and forceful character, he grumblingly did his best to help him.

Later in the morning of 8 July the burgomaster held a council of his own. The city fathers had a desperately heavy day in front of them, trying to organise the burghers, many of whom were making every effort to lock up and get out. They wanted to bring into the city a large amount of timber still stacked outside the New-gate; to redistribute the reserves of grain into stores of more equal size; and to arrange for guards at various points. But above all, for the most obvious reasons, an immediate increase in the numbers of men at work on the fortifications was required. While the burgher companies of militia were ordered to assemble at one o'clock outside the town hall, a summons went out to the rest of the male population to attend in the square 'Am Hof' at three o'clock, outside the civic armoury. Here Nicholas Hocke, the syndic, mounted the steps of the building. In a powerful speech he tried to stir up enthusiasm for the good cause, pointing out that ordinary employment would necessarily be interrupted or suspended during the coming crisis. He offered decent wages to all who went to work on the fortifications of the city. Not far off, in the Bishop's palace the Vicar-General was telling the clergy that they also must take their turn at the works. Soon afterwards the sound of drum and trumpet was heard; and Lorraine's cavalry appeared, riding past the city-walls, and over the Canal through Leopoldstadt, to an encampment on the Danube islands. In the evening, both Lorraine and Starhemberg entered Vienna, and almost their first recorded action tightened the pressure on the townsfolk. They threatened the use of force unless sufficient numbers were ready and present for duty, on the defence-works, at four o'clock the next morning.

At dawn the burgomaster himself was there, shouldering a spade. Hocke enrolled the workers. Starhemberg demanded another 500 within twenty-four hours; and more workers were brought in during the day. For almost a week the burghers, the casual labourers, the substitutes paid by burghers who preferred to avoid this strenuous drudgery, the soldiers detailed for the same duty by Starhemberg as they reached the city, and members of the City Guard all made great efforts. In spite of gloomy comments from some experienced observers, they managed to get the bastions, the moat and counterscarp into reasonable condition. At this stage, what was essential were improved earthworks and adequate timbering. By digging hard under competent direction it proved possible to buttress weak patches in the stone revetments of the curtain-wall and the bastions, and to deepen the moat. New palisades now shored up the counterscarp, and a fairly usable 'covered way' along it protected the outermost position which the garrison would have to try and hold. In the moat – separating the counterscarp from the walls and bastions – excavation was still needed. Additional barricades were set up in various parts of it, while at other points new wooden bridges were built to link bastions to ravelins, and ravelins to the counterscarp.

Important conferences were held on 9 and 10 July; Starhemberg and Lorraine elaborated their plans. It was then for Starhemberg to settle details with Breuner of the commissariat and Belchamps of the Treasury. He told the first that soon they could count on a garrison of 10,000 troops, together with the City Guard and the civilian companies; and that they must be ready to face a siege lasting four months. Happily, food was not a difficult problem. The officials of the commissariat confirmed that there were stores of grain in the city large enough to feed a force of this size until November.

On the next day, the 10th, finance was discussed, a much more difficult matter.[26] Starhemberg insisted that the punctual payment of the soldiers throughout the period of siege, and generous treatment of labour squads in the works, were absolutely essential if the Turks were to be resisted with any chance of success; but he was told that only 30,000 florins remained in the military treasury, none of which could be spared for pay. It was calculated that the wages of the troops alone would amount to 40,000 florins a month. But Belchamps had been looking into the question, and was earlier in touch with the Hungarian Bishop of Kalocza, George Széchényi, who had lent a large sum to the government in 1682. In 1683 he brought his funds to Vienna for safe-keeping, and then sought refuge farther west when the Turks advanced, but before leaving the city he agreed to place 61,000 florins at Belchamps's disposal. On 9 July Prince Ferdinand Schwarzenberg, having reached Vienna after Leopold's departure, offered a loan of 50,000 florins and 1,000 measures of wine, which he had in his vaults. He then left the city. His negotiation was not with Belchamps in the first instance, but with his friend Kollonics,[27] the Bishop of Wiener-Neustadt, who was determined to remain behind and fight for Church and Emperor.

A Knight of St John who did not forget the bravery of his youth when he served in Crete, Kollonics felt little sympathy for anyone hesitating to make sacrifices at this critical hour. So, a few days later, he turned his attention to the property of the Primate of Hungary; for the Archbishop of Esztergom, George Szelepcsényi, had brought to his Vienna residence, No. 14 in the Himmelpfortgasse, between 70,000 and 80,000 florins in money, together with ecclesiastical plate, crosses and similar precious objects which were later valued at over 400,000 florins. The Archbishop himself took refuge in Moravia. On 19 and 20 July, after the siege began, the administration impounded his assets. By melting down a part of the treasure, the mint in Vienna solved the purely financial problem for the duration of the siege. It seems probable, although there is no direct evidence to prove the point, that Belchamps knew well enough that a few outstandingly wealthy individuals had deposited money and plate in the city for safekeeping earlier in the year. For various reasons, lack of transport or lack of instructions, these could not be removed fast enough, when it abruptly and unexpectedly became clear that Vienna was not (as it had been, up to date) the surest refuge within hundreds of miles. But the size of these sums belonging to a nobleman like Schwarzenberg, or to clerics like the Hungarian episcopate, when compared with the poverty of the government, is very remarkable.

Money without manpower was useless. Lorraine and Starhemberg had immediately agreed that the infantry regiments marching up the Danube from Pressburg should move at once into Vienna. On 10 July, troops of the vanguard first appeared. More arrived on the following day, and on the 13th the mass of Leslie's command completed their long journey from Györ; the great majority of his infantry regiments were sent over the river with the utmost despatch. Early that day, therefore, Starhemberg commanded 5,000 men. By evening he had some 11,000.[28] The prospects were at least less dismal than the week before, when the Turks were expected to invest or storm a city held by no more than the ghost of a garrison.

Yet the foremost Ottoman raiders now appeared, and in the distance the smoke of burning villages in the neighbourhood rose skywards. Starhemberg did not dare delay in performing one of his most disagreeable duties: the speedy and forcible clearing of the glacis. Since earlier demolition orders had not been obeyed, he began – on 13 July – to burn down everything in the area outside the counterscarp which would obviously hamper the garrison. Most of all he wanted to clear the ground west of the city, where suburbs came closest to the moat. More smoke rose skywards. The sparks flew. They flew over the walls as far as the roof of the Schotten monastery by the Schottengate, where a fire broke out in the afternoon of Wednesday, the 14th; and it almost altered the course of history. The wind blew sparks against the neighbouring buildings, an inn, and from the inn to a wall of the Arsenal, where supplies of every kind were stored, including 1,800 barrels of powder. Nearby, other powder magazines adjoined the New-gate. If the defence-works here were seriously damaged by explosion, or the stores lost, resistance to the Turks was hardly thinkable. The flames moved along a wooden gallery into the Arsenal. Townsmen and soldiers gathered, there was a muddle about keys which could not be found, but soldiers broke through a door and cleared the points of greatest danger. A hysterical mob, looking on, smelt treason at once and lynched two suspects, a poor lunatic and a boy wearing woman's clothes. It also destroyed the baggage which an inoffensive mining official from Hungary, then in Vienna, was trying to get out of a second inn near the Arsenal; and it panicked at the sight of a flag flying unaccountably from a roof close to the fire, fearing some kind of a signal to the enemy. More effectively, the wind then veered. Flames swept towards and into aristocratic properties on the other side, away from the Arsenal, and proceeded to burn out the Auersperg palace where the ruins went on smouldering for days. The crisis had passed before the arrival of the Turks; but the danger of yet more fires, set off by Turkish bombs or by traitors and spies inside the walls, was to be a constant nightmare in Vienna later on.

Starhemberg very properly ordered the municipality to requisition cellars for the storage of powder. It took over a number of crypts or cellars under churches and convents for this purpose.

On the same day, the 14th, Lorraine began pulling his cavalry out of Leopoldstadt and the islands.[29] Breaking down the bridges as they went, they crossed right over the Danube and took up a new position on the north bank. Only the final bridge was left intact, guarded by a small force. Leslie's infantry continued to move into the city. Stores, coming downstream by boat and raft, were still being unloaded by townsmen and units of the garrison.

III

On the evening of 7 July the Emperor had got as far as Korneuburg, nine miles from Vienna. The grandest persons in the realm slept that night on bolsters and rugs taken from their carriages; their attendants meanwhile stood at the gate of the little walled town, on the lookout for fires in the distance. Harrach, the Master of the Stables, on whom a most arduous administrative burden fell in the course of the journey, could only see one, and a long way off. The papal nuncio says that he saw many fires.[30] Harrach, a sober observer, paid more attention to the unfriendliness of the peasants: it seemed that countrymen cursed citydwellers, for squeezing them in normal times and then flying headlong to safety when a crisis broke. Partly for this reason he lamented the absence of a proper military guard. The troop of 200 cavalry which had brought the Hungarian Crown from Pressburg to Vienna was next detailed to accompany the court; but in accordance with instructions given before the afternoon of the 7th, it went first into the Wiener Wald to protect the route originally chosen for the Emperor's children. Cavalry only came up with Leopold, beyond Korneuburg, on the following day.

He spent the next night at Krems, when a report came in that Tartars were on the other side of the river. They threatened the bridge at Stein, a mile away!* This was soon contradicted, so that the carts and wagons of the court's gigantic transport crossed to the south bank of the Danube and straggled on to Melk. The Emperor, still at Krems, gave orders for the despatch of more gunpowder from the stores there to be sent downstream at once.[31] He then began his day's journey, travelling by water to Melk until midnight with the wind and current both against him.

One of our most useful diarists, Justus Passer, the Hesse-Darmstadt envoy at Vienna, had managed somewhat differently.[32] He could not arrange to leave the city before the 8th, and then only on foot. He walked a good way into the Wiener Wald but was later lucky enough to get a lift as far as St Pölten. Here he at last secured horses and rode off to Melk, where he arrived very late on 10 July to find Leopold and the court, with all accommodation taken and most people spending the night in the open, next to their own precious horses and carts. So Passer continued on through darkness and dawn to Neumarkt where the dowager Empress had found quarters, and finally to Enns – after paying money to bands of cavalrymen, who demanded it with menaces. He was now ahead of the Emperor and court, but they soon passed him again and reached Linz first.

Another of our few witnesses had anticipated even Leopold. Pucci, the voluble representative of the Grand Duke of Tuscany, in fact began careful preparations well before that afternoon of panic in Vienna.[33] He got a wagon and horses for the purpose of carrying all his household goods to some place of safety. When the crisis broke, almost everything had to be left behind at the envoy's lodging in the Herrengasse, as many people as possible scrambled into the wagon and he left the city. Arrived safely at Linz, he reported that the court and government intended to fix their headquarters there. The overcrowding

---

*This was the first bridge over the Danube, upstream from Vienna.

was dreadful but it seemed that the Empress, for one, was anxious not to travel farther as her pregnancy advanced.

A few days later (at about noon on the 14th), a frightening rumour swept through the town of Enns that the Tartars were coming up fast. By 2 a.m. next day this news reached Linz, and caused first an alarm and then a hurried departure as panic-struck as the flight from Vienna a week earlier.[34] Some forty craft were commandeered, the court went safely upstream along that perilous stretch of the Danube that coils through the mountains, and arrived at Passau two days later. Pucci and a Danish envoy travelled by land. Justus Passer, coming up behind, discovered that everything and everybody were in complete confusion at Linz. All the richer burghers had left but refugees poured into and through the town. He himself finally hired a boat, it was nearly wrecked above Aschach, and he too got to Passau. Not surprisingly perhaps, he detected a melancholy in the Emperor's features during vespers in St Paul's church on the evening of the 18th; and one of the questions of the hour was whether the court should move still farther up the river, possibly as far as Regensburg. An alternative discussed was a removal to Prague but at the same time there were disturbing rumours of peasant risings in Bohemia.

The manuscripts from Leopold's library in Vienna reached Passau on the 18th, the archives of the Imperial Chancery on the 21st, and the valuables of the treasury (the *Schatzkammer*) on 22 July.[35]

Earlier, the choirmaster of Heiligenkreuz had been in St Pölten.[36] He tells of his difficulties in trying to travel farther west and of his meeting with Jesuits, some disguised, who admitted that their most serious danger was the embittered peasantry. At Melk he saw Leopold on the point of departure for Enns and Linz, and the little Archduke Joseph given the Abbot's blessing in the courtyard of the abbey. The first standards taken from Tartars were being set up in the church. Returning to St Pölten he found his own freedom of movement, and that of many other travellers, strangely affected by the mixture of hearsay and news handed from knot to knot of people. The Tartars were over the Wiener Wald, it was said, and they were trailing the Emperor's treasure which a strong guard was bringing from Krems to Melk. It was therefore too dangerous for civilians to move, because of the Tartars. No, said others, the real risk came from soldiers convoying the treasure. And at the same time the truculence of the peasants appeared as serious an inconvenience as anything else during this intolerable week, in the experience of such as the choirmaster of Heiligenkreuz.

While refugees had been fleeing up the Danube from Vienna, on a course roughly parallel others were in flight from Graz and the lowland towns of Styria up the valley of the Mürz.[37] North of the Mur and Mürz, the miners of Eisenerz mobbed Jesuits. Away in the eastern areas of Styria defence measures were hurried on, beacons were prepared and stockades built; the Hungarian frontier was manned. Because Batthyány had submitted to Thököly, his villages just across that frontier were raided by the Austrians. There were reprisals, devastation, and terror in all this part of the world. For a moment it looked as if Fürstenfeld, a border town of some importance, would fall to the Magyars although an expeditionary force from Carinthia and Carniola later came to the rescue and occupied it. Just as a thin screen of troops under Lorraine's command was to protect Moravia, north of the Danube; so here in the south Wiener-Neustadt held out, and beyond Wiener-Neustadt a few companies and squadrons covered the approaches to Styria. The dragoon regiments of Metternich, Aspremont and Saurau were there. Further support was looked for from Nicholas Erdödi, the Ban of Croatia. All the same, throughout a vast area south of the Danube government had collapsed in mid-July, and the populations were helplessly on the move.

5
The Siege

On the day the choirmaster first came to St Pölten, 100 miles distant to the east Kara Mustafa was in Ungarisch-Altenburg; and his Master of Ceremonies speaks of the dust rising thickly as the troops marched, so that one man could not recognise another.[1]

Three days later the Grand Vezir reconnoitred the ground between Schwechat and Vienna. He made his way first to the Neugebäude, a palace built by the Habsburg emperors on the spot where Sultan Suleiman the Lawgiver was believed to have camped during the siege of 1529. For this reason, and because it faintly imitated the Turkish style of architecture, and overlooked superb gardens with clipped alleys, with aviaries orchards and a menagerie, Turkish travellers in the past had greatly admired the palace.[2] Kara Mustafa may have wished to show his respect for that mighty predecessor whose venture against Vienna he hoped to surpass, but he also quite certainly regarded the building as a prize worth protection. There could be no question of sacking or despoiling it; and a strong guard was put there. He enjoyed his siesta, he rode forward to look at the city ahead, and then returned to Schwechat. But he was not a wise commander and it was already clear that he was unable to control his forces. The same day, and only a few miles off to the right, Fischamend on the shore of the Danube was raided and, according to the Master of Ceremonies large stocks of timber were utterly destroyed: but a siege of the kind which Kara Mustafa had in mind required timber for the galleries and trenches of the miners.

On the next day, Wednesday 14 July, he moved forward to the slopes which look down towards the city from the south; the valley of the Wien was immediately in front and farther back were all the other features of military significance – the Canal, the Danube, the hills of the Wiener Wald behind the city, and the contours around the suburbs.* Here he called his council. Obviously, his lieutenants and engineers had been making their plans, and the

---

*See illustrations IX and XI.

time had come to settle finally and formally the dispositions for an assault on Vienna. They were based on a conviction (which appeared to justify the whole general strategy of an attack), that the fortifications could be breached in the sector adjoining Leopold's palace, the Hofburg.[3] Here the Wien curved away from the walls. From the higher ground on its left bank there was a fairly gentle gradient down to the glacis and counterscarp; the drainage appeared good; and from this point the approaches could conveniently be dug. Kara Mustafa had been told all this before. Now he was able to see for himself the force of the proposal. Even while he stood viewing the scene, the enemy tried frantically to destroy the buildings and garden-walls of the suburb, where they came closest to the bastions opposite the Hofburg; but the chances of exploiting so favourable a site remained very high. Moreover, the arguments against any other course of action were strong. If he made his approaches opposite the eastern wall of Vienna, they would have to begin close to the waters of the Wien, which would be likely to seep into them; if it rained hard, mining in this area would prove impossible. Farther round, the terrain favoured diggers and miners, and the rising ground at the back provided a good site for artillery. Engineers and gunners here had a chance of combining and concentrating their power to the best advantage.

Without hesitation the Grand Vezir instructed the main force of his army to camp on the other side of the Wien, between the villages of Gumpendorf and Hernals. Many detachments were sent further, to settle along a broad band of ground (as far as the village of Döbling), in this way circling round the city west and north. Other troops would be stationed in the suburb of Rossau,[4] adjoining the canal and relatively close to the city defences.* The pasha of Timisoara commanded his contingents here, together with Janissaries, with units from Anatolia and a whole miscellany of remote Ottoman provinces.[5] A smaller if still formidable, division stayed on the right wing, east and south-east of Vienna, at St Marx and elsewhere.† The Viennese observed with dreadful anxiety their opponents' swarm of tents, now being placed in a grand if irregular crescent which gave an appalling, exaggerated idea of the total force of effective fighting men encamped around them.[6]

Kara Mustafa sent in a summons to surrender, framed in accordance with the customary Ottoman demand on such an occasion.[7] A Turkish officer rode up to the counterscarp with a document, handed it to a Croat soldier and awaited a reply. 'Accept Islam, and live in peace under the Sultan! Or deliver up the fortress, and live in peace under the Sultan as Christians; and if any man prefer, let him depart peaceably, taking his goods with him! But if you

---

*These villages and suburbs are named or numbered in illustration IX. Beyond Gumpendorf the ceremonial tents of the three headquarters in the Ottoman encampment are conspicuous, and the suburb of St Ulrich lies in front of them. The houses of Rossau surround no. 26
†See illustrations VII and IX.

resist, then death or spoliation or slavery shall be the fate of you all!' Such, embroidered in rhetorical language, was the message. But Starhemberg curtly dismissed the messenger and continued to wall up the gates. Kara Mustafa, says the Master of Ceremonies, bade the guns speak.

The defenders were now compelled to reckon with a whole set of possibilities: an immediate general attack, feint assaults at certain points combined with real attacks on others; or a gradual and systematic destruction of the defence-works. But the enemy's preparations soon gave away clues which became progressively easier to interpret.

On that first day the Turkish command, bringing up quantities of men and a tremendous train of baggage, horses, camels, guns and equipment of every kind, seemed occupied in building a new city of their own. Only a few roving detachments ventured close to old Vienna, to be smartly repulsed. The focus of Turkish activity lay south of the Burg. Well to the rear, the Grand Vezir's tents were placed, and accommodation was prepared for treasury, chancery and offices of justice. The stores accumulated. Large forces were close at hand, and grouped into three divisions; to each was assigned a frontage for their approach to the city, in an area which lay on both sides of the road leading from the village of St Ulrich to the Burg-gate. This road sloped gently down, and then crossed the glacis to the counterscarp. At intervals there were walls and buildings still standing, also walled pleasure-gardens, and among them a building named the Rotenhof next a garden which belonged to Count Trautson. Here Kara Mustafa put his own forward base, within gunshot – about 450 paces – of the walls of the city. The Turks were delighted by the shelter to be found in so advanced a position. One of them believed that there was no precedent, in the long and glorious history of the Ottoman empire, for a siege in which the soldiers of Allah could actually ride under cover in this way as far as the points of entry into the trenches.[8]

In this advanced position, Kara Mustafa naturally assigned himself the place of honour in the centre; he was to be assisted by the Aga and Prefect of the Janissaries with the troops under their command, and by the *beylerbeyi* of Rumelia with his. On the right he put the pashas of Diyarbakir and Anatolia with Asiatic contingents, and some more Janissaries. He gave the command of the left to the pashas of Jenö and Sivas, led by the Vezir Ahmed. On the same day, Wednesday the 14th, he himself crossed over the Wien to his ceremonial tent in the main camp; and during the night the troops of the centre, right and left, began digging their approaches towards the fortifications of the city. The centre faced the projecting angle of the counterscarp opposite the Burg-ravelin; the right wing of the Turkish position around St Ulrich faced the Burg-bastion; their left faced the Löbel-bastion. Early next morning batteries started firing from the height immediately behind them.

Leopold's envoy Kuniz and his band of interpreters, after their long journey from Istanbul, found themselves assigned a pitch only a few hundred yards from St Ulrich. They would soon be scheming to get into touch with the garrison, not much farther off. Serban Cantacuzene, Prince of Wallachia, took up his quarters in the neighbourhood of Schönbrunn. Our poor friend Marsigli, who had been captured by Tartars and sold by them to Vezir Ahmed, was now a cook-boy and drudge at Hernals.

The defenders continued to palisade the counterscarp. Now that Starhemberg understood the enemy's tactic he had his own artillery moved into position, with the strongest concentration of pieces near the Hofburg. Other matters absorbed the councillors assembled in the town hall. The number of strangers in the city still frightened them, the scare of the Schotten fire suggested that traitors were at large: they wanted a complete census of the population household by household. The storage of the ammunition had not yet been settled. Next, they tried to decide how to use their manpower, and allocated 800 men to the burgher companies under arms, 120 to the watch, 180 to duties on the Dominican-bastion,[9] and another 180 to assist their Junior Treasurer George Altschaffer in his multifarious duties. His office was indeed the chief executive agent of the city councillors. As the siege continued, both they and Starhemberg used it unsparingly for a miscellany of civilian and semi-military chores.[10]

During the day a fragment of brick or stone, dislodged by an enemy shot on the Löbel-bastion, hit Starhemberg on the head but he soon returned to work.

After dark the garrison tried its first sortie. The men were frightened, some turned back without leaving the shelter of the counterscarp although the others pushed forward. Casualties were few and the experiment was not discouraging, with a certain amount of damage done to the enemy works. It was therefore repeated more confidently twenty-four hours later. Nevertheless, by the morning of the 16th the Turks had already advanced so fast that they were only 200 paces from the salient angles of the counterscarp. Fortunately the preparations to resist them were also nearly complete. The Burg-gate, adjoining one side of the bastion, was being dismantled and the timber removed. A gallows was put up, as a warning to lawbreakers at a time of siege. The re-storage of powder continued. A new mill to make it was started in the moat itself. On the whole the defenders began to settle down, although depressed by the speed and scale of Turkish activity.

They had good reasons for their fears. Kara Mustafa began to carry out his next great move, a total encirclement of the city.[11] He went himself to survey the whole position, first from a point somewhere on the lower slopes of the Wiener Wald, and then from a suburb nearer the walls. He gave fresh orders to Hussein of Damascus, and to the Princes of Wallachia and Moldavia. In consequence, a strong force crossed the shallow waters of the Canal into Leopoldstadt and the islands. They drove back Lorraine's rearguard under Schultz, which retreated towards the last of the Danube bridges. The Turks fired the buildings in Leopoldstadt and took up new positions in order to face Vienna from this side. Shortly afterwards they built bridges of their own, above and below the city's fortifications, to connect Leopoldstadt with the right bank of the river; they constructed various batteries and breastworks opposite the north wall held by Starhemberg's men.* As a result, when the defenders had dismantled the bridge which in normal times linked the city and the suburb, Vienna was completely cut off and surrounded. Supplies coming downstream were barred by the Turkish bridge crossing the Canal to Rossau. A bombardment at close quarters from the north was inescapable. If they wished, the Turks could try an assault from this side while pressing towards the Hofburg from the south at the same time. It had also to be considered that if Thököly ever came up along the farther bank of the Danube, he would find it easier to reinforce the Turks for any action against the city; while the Turks could then assist him against Lorraine's troops. A minor consolation for Starhemberg was that the ground rises fairly sharply from the bank of the Canal towards the centre of the town (as the Romans had noted centuries earlier, when they settled here), which made any attack from the north more difficult. Indeed, Kara Mustafa had already committed his main force to the approach from St Ulrich to the Burg; and throughout the siege the Turks never in fact tried to feint, or to mask their plans. The Grand Vezir was a bold and thoroughly unimaginative commander. As time passed Starhemberg must have realised this weakness in his opponent.

Kara Mustafa, on the Saturday, was able to visit Leopoldstadt. He siesta'd amid the ruined splendours of a Habsburg residence, the Favorita, and returned over the new bridge to Rossau. With the total encirclement of Vienna, the Turks were jubilant. They already spoke of a 'final victory' as something in the hollow of their hands. They felt the rhythm of their own triumphant advance; the batteries fired, the working-parties pushed forward the trenches and galleries, the guards took turn and turn about; while the musicians of the Grand Vezir, of the Aga of the Janissaries, and of all the pashas, began to play at every sunset and dawn.

Indeed the rhythm of a routine was quickly imposed on assailants and defenders alike, to be repeated daily for a week, until 22 July. It was felt in all the sectors into which the siege divided: behind the Turkish approaches, in the approaches themselves, along the counterscarp and moat and walls held by the garrison, behind the walls and in the streets of the city, and finally in Leopoldstadt. It affected somewhat less the Turkish detachment and the cavalry regiments of Lorraine which faced one another, at a considerable distance from Vienna, across the main stream of the Danube. Each of the sectors deserve attention, in order to grasp the complexity as well as the general pattern of these grim proceedings.

The initiative stemmed from Kara Mustafa. His headquarters were those splendid tents erected in the centre of the main Turkish encampment, and here

---

*The Leopoldstadt suburb is visible in illustration IX, between the Canal and one of the main channels of the Danube.

he lived in ostentatious luxury. He gave formal audiences, to the envoys of the Magyar lords Batthyány and Draskovich on 15 July,* or to the Aga who came direct from the Sultan on the 19th. Here also he honoured men with the robes which signified promotion in the Ottoman empire. Close by were the other centres of administration, judicial and financial. But of greater immediate significance was Kara Mustafa's forward base, in the Trautson garden. It was set up in the shelter of the garden wall, a timber structure strengthened with sandbags. A little farther forward a hole was knocked through the wall, giving the Grand Vezir direct access to the trenches. As the days passed it seems as if more and more of his personal equipment was brought from the camp to the garden. From here he made his periodical tours of inspection in the Turkish trenches.

Christian surveyors who later examined the site gave unreserved praise to the layout and construction of these siege-works.[12] They found that, with all its appearance of bewildering elaboration, the system of approaches and parallels was admirably suited to the ground. Approaches led more or less directly across the glacis towards the three salient angles of the counterscarp in front of the Burg-bastion, the Burg-ravelin and the Löbel-bastion.† The Turks naturally describe the force aiming at the Burgbastion as their right flank; and here the approach began from the so-called Rakovitsch garden and was duplicated on each side, half-way along its course, by other trenches which proceeded in the same general direction. Parallels were thrown out to the left and right; on the extreme right, they were connected once more by another approach. This was one wing of the main Turkish front. Its parallels were linked with the system of approaches, even more elaborate, in the centre of the whole position. Here three main avenues, one of them coming direct from Kara Mustafa's entrance by the Trautson garden, converged towards that part of the counterscarp opposite the Burg-ravelin. They were linked by a similar dense series of parallels, which extended towards the approaches on the left wing. One of the latter likewise began its course by branching off from Kara Mustafa's main access to the central network; then, having gained sufficient ground to the left, it turned direct to the Löbel-bastion. Two more approaches followed the same course; one was the route which connected the parallels at their farthest extension on the left.

In the construction of this astonishing warren the Turks complained of the stoniness of the soil, but the corps of labourers worked (or were forced to work) extraordinarily well. They dug deep, and were therefore protected by high entrenchments as well as by the timber roofing inserted at many points. Much larger spaces were hollowed out at intervals in order to accommodate large bodies of troops. Batteries were installed and, when the system was

---

*An important point connected with the submission of Batthyány and Draskovich was that they undertook to send large stocks of provisions from their lands to the besieging army at Vienna.
† see illustration VII

complete, more guns and timber and ammunition were brought right forward
to the edge of the counterscarp. Sorties of the garrison were not only
hampered by the soft earth thrown up in digging the trenches, but by the
soldiers in the parallels, who protected the labourers as they pushed forward
the various approaches.

An important but less effective part of the offensive was the artillery. It had
started firing from the slopes behind the Trautson garden. Batteries were then
mounted farther down and to the right, very near to where the approaches to
the Burg-bastion began; then, below the Trautson gardens by the Rotenhof, as
well as away to the left; then, closer and closer to the city. A cannonade was
kept up intermittently throughout the siege, though it was apt to be silenced
by rain. Its main defects, judged by the best standards of the period, were the
lightness of the calibre and the poor quality of ammunition. There can be
no reasonable doubt that Turkish artillery of the seventeenth century could
not damage the stronger fortresses of Christian Europe with sufficient severity
or speed. It has been suggested that the Ottoman officers did not bring their
heaviest pieces with them, because the Sultan had originally agreed to have
Győr besieged, or possibly Komárom, but not Vienna. More probably they
never dreamt of transporting guns of the largest size across the Balkans, while
they lacked the resources or expertise to have them manufactured at Buda,
the obvious advanced base for all supplies. (From Buda, they actually received
much of their very unsatisfactory gunpowder.) Turkish authorities distinguish
between weapons of middle and heavy calibre, throwing balls from ten to forty
okka[13] in weight, and those of light to medium throwing balls between three
and nine *okka*. Others were still lighter. At Vienna Kara Mustafa apparently
had none of the heaviest type, reckoned essential for the effective battering
of properly built defence-works from a reasonable distance; he had to use
seventeen of the medium weights, and ninety-five lighter cannon. There were
also no mortars available. In fact his artillery could slaughter men, but do no
more than dint the fortifications. In spite of this the Ottoman commanders
were convinced that the trench and the mine were the fundamental siege-
weapons; gunfire was an auxiliary. For them, this had been the lesson taught
by their ultimate success in taking Candia in Crete, in 1669.

The transformation of the glacis by a network of tunnels and trenches, the
Turkish battle-front, had its counterpart in the defences of their opponents.[14]
If it was earlier hoped to obstruct the Turks by burning down the suburbs and
clearing the glacis, and this had failed because nothing seemed to halt their
progress forward from St Ulrich, it became the more essential to convert the
great moat into the most formidable barrier that men could contrive. First of
all the Habsburg engineers turned their attention to the counterscarp again,
reinforcing it with iron spikes, and with timber baulks set crosswise. At the
salients, entrenchments were thrown up behind the area created by the angle,
converting these vulnerable points into stockades of peculiar strength. The
covered way along the counterscarp was sealed off into sections by building

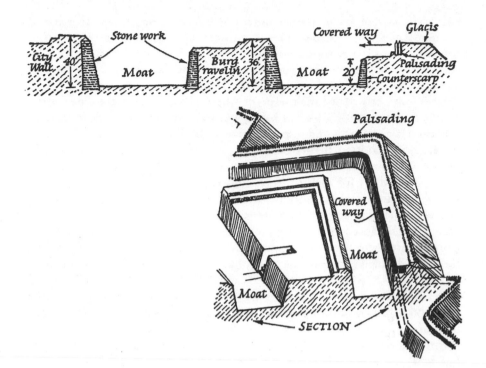

walls across it at intervals so that the attacker would be forced to take them one by one, after prolonged resistance in each. Behind this line of defence, and at a lower level, Starhemberg began to complicate the hazards on the floor of the moat. George Rimpler was his chief technical adviser here. More entrenchments were made, to connect the ravelins with the flanks of the bastions; half-way along such entrenchments block-houses were set up, projecting slightly forward, to enable their fire to command the ground in front of the ravelins. These defences were the so-called 'caponnières' of contemporary writings on this abstruse but practical subject. The engineers also paid particular attention to the Burg-ravelin itself, which faced the centre of the Turkish advance. Inside its walls more trenches were dug, and ramparts thrown up; the covered way connecting the ravelin with the main city-wall was strongly palisaded. One flaw in the original design of this ravelin worried the experts, but at this late stage it could hardly be remedied: a plinth projecting from the base of its outside wall, intended to prevent falling stone or earth from filling up the ditch, was too high and blocked a clear view of what might be going on at the foot of the wall. It proved a godsend to the miners of the enemy later on.

Lastly Starhemberg looked at the two bastions; he had to anticipate that these would in due course be exposed to powerful Turkish attacks.*

---

*see illustration VI.

His advisers were fairly satisfied with the Burg-bastion, except that it was ill-equipped with casemates for the purpose of counter-mining, and they contented themselves with throwing up inner works in the usual form of entrenchments and traverses. The Burg-gate was blocked. Then, along the foot of the curtain-wall running towards the Löbel-bastion, a secondary line of defence was constructed; at the point where it approached the Löbel itself an additional piece of work was hastily put in hand. This was an improvised extension of that bastion, designed to give more elbow-room to the defenders there, and to shorten the length of the curtain-wall, making this easier to protect. Even with these alterations there was still wretchedly little space on the Löbel-bastion for men or guns; and the lofty bulwark capping it, the 'Katze', remained very exposed to Turkish fire.

The defence was able to concentrate on this stretch between the Burg and the Löbel, because the enemy never made any serious attempt to test the garrison elsewhere. In a single 'watch' on 9 August (the only date for which there is a detailed list), out of a total of 2,193 officers and men at the twenty-two guard-posts round the city, over 1,000 held the line between Burg and Löbel.[15] Old maps show that elsewhere the counterscarp was reinforced by new works thrown out towards the glacis, but they seem never to have been used or needed. On the other hand, detachments of the garrison tried on 18 July to bring into the town some of the wood stacked outside the New-gate, but were not successful. The Turks, taking cover in the ruined buildings of Rossau immediately opposite, shot down the men who sallied out from the counterscarp.

While the ring of fortifications buzzed with activity, inside Vienna the civilian world struggled to survive under conditions of siege.[16] If the schools had closed, the churches soon opened again. Stocks of food were still ample, and prices steady. The flurry of excitement which had first called out the burgher-guards and companies recruited from the artisans, died down when the siege began to follow an orthodox course. The garrison of Lorraine's infantry was large enough to hold the defences; neither the fighting, nor the spread of illness among the troops, had yet taken such toll that Starhemberg was compelled to use untrained auxiliaries, except at a few points of little importance. The civil administration was gradually being pulled into shape by the commander himself, by Caplirs and burgomaster Liebenberg. A number of useful measures were agreed, and to some extent carried out. Fire-brigades, when incendiary bombs began to fall in quantity, began to do their work admirably; they arrived promptly when a stable caught alight near the Löbel on 19 July and though a quantity of straw blazed away little damage was done. Persistent official pressure now forced all householders to provide themselves with buckets, barrels or skins, kept filled with water; and they had to dismantle roofs made of shingles, in order to lessen the risks of fire. But there were fires, and more companies of fire-fighters were formed to deal with them. Other instructions dealt with the scouring of the streets, the removal of refuse and of dead animals; while paving-stones were dug up, partly for the reason that Turkish shot did least damage if it fell on soft earth, partly because more stone was needed on the fortifications. At the same time timber was taken from damaged buildings. Long lengths made extra palisades and baulks for the works. Smaller pieces increased the supply of firewood, or were dipped in tar for flares to illumine the moat and counterscarp at night, so that the enemy could not creep forward under cover of darkness. In addition the municipal authority organised the inspection of all properties, for a variety of reasons. It wanted to draw up a schedule of the total supply of straw in the town, because the wounded soldiers and civilians needed straw. It wanted all the fodder available, for the horses which were essential for the transport of supplies from one area to another. It wanted a census, to identify idlers and suspects. It again wanted full information about cellars for storage, and empty premises for the accommodation of the sick. Individual members of the inner council of the burghers were charged with these assignments, while the tight little municipal bureaucracy of inspectors and tax-collectors found themselves busy on novel and unfamiliar work.

Some problems were almost insuperable. The administration could not easily get rid of garbage, or even find sufficient burial-grounds for the dead. The Turks cut the conduits of fresh water leading into the city. In spite of orders and plans the growing number of sick and wounded caused terrible hardships, and the apothecaries and the nursing nuns and the City Hospital itself were unable to deal with the casualties of the siege. One strong man did his best to come to the rescue: Kollonics. This churchman had solved the financial problem by putting pressure on the clergy, as we have seen. In the sphere of hospital and medical organisation, he likewise swept aside clerical immunities which in any way hampered the arrangements which he sponsored for the treatment of the sick. He allotted accommodation in different religious houses to the sick or wounded of various units of the garrison, and to the civil population. He called in the help of all the physicians whom he could find in Vienna to assist the regimental doctors. He did in fact improve the medical services, in his own way strengthening the will to resist in the more critical weeks ahead.

The completeness of the siege gradually increased. On two consecutive nights, early on, detachments of the garrison sallied out from the walls. The first, a troop of 80 men, was severely handled by the left wing of the opposing army. The second, of 500, was the last of its kind for many weeks. The main purpose of such raids had been to smash the approaches to the counterscarp, but it was found that these were too well protected by Turkish infantry in the parallels. Cattle raids were of course a different matter; they occurred on a number of occasions, sometimes with official consent. In addition, on 23 July Starhemberg warned the municipality that women were going out of the town to barter their bread with the Turks in exchange for vegetables: too many persons, he said, were climbing across the fortifications. He viewed this with great suspicion, because security was in fact more important than the food supply. Not only by the enemy, therefore, but by a grimmer consideration of their own interests, the Viennese were barred in. The troops on duty had instructions to fire at all trespassers on sight. Even so, private forays by a few who knew the ground must have continued, men scrambling at night along ruined boundary walls to caches of supplies still buried and hidden in the burnt-out suburbs. These would be the routes followed by Starhemberg's messengers sent out to Leopold and Lorraine later on.

Life was intensely uncomfortable everywhere in Vienna, especially in the quarter bordering the Canal at the commencement of the siege. The enemy guns fired furiously from Leopoldstadt; houses and churches facing them were badly damaged. It was decided to wall up the windows in the neighbourhood of the Rotenturn, the city gate, and Starhemberg placed a heavier armament on the adjoining bastion, which replied very effectively to the Turks. He and his colleagues believed that any embarrasments in this quarter were annoying but not dangerous, so long as Kara Mustafa refrained from a serious attack across the Canal, under the protection of his batteries in Leopoldstadt.

This survey has moved gradually north from the Grand Vezir's base, across the Turkish works and the Christian defences adjoining the Burg, then to the northern part of the town and to the Turks in Leopoldstadt. East and west, beyond the glacis, other sections of the besieging army were stationed, but inactive most of the time. Still further off, and north again from Leopoldstadt a series of broken bridges blocked the usual crossing of the Danube: here one more Ottoman force stood on guard, facing their enemy. Across the water the Habsburg cavalry would be stationed, but powerless to help the Habsburg infantry locked inside the city.

This garrison was now composed of the regiments (with ten companies each) of Alt-Starhemberg, Mansfeld, Souches and Scherffenberg; half or more of the companies of Kaiserstein's, Neuburg's, Heister's and Württemberg's; three companies each of Thim's, and of Dupigny's dragoons. To these must be added the City Guard. The nominal total of the seventy-two companies amounted to 16,600 men, but their actual strength was approximately 11,000.[17] Useful, but of slight military importance, were the civilians who could be mobilised. The most plausible estimate of the size of the ancient burgher-companies from the eight city 'wards', each led by a captain, lieutenant and ensign, allows them a combined total of 1,815 excluding their officers. But in this supreme emergency, when all ordinary business came temporarily to a standstill, public-spirited individuals took the lead in organising groups of volunteers and employers recruited their work-people. One prominent company was formed by Ambrosius Frank, a well-known inn-keeper, a member of the outer council of burghers. The butchers and brewers joined forces and raised a company, the shoemakers and bakers each raised one. Other artisans were grouped together, first in one large unit, and then later into two. Such were the six so-called 'free' companies of the city, estimated – at one count – to number 1,293 men. The university authorities, meanwhile, were mustering the students, together with the printers and booksellers, perhaps 700 in all. The big import-export merchants raised 250; they paid their men, and tended to attract recruits from other companies. Craftsmen, office-holders, and servants connected with the court – the 'Hofbefreiten' – were also organised; and with some hesitation their total manpower can be recorded as 960. Finally, a very useful small group of eighty huntsmen and sharpshooters was ready to serve. The municipality could therefore put about 3,000 at Starhemberg's disposal, the university and the merchants and the court about 2,000. The organisation of these 5,000 was always rudimentary, nor is it clear how many of them were available in the very early stages of the siege. But the civilians helped with guard-duties, and they did much of the repair-work.

In status the first citizen was the burgomaster, John Andrew Liebenberg.[18] He is a puzzling character and, unfortunately for patriotic Viennese chroniclers, not an ingratiating one. Although he had played a very honourable part during the plague-year of 1679, he subsequently found it difficult to clear his financial accounts with the Treasury. He filled all the important city offices in turn, before becoming burgomaster, but did not seem to enjoy sufficient private revenues of his own to free him from a suspicion that he was somewhat mean and unscrupulous in money matters; yet there can be no doubt that he died in considerable poverty, from which his family suffered later. His house, facing on to the square of Am Hof, close to the administrative office of the city treasury and the municipal armoury, was a business centre of the highest importance during the crisis. The town hall stood a little farther north in the Wipplinger Strasse, the ordinary meeting-place of the city councillors. A large proportion of the members of the inner council were even older than Liebenberg and, like him, died of illness and strain before the Turks were finally driven off. They all, or nearly all, were assigned duties of considerable responsibility. They supervised the distribution of bread or wine. They were captains of the burgher companies.

On 10 July, shortly before the Turks reached Vienna, while so much still needed doing if they were to be resisted at all, it was decided to amalgamate the inner council with the municipal tribunal, the *Stadtgericht*. The members of the court, headed by wealthy Simon Schuster who lived on the main street leading down to the Rotenturm and the bridge over the Canal, were brought in to share the duties and responsibilities of the senior councillors. But the outstanding citizen during the crisis was Daniel Fotky, the rich and energetic senior treasurer who was often sent by the townsmen to settle difficult matters with Starhemberg or Caplirs. He handled every kind of business, and in the intensely anxious weeks of August seems to have deputised for Liebenberg, whose strength failed rapidly. When the burgomaster died on 9 September Fotky took over all his duties. A worthy colleague of these men was Hocke, the syndic. Not a Viennese by birth, he had come to study law at the University there in his youth. He now proved a tireless and conscientious official, and later wrote what was certainly the best contemporary history of the siege. Posterity is indebted to him on both counts.

II

In the third week of July, Kara Mustafa still had every reason to be satisfied. The army of his opponents was sealed off from Vienna along the length of the Danube from Krems to Pressburg, and their reinforcements were clearly very far away. His own forces encircled the city, of which the main line of defence had now been reached; and surely his men would soon move across the counterscarp into the ditch beneath the curtain-wall. The garrison, no doubt, was full of fight. It might continue to struggle against overwhelming odds for a week or two longer, but with every day that passed it would get less effective. Everything, so far, justified his own actions during the previous six months; nothing suggested that he was open to a serious attack from any quarter. The siege could proceed systematically, without running unnecessary risks a thousand miles from Istanbul. His men, Kara Mustafa recognised, had not shown themselves able to rush the counterscarp. Attacks made under cover of darkness, and the impact of Turkish mortar-fire and grenades, were insufficient to help them forward. The Grand Vezir therefore sanctioned the next stage of an assault, the laying of mines to force entry from his approaches into the counterscarp. These approaches, and the whole complex of lateral communications, came nearest to the defences at three salient points, in front of the two bastions, and also in front of the ravelin which stood between them. Here, after much hard digging, the Turks prepared to mine; an officer was sent forward by Kara Mustafa to inspect, and to report back to him. For some unexplained reason, the miners in the centre lagged behind their colleagues to left and right, and did not complete their preparations so quickly. On 22 July the Turkish artillery bombardment suddenly became tremendous. Kuniz heard what was afoot, and tried to send a warning into the town. The Austrian command, even without this intelligence (which only arrived two days later) guessed enough to know what was coming. Starhemberg ordered every householder to arrange for the inspection of his cellars, and to report immediately if sounds were heard underground; and he considered the possibility that traitors in Vienna might tunnel out towards the Turkish lines. Most of Friday 23 July things were quiet, unusually quiet;[19] then, between six and seven o'clock, two mines, opposite the two bastions, were exploded by the Turks who immediately stormed the palisading which protected the counterscarp. But these mines were ineffective, and after violent fighting the position hardly altered.

Next day the bombardment paused towards the evening, when rain fell. During the lull the defence brought up new, and removed faulty, guns on the bastions; but at the same moment some citizens were shuddering over the rumour that enemy soldiers were creeping up a sewer. Others boldly re-opened their shops, closed during the day. Others again went to church; and in St Stephen's the congregation and preacher were startled by a ball which burst into the building and struck the organ.

On Sunday the Turks at last exploded their mine opposite the ravelin. It knocked down part of the palisading, and 'volunteers' poured into the attack while the garrison rallied to drive them out. It was a serious moment, and a number of high-ranking officers were wounded before the enemy moved back to the shelter of their trenches. In fact this assault set a pattern for a whole series of explosions, attacks and counter-attacks in the course of the following week. The other novel element, introduced on 26 July, was the countermining of the defenders, an art which they only mastered gradually. A few bold improvisers had offered their services to Starhemberg, especially Captain Hafner of the City-Guard, but they needed practice and experience before becoming efficient. The garrison relied more on their artillery, and on the bombs or grenades which they threw from the counterscarp into the Turkish works and the Turkish squads of labourers. On 27 July, at last, some attackers jumped into the covered way opposite the Burg, but were promptly thrown down into the moat and slaughtered by Christian troops at this lower level. On every one of three days following, the battle was furious. Inch by inch the Turks broke down the defences of the counterscarp. The effect of their bombs was to destroy the palisading, and after an expensive counter-attack had managed to drive back the troops which stormed in after the explosions, it was necessary on each occasion to repair the breach with more timber and fresh digging; but a stage had now been reached when these outer works could no longer be strengthened, and they could only be patched with great difficulty. It seems premature, but Starhemberg was already at this time making arrangements to fight inside the walls. He listed assembly-points for the burghers and other untrained forces, he silenced all bells and chimes except for the striking of the hour from the church towers, he decreed that the great bell of St Stephen's should only sound to summon the citizens if the worst of all emergencies should befall and the Turks entered the city.

Occasionally there was good news. The Danube rose a little, which made an attack across the Canal less likely. A large band of students from the University and men from the corps of butchers once sallied from the defences into the open country and brought back cattle; fresh meat had been getting scarce and dear. Unfortunately dysentery spread fast among the troops and civil population. It was the Turks' strongest ally. The town council set aside the Passauerhof, the property of the Bishop of Passau, as a hospital for these patients. The military authority, anxiously totting up the losses caused by mining and storming, now saw them multiplied by this new factor, and began to look around for reserves. The companies of 'Hofbefreiten' were deployed for the first time, and posted to the ravelin by the Stuben-gate. It was not a post of great significance, but they freed better soldiers for use elsewhere. This was the period of Vienna's greatest isolation. Starhemberg, from 24 July to 4 August, was in touch neither with Kuniz nor Lorraine. It hardly mattered, provided that the Turks continued to stand in front of, and not in or under the counterscarp. The defenders of the city also pinned their hopes to earlier reports that a relieving army would arrive in Austria in the fairly near future, and they still enjoyed plentiful supplies of bread and cash. The troops had been paid punctually, and large quantities of corn were ground. But if disease continued to spread and stocks dwindled and the enemy advanced, which all appeared probable, then the morale of even the commanding officer was vulnerable. The inveterate pessimism of Caplirs would prove as infectious as a bout of plague.

On 31 July the Christian forces listened to their own bands making excellent music, so they said, with drum and pipe. In the Turkish camp the Sultan's special envoy Ali Aga took his leave of the Grand Vezir before returning to Belgrade, and the Turkish musicians were also commanded to strike up.[20] The accounts of the besiegers and the besieged serve to show that the enemy's music roused scorn on both sides, while each continued to fight desperately in front of the Vienna Burg. Every foot of this small area was disputed, in the first week of August as in the last week of July. The Turks, having brought their foremost trenches as far as the palisades guarding the counterscarp, now threw up the earth to such a height that they gradually raised themselves sufficiently to command a partial view of the defence works, while at the same time they also tunnelled underneath their own entrenchments. They tried to set fire to the timbers which barred them, and the garrison countered by taking water from the ditch in the moat to put out the fires. Arrows and grenades flew about, as well as bombs and balls and stones. The Christians sometimes fixed scythes to long poles, to strike at the enemy through the palisades. On 2 August for the first time Starhemberg's men sprung a mine effectively, to the heartfelt satisfaction of the commander who congratulated the officer in charge, Captain Hafner. Arms and legs mingled with the smoke and falling rubbish opposite the Löbel-bastion. Artillery fire normally dominated the forenoon, while in the afternoon and during the earlier part of the evening the mines were exploded, to be followed by one or more assaults immediately afterwards and in the course of the night. At night, too, repair work was carried out by both sides. The Turks began to get into the defences on the counterscarp opposite the Burg-ravelin, because here their tunnelling and their mines had practically obliterated the angles and entrenchments which alone made effective resistance possible. Misdirected countermines at a critical time had even helped them. By the night of 3 August they were at last fairly in control at this point; and a new phase of the siege began when they started shooting down the ditches in the moat on both sides of the ravelin opposite them. The most desperate attacks failed to drive them back, and Habsburg losses were very heavy. One of the most serious was the death in action of Rimpler the engineer. The defenders, retreating from the lost section of the counterscarp, tried to bring back the timbering of the palisades with them, or to burn it; while the Turks dug and mined in such a way that earth fell from the counterscarp into the moat and partially filled it up. Their intention, naturally, was to raise a barrier protecting them from the marksmen posted in the 'caponnières' recently constructed to left and right of the ravelin, and so to ease their progress towards the ravelin itself. This obstacle required an assault at various levels, with miners attaching themselves to its base while storm troops mounted as near as they could get to the top of the outside walls.

This descent into the moat, and then the move forward as far as the ravelin, cost the Turks nine more days of furious fighting. While they piled up their earthworks, Starhemberg's men managed to come along with barrows and trundled earth away. Then the Turks would sally out from their cover in great force, and the garrison came out likewise to repulse them. The Turks dug galleries and boarded them over; in the night of 8 August Daun and Souches with 300 men set fire to some of these galleries. On the 9th, the Turks destroyed a wall connecting one corner of the ravelin with the Burg-bastion. On the 10th they sprung a new mine at the forward point of the ravelin, but it misfired and they had to begin again. The losses on both sides were very severe and, as officers fell, promotion was rapid. In Vienna a new graveyard was opened in the old cemetery of the Augustinians. While one popular officer, Kottoliski, died on the Löbel side of the ravelin, his brother was wounded on the other side in the course of the same night's fighting.[21] The Turks continued to work forward into the counterscarp opposite the bastions, and from the counterscarp into the moat. The cannon from the bastions played on the batteries which the Turks themselves gradually moved forward; bombs sometimes exploded on guns opposite, and fired them off. Yet the brunt of the fighting was in the central position, at the forward tip of the ravelin. The garrison had at length to withdraw its heavier pieces from this area to the main city wall and to the bastions; but at the same time, along the stoutly protected causeway which led forward from the wall to the rear of the ravelin, detachments of troops periodically advanced to mount guard – one detachment relieving another at fixed intervals – in that crucial, most exposed of all positions. As long as possible, also, they held on to points in this section of the counterscarp, and to the caponnières in the moat. Slowly they were forced out. The Turks edged in, were pushed back, and edged forward again. The interminable rota of watches in the ravelin still continued.

The monotony, as always in crises of this kind, matched the suspense. It was difficult to distinguish one mine, one sortie, from others. But in the early afternoon of 12 August, since nothing of note had occurred earlier in the day, something serious was expected. The officer commanding in the ravelin was warned by his men that they could not locate the spot where the Turks were obviously preparing their next mine on the grandest scale. As a spectator observed, even the attackers seemed to pause and wait anxiously. Then, abruptly, the mine was sprung. It was said to have shaken half the town.

When the smoke cleared, the same spectator was horrified to see that the combined result of previous Turkish works and the new upheaval was to raise a sort of causeway to the level of the defenders' first entrenchment on the ravelin, wide enough for fifty attackers abreast. Soon eight Turkish standards were fixed there. The fighting was intense; the garrison recovered some of the ground lost, but at the end of the day Starhemberg had to recognise that his opponents now held a small part of their immediate objective, the ravelin, and could not be driven off. The 12th of August, like the 3rd, was an epoch in the siege of Vienna.

1. The Ottoman Frontier: *above*, Esztergom; *below* Neuhäusel

Edward Browne, the English traveller who made these pen-and-ink sketches in 1669, wrote a few years later of the frontier between Christendom and Islam in Hungary:

A man seems to take leave of our world when he hath passed a day's journey from Rab (Győr) or Comorra (Komárom): and, before he comes to Buda seems to enter upon a new stage of the world, quite different from that of western countries: for he then bids adieu to hair on the head, bands, cuffs, hats, gloves, beds, beer: and enters upon habits, manners and a course of life which, with no great variety but under some conformity extend unto China and the utmost parts of Asia

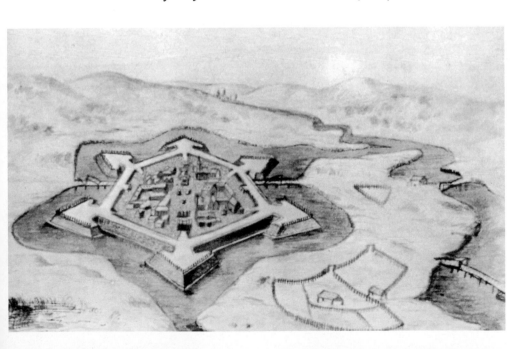

II. The Habsburg Frontier: *above*, Komárom, a fortress on the Danube; *below*, Petronell, a nobleman's mansion east of Vienna

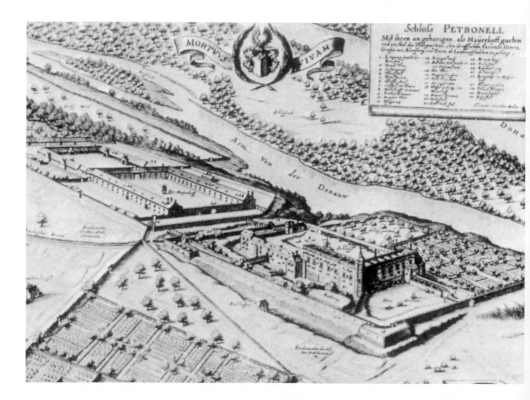

III. Emperor Leopold
in Youth and Old Age

iv. Charles V, Duke of Lorraine

v. The Burgplatz

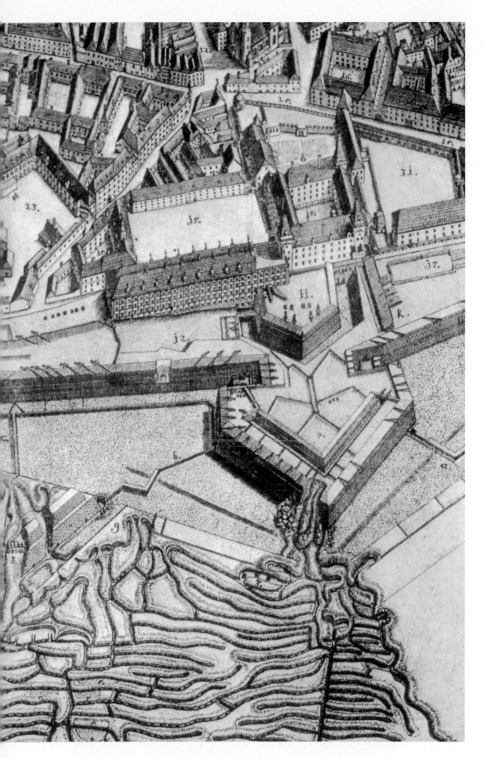

VI. The Hofburg and the Turkish Siege-Works

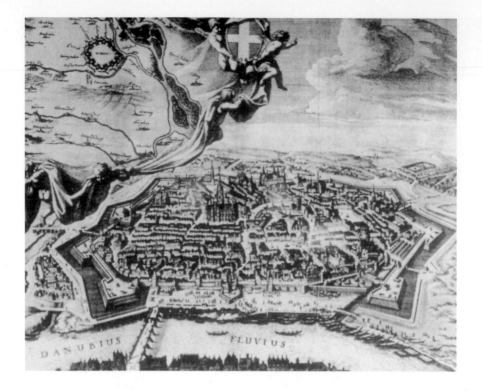

VII. *Above*, Vienna in 1649; *below*, a plan of the City in 1683

In the older print (much of it based on a drawing made in 1609)
a mediaeval wall still defends the city along the Canal. The plan
of 1683 shows the new bastions on this side, and the destruction
of the bridge over the Canal by the garrison.

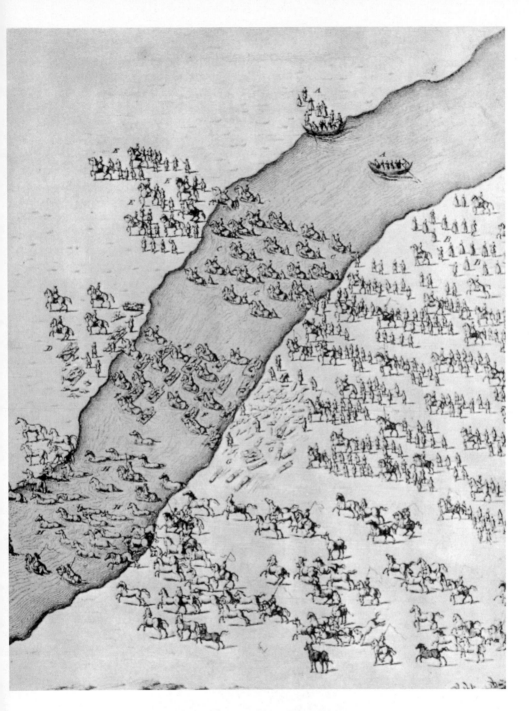

VIII. The Tartars Crossing a River

A, B: women captives; C, E: other prisoners, tied to the tails
of the horses; D, F: Tartars getting equipment across on bundles
of reeds; G: extra reeds; H: spare horses

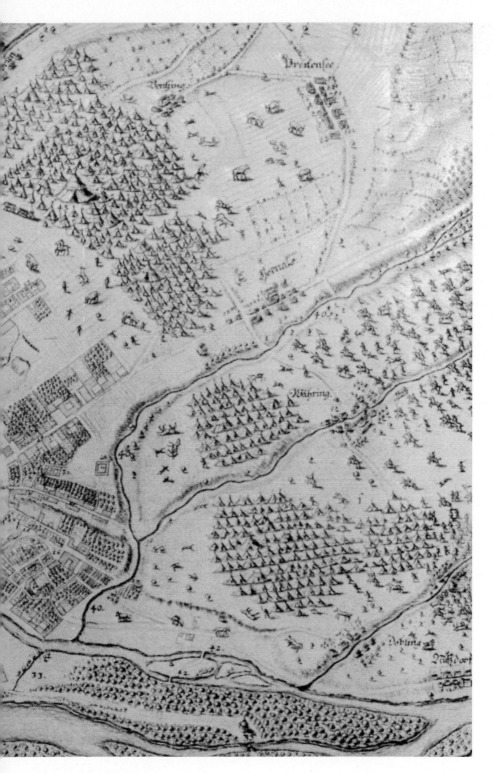

IX. The Siege of Vienna

x. Koltschitzki in Disguise

XI. The Danube and the Wienerwald: *above*, the ascent to the Wienerwald from St. Andrä; *below*, upstream from Vienna

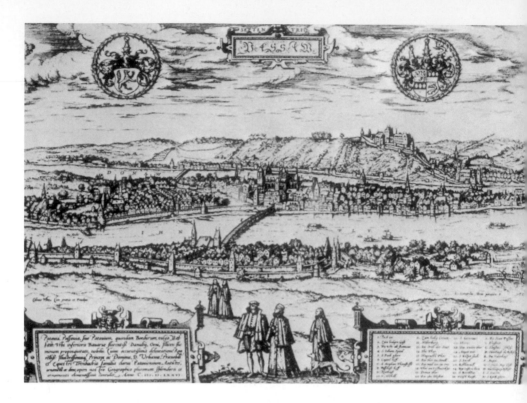

XII. Passau

VIENNA

XIII. Ernest Rüdiger von Starhemberg
The contemporary idea of a triumphant commander

xiv. John III Sobieski, King of Poland
Another contemporary version of the hero in action

6

Outside the City

I

In the broad landscapes outside the city there was warfare of a more savage, less organised kind but it is extraordinarily difficult to give an account of the movement of the Tartars, Magyars, and other irregular forces which accompanied the Ottoman army. Kara Mustafa had no control of them, and they appear to have advanced at their own pace, and in whatever direction seemed open to them. Their devastations were probably the greatest single handicap suffered by the Ottoman high command, once it had been decided to attempt the siege of Vienna; it became much harder to feed the standing troops outside the city walls. The most obscure period of all is the week before the siege began, partly because neither the Estates nor Leopold's government had bothered to put into working order the ancient defence-system, which flashed warnings of an enemy attack from beacon to beacon across the hills. The beacons were not laid, so that no one knew and no one could record the routes followed by the Tartars. After 7 July the foremost raiders certainly pressed on unopposed over the Wiener Wald, almost keeping level with Leopold and his court on their journey up the Danube. When the main Ottoman army reached Vienna, on 14 July, a cluster of Tartar bands was near Melk fifty miles ahead, and during the next few days they moved still farther west until they came to the River Ybbs. They went upstream, and a few of them got across the river, but were at last roughly handled by the peasants and forced back. They proceeded to ravage the extensive lordship of the Auersperg family round Purgstall. If a later account can be trusted, they tried to advance from this area up a road which led through the hills to the industrial and mining district of Steyr, but were again stopped by peasants whom they had themselves pushed out of the villages on to higher ground.[1] We cannot say when this section of the enemy finally withdrew eastwards again.

After 7 July, on the border of Hungary other Tartars and Turks turned south from the Leitha valley. Breitenbrunn by the Neusiedler See was burnt, and

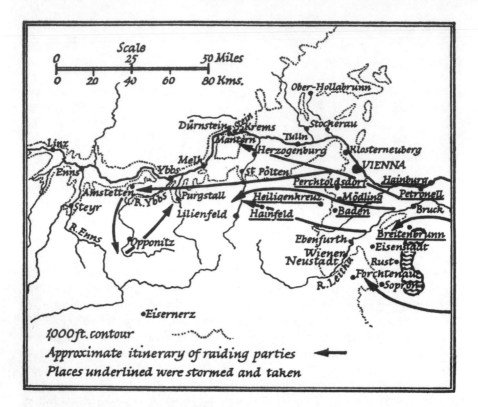

they continued on their way to the towns of Rust, Eisenstadt and Sopron. The citizens of Sopron, as their worthy chronicler Hans Tschány records, had been troubled by every kind of rumour for weeks past.[2] From the beginning of the month their workers in the fields gave up reaping. Turks and Magyars were already across the Rába east of them when these new bands approached, and they felt compelled to seek a negotiation which would stave off the worst horrors of invasion. At this moment, Thököly was popular in Habsburg Hungary because he alone appeared able to act as a shield against the Moslems, while the Moslems used him to gain sufficient control of new territory as quickly as possible. The townsmen of Sopron soon admitted the 'king's' commissioners. They took an oath of obedience on 16 July in return for an assurance of good treatment, and their neighbours in Eisenstadt and Rust followed suit. A Turkish commander quartered in the Esterházy palace which overlooks Eisenstadt. By then Paul Esterházy himself, who had earlier withdrawn from an untenable position on the frontier to the strongest of his private fortresses, was safely in Austria. But his men remained in Forchtenau.* Together with the Habsburg garrison at Wiener-Neustadt, and another handful

---

*Forchtenau (Forchtenstein) is on high ground midway between Sopron and Wiener-Neustadt.

of supporters in Eberfurth, they now confronted the Turks and Tartars camped along the shore of the Neusiedler See.[3] The stage was set for a long series of bitter raids and counter-attacks, of burnings and sackings, in this otherwise smiling countryside.

Meanwhile the main Ottoman force was advancing on Vienna. On its way, some troops turned aside to storm and destroy Hainburg on the Danube (12 July). Bruck-on-the-Leitha had repulsed the Tartars five days earlier; the castle near-by, belonging to the Harrachs and garrisoned by Croats, also resisted them. But the Bruck townsmen could see little point in trying to defy a more formidable attack, and were soon aware that Eisenstadt and Sopron had come to terms. They decided to accept Turkish (not Thököly's) jurisdiction,[4] and gained a measure of security at the price of heavy requisitioning; by the time the negotiation was complete they were more or less quit of the menace of depredations by Turkish irregulars, who had moved farther forward. Apart from the marauders already across the Wiener Wald, there were now many others in the region immediately south of Vienna, where they seem to have killed more, captured more, and burnt more than anywhere else in Austria. Between 12 and 16 July they took Mödling, Baden and Perchtoldsdorf.[5] If a majority of the inhabitants had fled, just in time, sufficient remained to be the victims of undoubted savagery. Almost more frightening were the endurance and persistence of the raiders, who pushed up into the hills unhesitatingly. On 13th and 14th places twenty miles west of Mödling had been stormed; Hainfeld, another fourteen miles farther, was destroyed on 18 July. The countryside seemed utterly defenceless for the moment. But beyond Hainfeld the monks of Lilienfeld were preparing successfully to meet enemy attacks, and a little later and somewhat farther north – along the direct road from Vienna to St Pölten – the Countess Pálffy held out in her castle. On the Sinzendorf estates not far away, while barns and cottages were destroyed and livestock disappeared, the manor-houses survived intact.[6] Nonetheless, all contemporaries wrote and spoke in paralysed terms of a great tract of land rapidly filling up with hostile bands of Tartars and Magyars – who were more feared than any – while the immensely large Ottoman army battered away at Vienna. A relieving force, it seemed, faced the impossible task of first getting through an area ruined and dominated by the irregulars. Only a few cool-headed individuals realised that the success of the Tartars depended on the total lack of any system of defence organised to link the villages and valleys together, and that this had led to a panic which emptied the country of the more able-bodied, leaving it defenceless.[7]

II

Multiple disasters had pushed the remnant of the Habsburg field-army to the other side of the Danube. Its hold on that part of the country was in consequence all the stronger. On 15 July most of Lorraine's cavalry regiments withdrew from the islands which gave access to Vienna. On 16 July, after a sharp encounter with the Turks in front of the last of the bridges leading from one island to the next, his rearguard also retired to the north bank of the river. It was a major defeat, and resulted from a major miscalculation. Lorraine at first undoubtedly hoped to keep in touch with Starhemberg, holding a position from which he could threaten the besiegers. But Le Bègue (his secretary) is emphatic that lack of forage made it impossible to leave cavalry on the islands; and he says also that such a position could not be maintained without the help of infantry.[8] Conceivably Lorraine gave up (as he had given up behind Györ) too easily, and certainly Herman of Baden thought so. But on this occasion he had at least avoided a division of his forces. His new camp at Jedlesee contained about 10,000 men, mostly cavalry, in the third week of July.*

For the next nine days he was stationary, almost powerless. His measures were modest but useful. He threw a few troops back across the Danube to stiffen the defences of Klosterneuburg, where fortunately the clergy and townsmen of this great monastic stronghold only six miles upstream from Vienna, and close to the high ground of the Wiener Wald, had in any case determined to resist the Turks. Colonel Dunewald and a majority of the dragoons were sent to Krems, another forty miles up the Danube; from here they too crossed to the south bank, and checked further raiding by enemy irregulars in the wide plain which stretched away eastwards towards Tulln – about half-way between Krems and Klosterneuburg. Dunewald soon reported a successful encounter, and the repulse of perhaps 800 Tartars.[9] Moreover Lorraine was still in touch with the garrisons at Györ and Komárom, and ventured to bring back from Györ two more infantry regiments, those of Baden and Grana; they arrived safely at the camp on 24 July. Prince Lubomirski had by then reached Olomouc with six companies of Polish horse. Lorraine summoned them at once, apparently intending to send their commander on an urgent mission to Sobieski, in order to beg the King to march south at top speed. Lubomirski duly came – but despatched a deputy to Sobieski. He himself wished to stay in the theatre of active warfare.[10]

Lorraine also sent off Taafe, followed by other officers, to Passau; and the Duke of Sachsen-Lauenburg to the Saxon court at Dresden. All were to plead for the instant departure of more troops, so that the relief of Vienna could be attempted with the least possible delay.[11] In particular, the messengers to Passau were instructed to raise the fundamental strategic problem of the day by firmly stating Lorraine's opinion that a relieving army could only approach the city by a route through the Wiener Wald. Members of his staff also considered that it might be necessary to build a fortified camp somewhere in that steep and wooded country, from which to try to strike at the Turks.

At this point news arrived from Hungary. On 11 July, Thököly had broken

---

*For Jedlesse and other points north of the Danube, see the maps (pp. xiv–xvii).

up his quarters near Miskolcz, about 200 miles from Vienna, and begun to ride with his followers through the Slovakian hills.[12] Ahead of them, his agents summoned the larger towns to promise obedience to the new Magyar 'king'. The citizens of Trnava took an oath of loyalty on 19 July and Géczy, the most active of these envoys, negotiated with the burgomaster of Pressburg. The Habsburg garrison in the citadel there was completely isolated by then; and the townsmen had to reckon not merely with the menaces and blandishments of Thököly who appeared on the scene in person on the 27th, but with the Turks. While the main body of the Ottoman army advanced on Vienna, and other troops blockaded Győr, a third force of possibly 7,000 men under Abaza Kör Hussein – the 'One-eyed' – wheeled from Győr to Esztergom and crossed the Danube.[13] The Turkish commander and Thököly soon quarrelled, but jointly they threatened Pressburg. There were signs that the Turks intended to build a pontoon bridge from a point opposite the town in order to get additional troops over the Danube, and by this means give further assistance to Thököly in driving forward right up to Lorraine's encampment opposite Vienna. Their adversary would then be compelled to withdraw once again to the west. It would become exceedingly difficult for the Poles to enter Austria by the direct route through Moravia. The area from which the Habsburg army continued to gather food and taxes would be diminished, and the garrisons at Győr and Komárom totally cut off from their comrades. But at the end of July Lorraine reacted violently to the danger, and won his first positive victory since the beginning of the campaign.[14]

A small force, under Major Ogilvie of the Baden regiment, went ahead to try to stiffen the Pressburg garrison. It was unfortunately cut to pieces by Thököly's men and Ogilvie had to return. So Lorraine, leaving only a few companies of dragoons behind him, moved east to Marchegg on the Morava, ten miles from the point where this river meets the Danube and twenty miles from Pressburg. There he learnt that the burghers had allowed a small troop of Thököly's supporters to enter the town, that Thököly himself was now coming up fast with very large numbers – possibly 25,000 Magyars and Turks. The enemy had begun to build his bridge. In spite of the appalling consequences of a defeat at this stage, Lorraine forded the Morava in the late afternoon of 28 July. His forces, first his dragoons, then the Poles, and finally the main body of cavalry, rode through the night up the narrow valley leading to the crest – and to the vineyards – which overlook the citadel and city of Pressburg. Almost at the beginning of this march his van frightened off a few enemy outriders; and Lorraine could not know that these gave the alarm to Thököly who determined to withdraw at once, with many of his followers. Thököly, like Lorraine, greatly over-estimated the size of the force opposed to him.

In the last hours of darkness, the dragoons under Lewis of Baden were posted in the vineyards close to one of the suburbs and the citadel. Lorraine himself came forward to inspect, and saw below him the town, and beyond it two of the enemy's principal camps, apparently some miles apart. Then, easily,

Ogilvie and 200 foot got inside the walls of the castle and strengthened the garrison. At dawn Baden occupied a part of the suburb and summoned the town to surrender. The townsmen speedily gave way to him; but first giving 300 of Thököly's soldiers sufficient time to escape.

The accounts of the battle which followed are very confusing.[15] It seems probable that Lorraine doubted whether he was strong enough to attack the main body of Magyars and Turks outside the town. Luckily Baden and other officers argued boldly for an assault, and he finally agreed. The dragoons were spread out on a broad front between the hill-slopes and the Danube, while the heavier cavalry was being ranged into battle-order; then the dragoons were concentrated on the wings. The Poles under Lubomirski's command were nearest the river. Other Poles under Tetwin, with the Veterani and Pálffy regiments, stood on the far left. The attack commenced and it soon became clear that most of the Magyars present felt unable to resist. The Turkish units alone were not strong enough to do so, and the reason for this weakness was almost certainly that Thököly and many other Magyars had already withdawn. The Habsburg victory of 30 July was a chase rather than a battle. Even Lorraine lost control of the situation for several hours whilst Lubomirski and Tetwin, their men and those of the Veterani and Pálffy regiments drove across the plain and then slowly returned, loaded with spoil of various kinds, tents, baggage, horses and cattle. They were all – or nearly all – back by dusk; and in the camp that night there was drinking and congratulation, spiced with the envy of those troops who had gained less or too little in the way of plunder. But the Habsburg commanders had not wasted time: the materials for building a bridge over the Danube were either removed or destroyed; supplies were taken into the castle; and the municipality of Pressburg was roughly admonished for truckling to the rebels. It once again promised loyalty to Leopold.

The threat from Thököly had been promptly and successfully met. It was high time to hurry back to the scene of the siege which agonisingly continued its course. On 31 July Lorraine and his men were once more in Marchegg, across the Morava. He himself believed that it was essential to lighten the weight of Turkish pressure on Vienna at once. Conceivably he could have crossed the Danube at Pressburg and threatened Kara Mustafa from the east. The testimony of various prisoners in his hands suggested that the tension between Magyars and Turks had risen high. Messages from Györ and Komárom spoke of extremely effective raids made by Habsburg skirmishers in that area. Intercepted correspondence between the besiegers at Vienna and the authorities at Buda disclosed the tightness of supply in Kara Mustafa's army and grumbling in its ranks. But Lorraine had a diminutive force by comparison with his enemy's, whose cavalry enjoyed every chance of emphasising its superiority in the gentle plainland on that side of Vienna. A bridgehead so far to the east was both remote and vulnerable. Indeed the arguments in favour of a speedy crossing at Krems or Tulln, and the construction of a fortified camp in the Wiener Wald from which to try and regain contact with the beleaguered garrison, still sounded convincing to the members of Lorraine's staff. They were shocked when Taafe reached Marchegg with the gloomiest account of the mood of ministers in Passau. Leopold's government appeared to view the situation calmly, almost passively, and to insist that any move on Vienna depended on the prior arrival of reinforcements from Germany and Poland; while clearly such reinforcements were coming up at a slow pace. Lorraine was not prepared to accept this programme without protest.[16] He passionately wanted to anticipate what he considered the obvious perils of the immediate future. Pálffy was sent off to Passau to press his case once again.[17] Other messengers set out on longer journeys, to the King of Poland and the Elector of Saxony.

Fresh intelligence soon showed that the Habsburg cavalry still had work to do on the eastern front; the regiments could not yet be taken back to the Vienna bridgehead. Thököly's supporters, it seemed, were about to break across the Morava into Moravia, possibly into Silesia. Lorraine was on the point of moving up the river towards them, when he also learnt that the Turks had got over from the south bank of the Danube on to the islands opposite Gross Enzersdorf some miles below Vienna, a village where Habsburg magazines were stored. At the same time, they were adding to their strength on the islands which faced Lorraine's original encampment opposite the city. So he turned about, spent the night of 3 August at Enzersdorf, and pushed forward to the bridgehead.[18] The Turks were successfully dislodged from the islands lower down the river, and their chance of crossing the Danube was cut to a minimum. The troops then turned up the Morava to deal with the Magyar raiders.

The condition of the whole area round Pressburg had become anarchic; typically, on 8 August, an accidental but devastating fire reduced to ashes most of the town of Trnava. While Thököly himself kept close to the shelter of the Little Carpathians, and resided mainly in the castles of Czeklesz (about ten miles east of Pressburg) and of Vereskö farther north, some of his men moved forward again.[19] To oppose them the Habsburg headquarters were set at Angern from 6 to 20 August, from which troops would go at intervals to winkle out or mow down those wild incendiaries who were burning the villages of that unpretentious countryside. It was a merciless, sporadic form of warfare in which civilian losses of life and property were extremely high. The Poles once again, mobile and relentless, distinguished themselves; and Lorraine took care to inform Sobieski, while pleading in a sequence of dispatches for the King's speedy arrival, of the prowess of his countrymen. Privately he would have preferred the inhabitants to withdraw completely with their goods and livestock, rather than that he should be burdened with the impossible task of protecting them. This, in fact, he was not able to do; but he did manage to stop Thököly entering Moravia with a compact force which could threaten the main routes from Poland to Austria.

Meanwhile, his attempts to gather reliable information about the state of Vienna after four weeks of siege always continued. Le Bègue laments on 2 August: 'However hard we try to get news from Vienna and the Grand Vezir's camp, we can learn nothing at all.'[20] Peasants who had worked for the Turks were questioned, as well as a captured Turkish Aga, a burgher from Bruck-on-the-Leitha, a so-called 'Catholic Cossack', and a man who described himself as a German deserter from the Ottoman army and turned out to be an Italian Jew. Their testimonies were weighed, and the balance of probabilities estimated. They had to be compared with reports coming in from the commander at the bridgehead, Magny. How much could be inferred from the noise of successive bombardments and explosions? Or from the intermittent silences which followed them? The arguments, now becoming familiar to us, went round and round in a confusing circle. Kara Mustafa was well and truly pinned down, and undoubtedly expending his resources on the grandest scale. His convoys bringing up supplies from Buda were liable to attacks by the undefeated forces at Győr and Komárom; while farther south Wiener-Neustadt still held out. The enemy was apparently not strong enough to take Klosterneuburg, or to raid farther west than Tulln (after the first fortnight of the siege), or to get over the Danube at any point west of the Morava provided that Thököly could be prevented from helping him. Nor were there any reports that he had fortified his camps round Vienna or placed a guard on the heights of the Wiener Wald. Unfortunately, any optimism based on these facts was tempered by consideration of the one premise of supreme importance: they all depended on the continued resistance of Vienna. The Turks understandably bent all their efforts to this end, the capture of the city. If they succeeded, they could then strike at lesser objectives with every hope of victory in each case. So Lorraine and his staff were back again at the starting-point of their inquiry, their ignorance about the progress of the siege. After a fortnight at Marchegg and Angern they could still only conclude that the siege *was* making progress, but slowly. After listening to Taafe, and studying the dispatches which followed Taafe from Passau, they decided that powerful reinforcements were indeed coming up, but very slowly indeed. Nine thousand Bavarians and 8,000 Franconians would be within striking distance of Vienna by mid-August. A Saxon army of 10,000 was unlikely to approach before the end of the month, or a Polish army of perhaps 20,000 before the beginning of September; possibly the Polish vanguard under Sienawski would reach Austria earlier than the main body under Sobieski himself. The dilemma was obvious, but insoluble: the longer Lorraine waited, the larger and stronger the relieving force would grow, but the more likely a successful Turkish assault on Vienna. The maximum period of weeks or days was needed to give the Christian armament a chance of confronting the Turks on almost equal terms. To exceed that maximum by an hour was to invite a crushing disaster.

On 2 August he had sent Pálffy to Passau. The days passed, he received no reply, and was compelled to go on waiting at Angern anxious and frustrated.

III

Just then, the city re-established contact with the outside world;[21] for it is one of the more puzzling features of the siege that no arrangements were made, before Lorraine drew back from Leopoldstadt and the islands, for signalling of even a rudimentary kind across the river by the use of rockets. The soldiers camped at Jedlesee simply attempted to guess at the course of events from what they could see and hear of the rival artilleries. With the help of Prince Serban Cantacuzene of Wallachia and his Christian subjects, who always served the Turks half-heartedly, Kuniz from the besiegers' camp was able to send messages into Vienna during the first week of the siege – but this did not help the Habsburg commander on the other side of the river.

On the night of 21 July a bold cavalryman swam across the Danube from near Enzersdorf, bearing a letter from Lorraine which promised the speedy relief of the city. He (or possibly some other volunteer) left Vienna the same day, and the Turks caught him, but luckily they could make nothing of his dispatch which was in cipher. Brought before the Grand Vezir, he said that the losses of the garrison had already been so great that the city was likely to surrender in the very near future. Also on that day, the 22nd, Kuniz managed to get a warning through that the enemy had cut a large amount of timber from the woods round Schönbrunn, in preparation for the advance of their trenches and galleries – for which it was needed – as far as the counterscarp; from here they intended to mine a way through the remaining defences. Starhemberg replied at once, promising to resist to the utmost, and this messenger got safely back to Kuniz. Simultaneously another crossed the Danube to Lorraine, who had heard nothing from the city for eight days. He learnt that the Turks were approaching the counterscarp fast, and that it looked as if they next wanted to extend their trenches laterally from a point facing the Burg-ravelin in order to bring them opposite the Burg and Löbel bastions. Starhemberg repeated that he was determined to hold on.[22]

Kuniz again sent a servant, a man named Heider, to give warning of mines likely to explode (so he thought) close to the Schotten-gate. Heider entered the city safely, and began the return journey almost immediately, carrying a dispatch for Lorraine which the garrison hoped that Kuniz would be able to forward. No doubt Heider had described the envoy's contacts with the Prince of Wallachia, the Turks' unreliable ally; these could surely be used to transmit information through the Ottoman camp, from the city to the Christian world beyond the Wiener Wald or the Danube. But Heider was caught by the Turks. He loudly protested that his only business in Rossau – where he was taken – had been to look for supplies of wine for his employer, but it needed a handsome bribe from one of Kuniz's interpreters to save his life. On 26 July the Turks shot an arrow into the Burg-ravelin, having attached to it the intercepted letter in cipher of the 21st. They added a superscription, saying that the plight of the city was perfectly well-known to the Grand Vezir who once more promised mercy to the citizens if they surrendered immediately, or death and total destruction if they hesitated an instant. There was no reply, Starhemberg held firm, but for the next week Vienna was cut off from Kuniz, Lorraine and the government at Passau.

Lorraine soon had to concentrate on the threat from Thököly, while Kuniz was obviously vulnerable to Turkish reprisals after the arrest of his servant. The authorities in Vienna failed to find any more volunteers for an enterprise so manifestly dangerous as this journey in disguise through the dense numbers of the enemy. At last, on the night of 4 August a cavalryman who knew Turkish and was dressed in Turkish clothes got into Vienna, bringing with him letters from Passau.[23] Details were given in these about the size of the forces which it was hoped to assemble for the army of relief, although the government referred only vaguely to the timing of future operations. Caplirs and his colleagues drafted an answer, advising that they could not reckon to hold on much longer to the strip of counterscarp in front of the threatened bastions; but nobody was willing to take the message out of the city. Caplirs and Starhemberg wrote again on 8 August to say that the enemy was now in the counterscarp, and this time they found a volunteer, one Lieutenant Gregorovitz, to whom a company was promised if he succeeded in his mission and returned to Vienna. Recently a prisoner of the Turks, who had escaped, he claimed to know enough of the language to risk the journey. It was agreed that he should signal his arrival in friendly country from the beacon on the Bisamberg, the height nearest Vienna across the Danube, and easily visible from the city.

He set out, and there was great disappointment within the walls as one night passed and then another, and still the watchers in the tower of St Stephen's saw no beacon-light on the Bisamberg. In fact Gregorovitz was deviously doing his best, but took a long time to get over the Wiener Wald as far as Herzogenburg,* and from there to Mautern and Krems. Starhemberg (or Caplirs) had already decided to try again; and on this occasion a man of Armenian extraction, once an interpreter in Istanbul and Buda, and now a member of Frank's volunteer company of civilians, was brought to the notice of the burgomaster and sent by him to Caplirs. This person, named Koltschitzki, either had a flare for publicity or had fame thrust upon him by the pamphleteers of the period. By the end of the year he became easily the most famous of the messengers in the story of the siege, which makes it very difficult to distinguish between fact and fiction in the accounts given of his adventures between 13 and 17 August 1683. He and his servant named Seradly dressed up as Turks, and went over the counterscarp on the Rossau side of the city. They passed without incident through the Turkish guards and encampments, a little farther on climbed round the slopes of the hills which descend sharply to the Danube, and then

---

*Here, dressed in Turkish clothes and talking the oddest German, he had great difficulty in convincing people that he was not an enemy agent.[24] The Bisamberg appears in illustration xi.

themselves came down to the water's edge. Attracting the attention of peasants and boatmen who had taken refuge on an island in the stream, both were ferried safely to the north bank, and soon came up with Colonel Heisler and some of his dragoons. They hurriedly rode across the plain to Lorraine's quarters on the Morava, and reached him a few hours after the arrival of the dispatches brought out of Vienna by Gregorovitz.

At last the commander in the field had authentic information, even if a little out of date, about the condition of Vienna's defence and the progress of the Turks.[25] The text of one of Caplirs' letters survives, addressed to Leopold.[26] It states that the Turks had begun to mine and undermine the Burg-ravelin, that the defenders' supply of grenades was nearly exhausted, and that they were severely handicapped by the lack of trained miners. The numbers killed in the recent fighting were high. Disease took toll of many others. Starhemberg himself was ill. The immediate future was grim indeed, and particularly because the design of the Burg-bastion[27] made it peculiarly vulnerable to mines.

Almost at once Koltschitzki and Seradly started back. They followed much the same route, according to their own story coming very much nearer to arrest by the Turks in the no-man's-land outside the city, and by 17 August were safely inside the walls. Smoke was used to signal their arrival to the army in the field and, when night fell, rockets were sent up. The two men had earned the 200 ducats promised them; next day, they were paid. The actual content of the letters which they carried amounted, and could amount, to no more than a general promise from Lorraine to come to the relief of the city as soon as possible. Starhemberg replied in relatively confident terms,[28] because the Turks made slow progress from the counterscarp into the moat, and they were still a long way from capturing the ravelin. All their advances towards the two bastions had been repulsed, and their losses – to judge from the confession of prisoners – were very high, while they were running short of essential supplies. On the following day, 19 August, he added a postscript which stated that one more assault had been beaten back. The authorities meanwhile improved on their offer to any man who volunteered to carry the next dispatch. Koltschitzki and Seradly had been given 200 ducats when they returned to the city. Now 100 ducats were offered before the volunteer set out, with a promise of another 100 if and when he came back; and Seradly accepted the bargain – unlike the canny Koltschitzki, his master. He left on the 19th, a signal went up from the Bisamberg on the 20th, and he returned by the 23rd with the usual promise of a speedy relief, now planned to commence at the end of the month or at least early in September.

For the moment, there was little more that Starhemberg could say or do except continue his grim defence of the bastions, then coming sharply under attack. But he must have guessed that his dispatches played a useful part in building up the diplomatic pressure on Leopold's allies to hasten their advance to Austria, just as the messages from Lorraine helped to assure soldiers and civilians in the city that a powerful relieving army really was on its way to draw off the enemy from the siege. So he wrote again on 27 August, and Caplirs also.[29] A man named Michaelovitz took the letters and the ducats, and completed the double journey successfully. The two commanders pressed their case in much more urgent language than in earlier messages, referring to the sad loss of manpower from casualties and disease, together with the running-down of the stock of grenades; many, said Caplirs, who began the siege as corporals were now lieutenants. Their seniors had been killed in action. They would not be able to hold on to the ravelin for more than one or two days longer, and the Turks were beginning to mine the Burg-bastion. These ominous facts were promptly relayed by Lorraine to Sobieski, who appeared to the Austrian commander so agonisingly slow in his advance through Poland.

Starhemberg and Caplirs wrote once again on 1 September. They re-emphasised the fact, no doubt familiar to all military men who had visited Vienna, that the faulty design of the bastions under attack made it very difficult to defend them for any length of time, so that only an immediate attempt at relief could save the city. They lamented, as before, the shortage of skilled miners in the garrison, so that opposition to the Turkish workers underground was ineffective. At the very moment of writing, they stated, the enemy was *under* the Burg-bastion! They pleaded that they did not say these things for lack of courage, and would fight to the bitter end. Even so, they concluded, defeat was possible and the city might fall.

Michaelovitz was willing to transmit this solemn warning but raised his price, insisting this time on the immediate payment of 200 ducats. He left on 2 September and by the evening of the same day reached Lorraine's new camp at Korneuburg. Wisely, perhaps, he did not return to Vienna; he already had his money and preferred to save his skin. He set out on the journey home, but then vanished. Perhaps the risks were greater than ever before. Indeed, many contemporaries believed that the Turks captured and killed him, and few of them knew that he survived until 1699.[30]

Lorraine himself had by now marched westwards with his troops from the Morava, in order to be within reach of the Danube bridges upstream – the old bridge at Stein near Krems, and a new bridge rapidly being constructed from a point opposite Tulln, twenty miles from Vienna.

IV

At Passau, where the Inn flows magnificently from the south and the little River Ilz comes down from the Bohemian hills) and both join the Danube, Leopold's court was in residence from 17 July to 25 August. Quarters were difficult to find, and the Italian diplomats Pucci and Buonvisi preferred to live in the smaller towns nearby, Schärding and Braunau. Buonvisi hoped that from Braunau it would be easier to retreat farther into the mountains, if another emergency threatened and the Turks pressed forward to Linz or even to Passau.[31] Meanwhile the Hesse-Darmstadt envoy was unfeignedly thankful to continue his journey up the Danube to Regensburg and so home; unfortunately for us, he passes out of this history. But the court remained uneasily anchored at Passau. The officials tried hard to observe their normal calendar, to celebrate the birthdays and name days of princes and the festivals of the Church, lamenting that they had not with them the proper clothes.[32] They accompanied Leopold when he attended services in St Paul's and in the Cathedral – in which at least one of their number admired the new Baroque decoration just then clothing the medieval shell of the building – or crossed the Inn and climbed up to the pilgrimage church of Mariahilf. The wheels of government also began to revolve again. The Treasury, War Council, and Chanceries were soon hard at work.[33]

Their first obvious preoccupation was the question of reinforcements. They turned confidently to the Elector of Bavaria.

Max Emmanuel, travelling slowly homeward through Bohemia after his visit to Vienna and Kittsee in the spring, did not reach Munich before the beginning of June. Here he was careful to remain on friendly terms with Louis XIV, but the terms of his treaty with Leopold speedily committed him to send troops to the eastern theatre of war. The Turks advanced, and he readily accepted this obligation.[34] By the time the Habsburg court reached Passau the two governments had only to work out the details of an agreement, on such matters as the pay and supply of Bavarian regiments after their entry into Austrian territory; and a final treaty was signed on 6 August providing for the dispatch of 8,200 at once. Ten days earlier, the Bavarian foot regiments had already assembled at Straubing on the Danube. On the last day of July they, and also the Elector's horse, were reviewed by Leopold at Passau. Max Emmanuel himself arrived. Contingents from the Bavarian Circle of states came on a little later. The foot went down the river, the horse travelled overland. The total reinforcement of 11,300 men was quartered in the area south of Krems by the middle of August, under the command of General Degenfeld. It was the first undoubted and substantial contribution of Habsburg diplomacy and administration to the relief of Vienna.

Leopold's ministers were no less successful in Franconia and Thuringia. Their appeal for the instant dispatch of troops was discussed by the Franconian and Upper Rhine Circles during the second half of July at meetings in Kassel, Darmstadt, Schmalkalden, and Hassfurt-on-the-Main. Count Waldeck himself came from Holland and inspired the final decision. Soon 6,500 infantry and 1,500 horse made ready to go down the Danube from Regensburg to Krems.[35] It was a powerful reinforcement, swift and apparently generous. The sentiments of loyalty to the Emperor and fear of the Turk were no doubt effective strings for the Habsburg ministers to pluck, and they made good use of them during the crisis of the siege. The central German states had also another argument to consider. If both Leopold and Max Emmanuel were fully engaged in

Austria, and if in consequence Louis XIV took the opportunity to invade the Rhineland, they themselves could not hope to resist Louis unaided. But their troops had already been raised for the defence of the Empire. Unemployed, they were expensive. It was therefore expedient to lend them to the Emperor, and to quarter them in Austria. Motives were as usual mixed, but the action of the Franconian princes was pure gain for the hard-pressed administration at Passau.

The summons of Leopold's own soldiers from the Empire was also a relatively simple decision to take. Although the government's bias had earlier been to insist on the priority which their commitments in the west, and resistance to the claims of Louis XIV in Germany, should take over their commitments in the east and resistance to the Sultan in Hungary, the present crisis forced it to give way and to take risks. In consequence, although the diplomats were still instructed not to give way to French demands, the military administration quietly and steadily made arrangements to transfer regiments from west to east. On 1 August 1,000 men of the Lorraine regiment appeared at Passau, on the 5th Leslie's regiment, on the 12th the Neuburgers, all bound for Lower Austria. It looked to Pucci as if only the 'Jung-Starhemberg' would be left to hold Philippsburg on the Rhine, assisted by troops raised by the Circles in Germany.[36] The transfer, which of course involved a major administrative effort in the hereditary lands, as well as a real weakening of the military front against Louis XIV, was another solid addition to the army of relief on which the immediate future of the Habsburg dominion depended.

The government's relations with its commander-in-chief were much more complicated. From the middle of July until the middle of August neither party had any authentic information about conditions inside Vienna. Lorraine argued that Starhemberg could not hope to hold out for long, given the scale of the Turkish assault, and the limited amount of munitions and food known to be in the city when communications with it were cut off. Passau retorted that enough munitions and food were known to be at Starhemberg's disposal, that the garrison and the defenceworks were strong, while it would be madness to try and relieve the city without first assembling the maximum number of troops, drawn from all possible sources of manpower in Austria, Germany and Poland. This debate in fact continued week after week, carried on in a long sequence of reports, dispatches and instructions, which were taken to and fro between Lorraine's headquarters and the court at Passau.[37] Lorraine sent off five important and well-informed officers – Taafe, Welspurg, Rostinger, Pálffy and Auersperg – to Passau, and they reached Leopold on 20, 21, 26 July, 7 and 17 August. His written instructions to the second, third and fourth of these have been found, and we have Leopold's written response to the first and the third. References to other letters and reports also survive, so that it is still possible to follow the controversy, which was intensified by the perennial discord between Lorraine and Herman of Baden.

Taafe left the camp opposite Vienna on 16 July immediately after the Turks had cut the communications between Lorraine and Starhemberg. Lorraine, as we have seen, urged the maximum concentration of forces for the rescue of the city as quickly as possible, and also held that the relieving army would have to choose a route across the Wiener Wald. He quoted a letter from Caplirs, written a little earlier, which estimated the size of the garrison in Vienna at only 8,700 men (or even less)[38] and spoke gloomily of the shortness of all essential supplies in the city. There was a certain dishonesty about this, because Lorraine's staff knew well enough that there were over 10,000 men in the garrison; but it was ordinary good sense to favour the shortest possible route if the case for speed was proved. The government in Passau thought otherwise. It questioned the reliability of Caplirs and insisted on the Vienna garrison's will and ability to keep out the Turks. It felt that there were two important objectives, to raise the siege and to protect the hereditary lands from any further devastation by Turks and Tartars; it wanted to carry out the rescue operation in such a manner that the provinces surrounding Vienna were also saved from the Turk. Leopold therefore deprecated – he had already done so in a previous dispatch from Linz – the retreat of Schultz and his forces from the line of the Váh. He asked for a firm defence of the whole area north of the Danube from Pressburg to Krems, and insisted on the need to hold the bridge at Stein because 'the main army will probably have to pass over it to the south bank of the river'. But the question of the route to be followed by any relieving army was left over for more detailed discussion at a later date. The reply to Lorraine hints that it might be advisable to circle round farther to the south in order to give assistance to the Inner Austrian lands, and draw additional troops from that area. In any case the councillors at Passau believed that the suggestion, presumably also Lorraine's, that an attempt might be made to raise the siege as soon as the Bavarian regiments had reached Austria was impracticable and dangerous, and they would have none of it. Instead they wished to use any additional troops, first of all, to give greater security to the countryside both north and south of the Danube.

Taafe's mission, and the arguments urged by Lorraine and by the administration in Passau, anticipated the whole course of the debate during the next four weeks. Lorraine was certainly too nervous, but his fears may have spurred on the government sufficiently to bring together the force which saved Vienna just before it was too late.

Rostinger soon arrived at Passau with further memoranda. Lorraine once more assumed that the only possible route to Vienna lay across the Wiener Wald, but this time he said that the enterprise should be attempted as soon as an army of 50,000 German soldiers could be got together.[39] This implied that there was no time to wait for the arrival of John Sobieski and his Poles. It was also necessary to provide efficiently for the relieving army, guaranteeing the supply of forage and food, in order to cut down the time needed to move from Krems to Vienna; and both Lorraine and the officer in charge of his commissariat begged for more money in order to pay the troops. Their Polish auxiliaries were already two months in arrears, and grumbling in a way that threatened trouble. Leopold's reply simply avoided the principal point of the argument. It did not state clearly that a force of 50,000 was too small for an attack on the Turkish army, but informed Lorraine that the negotiations with other courts were designed to bring into Austria a very much larger force, that steps had been and would be taken to find sufficient supplies when they were needed.

Lorraine was not satisfied. After his victory over Thököly at Pressburg he sent Pálffy to Passau to press the view that, if Vienna appeared in obvious danger of falling to Kara Mustafa, an army of 25,000 infantry supported by cavalry should try to relieve the city.[40] A route over the Wiener Wald, 'or a little above it to the right', was again suggested; and the alternative of crossing the Danube at Pressburg and marching on Vienna from the east, which had been discussed after the recent victory in this area, was firmly rejected. Passau preferred to oppose Lorraine on this occasion by saying nothing at all; or rather, as Le Bègue sardonically noted, 'after 22 days' delay'[41] Pálffy returned to the camp with a message forbidding any attempt to take decisive action, before the German and Polish troops now on their way across Europe had joined the Habsburg force. Indeed, Vienna still held out. When the letters from Starhemberg and Caplirs were finally brought to Lorraine on 15 August and were then sent on to Passau, readers could interpret them as they wished: the position in Vienna was serious but not desperate, or it was desperately serious. Lorraine sent Auersperg – that incessant bearer of letters to and fro – to press the second view. The ministers in Passau took the first;[42] and for the next three weeks their veto forced the Habsburg commander to continue his many preparations for feeding, moving and guiding a confederate army, but not to anticipate the actions of such an army by acting independently.

The days of Wallenstein and Condé were over, fortunately for Leopold and Louis XIV. Lorraine, and after him Eugene of Savoy, loyally recognised the authority of the Habsburg ruler. In 1683 that loyalty helped to maintain a government otherwise discredited by an overwhelming temporary setback.

Meanwhile Passau had also to keep the civilian administration of the provinces going, more often by exhortation than command. Leopold, for example, wrote elaborately to the Estates of Croatia on 26 July thanking them for their services, informing them of the troops promised by the German princes, and stating that a substantial armament was being built up in Styria to protect the Inner Austrian duchies, and to collaborate in the rescue of Vienna itself. The Croatians were asked to give all the support they could, keeping closely in touch with the administration at Graz and with Lorraine.[43]

Much more important, at this time, was the correspondence with the Lower Austrian Estates and government at Krems, so much closer to the principal theatre of war.[44] The chief official here was Count Traun, assisted by the Abbot of Göttweig and others. One of Traun's first duties had been to try to enforce Leopold's order dated 13 July, that all shipping on the Danube in

Lower Austria must be moved over to the left bank of the river. Not everyone obeyed, and certainly not the Abbot of Melk, who was determined to defend himself against Turk or Tartar and at the same time wished to keep open his line of retreat across the Danube. The Abbot of Aggsbach was also a recalcitrant. Traun, authorised by the administration at Passau to use force, ultimately succeeded in getting his way; although the activity of the dragoons under Dunewald, who held the area south of the Krems bridge, no doubt did most to stop the enemy from raiding across the river. The security of the lands north of the Danube deeply concerned Traun, because devastation in that quarter would destroy the stocks of hay and corn needed to support the troops. Imports on the largest possible scale were needed, but the local supply was the obvious nucleus for Lorraine's commissariat, and a contractor named Kriechbaum signed an agreement with the Lower Austrian administration on 29 July to provide it with these commodities. For Traun, another worry was the attitude of the peasants. There were all the signs of total indiscipline in many lordships; rebellious groups of peasants refused to work, and resisted requisitioning. It looks as if a conscription order published at Krems on 28 July was an attempt to enroll a local police force, in order to restrain the subject populations; but Traun also asked Passau for a regiment of troops to assist this improvised militia.

In the middle of August he himself went up the river to Passau to discuss a different matter, of greater and growing importance: the building of a bridge across the Danube at Tulln for the use of Lorraine's regiments, and of the Polish troops when they arrived. Up to that time officials had been far more concerned about the existing bridge, connecting Stein (a mile away from Krems) and Mautern. When Leopold fled from Vienna, they at first wanted to build proper military works on the south bank, in order to protect it. But because the inhabitants of the little town of Mautern had almost all disappeared, while the Tartars' approach was strongly rumoured, they then decided to break the bridge down. Fortunately Lorraine's dragoons appeared in the nick of time, and Dunewald pushed the Tartars back. The bridge was saved. Then more troops, under Leslie, also reached Krems and from 9 August discussions were going on here about its repair and strengthening, and about the construction of a new bridge at Tulln, 25 miles down stream. The relief of Vienna, however slow the government's diplomacy and cumbrous its organisation of supplies in the Austrian provinces, had drawn a stage nearer. The great practical necessity of the immediate future was to provide for the safe and speedy crossing of the Danube.

Meanwhile certain stout-hearted individuals, neither helped nor hindered by politicians in Passau or Krems, began to take more positive action against the raiders along the south bank of the river. The Abbot of Melk, on 17 July, informed the Estates of Upper Austria that the devastation caused by the Tartars (and by Magyars) was above all due to a lamentable unwillingness to attack them. One of his officials, writing to a brother at Linz, adds that the enemy bands did not number more than fifteen men apiece. Sometimes only two or three horsemen swept up suddenly to set fire to barns and houses. They disappeared at once, if anyone dared to resist. It was, he said, as if the resident population were temporarily 'bewitched'; more probably they were just not at home, and like the government had fled in panic. The Abbot was made of sterner stuff, and enjoyed the great advantage of stone walls surrounding a stronghold. Equally, the authorities at the Herzogenburg monastery east of Melk did their best. With the help of fifty musketeers and a sergeant sent by Leslie, they kept the raiders out of most of their property. In fact, little damage was reported in this quarter of the plain.

An Austrian detachment continued to hold on at Tulln, although in the neighbourhood were not only Tartars and Magyars but Turks 'from Asia' – which we know, because during the second week of August a curious incident occurred.

Albert Caprara, dismissed by Kara Mustafa at Osijek, had been sent to Buda.[45] The Turkish assault on Vienna prospered, and the Grand Vezir could see no further advantage in detaining an ambassador extraordinary to whom he felt obliged to accord some of the privileges of his status. So Caprara was brought from Buda to the encampment outside the besieged city, where he conferred with Kuniz and saw for himself the desolation of once prosperous palaces and suburbs. He was next taken over the Wiener Wald. He records a dignified and philosophic conversation over coffee, with the Turkish officer in charge of an outpost near Tulln. They lamented together the illiberality of war in so noble a landscape. Then – we are not told precisely how this was managed – Caprara got over to the other side of the Danube, and went to report at Passau.[46] His journey, when it was first sanctioned by the Grand Vezir, must be understood as a sign of the Turks' confidence; by the time Caprara reached Tulln, Leopold's increasing armament had begun to tilt the balance of forces in central Europe to their disadvantage.

7

Warsaw, Dresden, Berlin and Regensburg

I

Administrative preparations to receive foreign armies in Austria were no doubt essential. The first duty of the ministers at Passau, as they saw it, was nonetheless the exercise of diplomacy. These armies would only move if the princes of Europe were brought to decide that they consulted their own best interests by coming to the rescue of the Habsburg Emperor. Treaty obligations, appeals to Christian sentiment, an analysis of the military implications if Kara Mustafa permanently lodged an Ottoman garrison in the heart of Europe: these were the major instruments to be handled by Stratmann and Königsegg in their unaccustomed quarters, as they looked to the world beyond the confines of the Danube.

They relied above all on Sobieski, bound by treaty to wage an aggressive war against the Turks in the campaigning season of 1683, and to help in the defence of Vienna if an emergency occurred.

In Poland the French ambassador had been heavily defeated in the course of the Diet's proceedings. He still hoped that three or four months would be needed to raise the taxes for a new army, quite apart from the time taken in raising and assembling the troops. In any case he believed that some of the Polish provinces, in meetings of their own 'diets', were about to mangle the recommendations of the national Diet.[1] Aristocratic assemblies, enjoying very extensive privileges, would always be unwilling to tax themselves or their tenantry for the sake of the state, and in particular (so he reported) the governors of Poznań, Vilna and Ruthenia continued in a mood of the utmost antagonism to their elected King. The ambassador admitted to Louis XIV that royal propaganda was active, and feared that too many of the smaller nobility were likely to listen to it, but he still pinned his faith to the slow workings of a political system in which the powers of King, Diet and Senate were held in check by the semi-independent status of the provinces. Time, the essence of the problem when armies had to be raised in the seventeenth century, appeared to be on his side. Yet on some important points de Vitry proved wrong. The provincial assemblies began to meet in the middle of May, and a fortnight later the overwhelming majority had accepted the proposals of the King and the national Diet. The Habsburg subsidy was also beginning to flow, and the military units to take shape.

But the weeks were passing swiftly by and, as they passed, the likelihood of an advance by the Poles into Podolia or farther east faded away. Here Sobieski ran into difficulties. He had intended to use the Church's money for the purpose of recruiting Cossacks. He greatly respected their military qualities, and wanted to coax them to attack the Crimean Tartars, those important auxiliaries of the Sultan. Innocent XI decided otherwise, and pressed for direct action against the Turks. He ordered Pallavicini, the nuncio, not to transfer any funds to the King unless the Cossacks were committed by the terms of their agreement to fight in Hungary; nor was he to do so before the Poles themselves actually began hostilities. Sobieski expressed immense annoyance at what seemed to him a fatuous denial of ready money, which in the end he secured by promising to get not less than 3,000 Cossacks into action in Hungary by mid-August.[2] In fact they never appeared, to his own bitter disappointment.

An aggressive Polish move in the south-east depended on the 'old' army of the standing troops. They were encamped under Field Hetman Sienawski within striking distance of Kamenets – which the Poles dearly wished to recapture. But in Warsaw it was reported, on 16 June, that the King himself proposed to move to Cracow at the end of the month, and had ordered Sienawski to withdraw from his advanced position and make Lvov his headquarters.[3] The shift of emphasis westwards occurred simply because the combined activity of Thököly and the Turks forced the Poles to mount guard along the Hungarian frontier. No one could be certain whether Kara Mustafa intended to halt at Györ, or march still farther up the Danube into Austria, or cross the Danube and threaten Moravia, Silesia and Poland. For the Poles, the very slow mobilisation of their 'new' forces increased the danger of the position. At the end of June Pallavicini almost felt tempted to hope for news of an immediate enemy attack in order to hasten the growth of the Polish army. Sobieski wrote a circular letter to all commanding officers to hurry them on, but clearly little or nothing had so far been done in many districts, above all in Lithuania. To this extent, de Vitry was right.[4]

Meanwhile the Habsburg army under Lorraine had retreated from Neuhäusel. The Vienna government feared for the security of Moravia, and for the fate of its inadequate force in northern Hungary. It tried to increase the numbers under Schultz's command by ordering Prince Lubomirski's men to join him, and also the 4,000 troopers promised by Sobieski in April.[5] There was no sign of the latter even towards the end of June, and urgent instructions reached Leopold's envoy Zierowski at Warsaw to press hard for another reinforcement. In response, on 4 July the King agreed to move Sienawski and 7,000 men still farther west. They would come as far as Cracow,[6] unite with the new companies assembling there, and be prepared to defend the upper reaches of the Váh if this proved necessary. It was considered vital to be ready for action when the truce between Leopold and Thököly expired on 21 July.

On the day after Sobieski's conference with Zierowski, unknown to them both, a messenger set out at top speed on the long journey from Vienna.[7] Count Thurn covered 350 miles in 11 days, and arrived at the royal residence of Wilanów outside Warsaw on 15 July. Austria was being invaded, its capital city was in danger, he reported, and the Emperor appealed to the King of Poland for help. In his turn the Count did not know that, while he spoke, Kara Mustafa was completing the encirclement of Vienna and Leopold was on his way from Linz to Passau.

At first Sobieski replied rather vaguely, promising assistance by the middle of August, if the Turks actually besieged Vienna. Much more detailed debate and discussion followed. Thurn gloomily told the nuncio that the facts were undoubtedly worse than anything contained in his dispatches, while the Poles had to weigh the view that the Sultan's army was now committed to a risky enterprise in an area mercifully remote from most Polish territory. At length the King announced his decisions: to send Sienawski and his 7,000 men to join Lorraine; to prepare to go himself to Vienna if it was besieged by the Turks; and if it was not, to fight in Podolia or possibly Transylvania. But most important of all, he determined to leave Warsaw at once. He had been meaning to go, he had delayed and dithered, and now it abruptly became clear to him that delay was dangerous. Illness, hunting, the birth of a son, the Queen's health, and purchases of property, had together taken up much of his time in the spring and early summer – the normal period of tranquillity between a winter of strenuous politics and a season of warfare in the late summer and the autumn. Now the sense of a gigantic emergency, and reasons of state, began increasingly to dominate his thinking again.

The King left Warsaw on 18 July and reached Cracow on the 29th.[8] The whole court with the Queen, Prince Jacob, the Austrian ambassadors, the papal nuncio, and an incalculable number of servants, carriages and carts went forward at an average speed of seventeen or eighteen miles a day. It was not fast going, nor was the road through Piotrków and Czestochowa the most direct to Cracow. But Sobieski had to allow sufficient time for the mobilisation of his army. He had to visit Our Lady of Czestochowa, then and now the greatest shrine in Poland, to beg her good offices for the coming campaign. He had to defer to his assertive wife, who wished to accompany him and to go to Czestochowa and Cracow.

At this point of time, when the fateful venture was just beginning to gather momentum, one circumstance strikes an observer very forcibly. No single

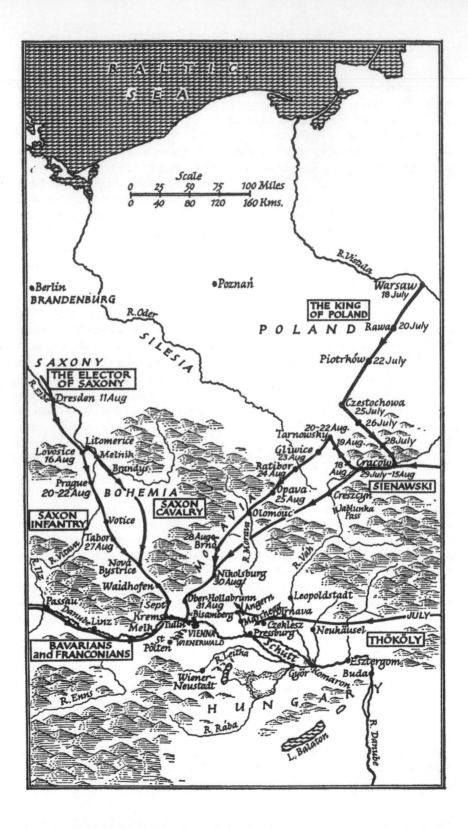

sensational report of a threatened catastrophe brought Sobieski to his feet, and made him ride from Warsaw to Vienna in order to honour his signature of a recent treaty. He was already preparing for the season's campaigning, when Thurn arrived. Already he had been forced by stages to move troops away from the south-east, the theatre of all his earlier exploits against the Turks, to the south-west. At Wilanów on 15 July he first realised that the enemy was across the Rába in force, and concluded that Polish military power would have to be exerted somewhere in the triangle of ground between the points of Győr, Vienna and Cracow; but news of the Ottoman advance to Vienna, the city's encirclement, and the state of siege involving the emergency clause in his treaty with Leopold, only reached him bit by bit. The distance from Warsaw to the Danube implied an equally disconcerting interval of time. Letters from Lorraine and Leopold to Sobieski were obsolete when they arrived, and his answers irrelevant. Then the gap narrowed. Vienna was ten days away at Warsaw, five at Cracow, and the news from Austria became clearer, fuller and more up to date. The King gradually elaborated in his mind a picture of the battlefield, drawn from the growing deposit of reports and dispatches which came in as he was riding south.

Piecemeal knowledge of the crisis hardly eased the strain which it imposed on the Poles. Their customary practice in the Turkish wars of the 1670's had been the leisurely commencement in August or September of warfare which lasted until December, and was fought in Ruthenia, Podolia and the Ukraine with the manpower assembled there in the course of years. Men from the rest of Poland were moved south and east at a very slow pace, and the votes of a Diet to raise taxes and troops in one year often took effect in the next (or not at all). In any case an uneasy peace prevailed after 1676, and the Diet of 1677 insisted on a radical reduction of the army. In 1683 the machinery required for warfare on the grand scale was only just beginning to turn again, and no Polish politician would have been surprised if a serious attempt to recover Kamenets were delayed for twelve months. There was, of course, the unhappy possibility of a Turkish attack; but at least Poland had a military frontier in the south-east, with the 'old' army permanently stationed there. Yet now, as early as July, they had to visualise the immediate dispatch of an army to a point 200 miles beyond the south-western frontier of Poland. The decision to bring the 'old' troops to Cracow in fact signified that the 'new' regiments were not ready; and as Sobieski told Innocent XI in August, the authorities were only beginning to levy taxes for their pay.[9] The chronic shortage of Polish men and money certainly accounts for his very great preoccupation with foreign subsidies[10] and auxiliaries, but probably the worst feature of the crisis of 1683 was that it broke so early in the year. Nothing can have perplexed Sobieski more as he pondered affairs on his journey.

There is no sign that the King repented or was reluctant to push forward to Vienna, and without doubt it was the one course open to him. Not only did the treaty bind him, a treaty which accorded with his own judgment on the strategic question, but the tremendous political struggle in the Polish Diet a few months earlier absolutely committed him to his present course of action. His party in Poland would have collapsed overnight if he had hesitated to support his allies at home and abroad on this issue.

On 19 July after the second day's advance from Warsaw, Sobieski wrote to the Elector of Brandenburg in his secretary's roundest Latin. 'Already the Ottoman fury is raging everywhere, attacking alas! the Christian princes with fire and sword . . .' Fresh news had come in, because he now referred to Leopold's flight from the threatened city. He announced the speedy concentration of all Polish troops at Cracow, and summoned the Elector to send an expeditionary force instantly.* The request went off to Frederick William's ambassador at Warsaw, but within twenty-four hours a special messenger followed with further news: a letter from Lorraine had just arrived.[11] This document, now lost, was the first instalment in a correspondence which has become one of the principal memorials of the time. Lorraine, it can be guessed, described how he was garrisoning Vienna with his infantry and placing his force of cavalry on the north bank of the Danube. A little later another letter reached the King. Its weightiest news was the withdrawal of the Habsburg troops under Schultz from the Váh valley.[12]

Replying to Lorraine on 22 July,[13] the King recognises that 'Vienna is really besieged by the Vezir'. Treaty obligations bound him to come to the rescue. He said that Vienna was more important to him than Cracow, Lvov and Warsaw – which meant, as always, that he preferred to defend these cities at the gates of Vienna. He was determined to overcome difficulties but complained that he had been left inexcusably ill-informed about conditions in Austria and Hungary. He asked for a detailed description of the Danube, its channels and islands; he obviously possessed no map of the Vienna landscape, nor did he even at this point specifically ask for one. He also criticised Lorraine for putting all his infantry into the city, thereby seriously weakening the army outside. He was all the more worried by this because his own infantry appeared dangerously inadequate. He hoped to use 4,000 Cossacks to cover the deficiency, and relied on the appearance of a strong Bavarian contingent of infantrymen. Further, he had not been told enough about the defences of the bridge or bridges which connected Vienna and its garrison with the field-army over the river. He recognised that the next bridge upstream, at Krems, might well prove of high military importance if Vienna were completely invested by the Turks, and Pressburg lost. But how strong, how large, was it? What was the character of the country ('*qui montes, quae planities, quae flumina, qui passus*') west of Vienna and south of the Danube?

To these queries, and a number of others, he expected full prompt answers.

---

*The Elector's obligation to send help to Poland was a relic, confirmed by treaty, of the old feudal dependency of East Prussia on the Kingdom of Poland which ended in 1657.

Meanwhile he was hurrying to Cracow, having placed detachments to guard the passes which lead from Hungary to south-west Poland and Silesia. He also asked Lorraine whether or not he should send Sienawski forward. By this offer, put in the form of a question, it looks a little as if he was delaying the Field Hetman's march southward to the battle-field although he had previously agreed to it; but perhaps he hoped to conceal the awkward fact that Sienawski could not have reached even Cracow by the time of writing.

Two days later, on 24 July, the King spent the night at Kruszyna, a property of the Denhoff family, where the palace and gardens were admired by a French contemporary as outstanding of their kind in Poland.[14] Here he wrote to his chancellor at Warsaw to inform him of the most recent news. A Polish officer had arrived with letters from Lubomirski and Lorraine describing the position at the bridgehead opposite Vienna.[15] The Turks were in Leopoldstadt, he learnt, and the men of the garrison were cut off from the field army. Too few defence-works protected the Habsburg encampment and a sense of gloom filled Lorraine's headquarters. The future depended, wrote Lubomirski (well knowing whom he addressed), on the King's speed and strength even though the Germans also promised help. The day after he had given this account to his chancellor, Sobieski replied to Lorraine from Czestochowa. He would advance at once, without waiting for the full concentration of either the Polish or the Lithuanian forces. He had sent forward a vanguard; and Sienawski followed. He begged Lorraine to fortify his camp properly and promised to do everything in his own power to further the common cause. After signing this vigorous but somewhat vague exposition of his plans, he resumed the journey to Cracow.

By now Polish statesmen could hardly complain that they were not being given detailed information. The worse the state of affairs at Vienna, the more Lorraine wished to impress on them his profound sense of alarm. During the next few weeks he answered Sobieski's queries and described what he had done to meet or anticipate his criticism. The bridge near Krems was strongly held, a new bridge to Tulln would soon be taken in hand. He reported the victory at Pressburg, praising to the sky the exploits of the Polish soldiers who fought there, and the march of the Saxons and Franconians from Germany. He forwarded copies of the letters received from Starhemberg and Caplirs in the city. He also sent a map of the theatre of war and this, on Sobieski's instructions, was thoroughly scrutinised by the French engineer Dupont, who had hurried from the distant front near Kamenets to southern Poland.[16] Lorraine, in fact, was doing his utmost to clarify the mind of the authorities in Cracow.

Two connected problems of great difficulty preoccupied the King. One was the mustering of his forces, the other the choice of a route to Vienna. At the end of June and the beginning of July, when the situation grew threatening in western Hungary, he naturally wanted to seal off the passes by which Thököly or Tartar raiders or even the Turks could enter Silesia and Poland, while he reckoned to leave responsibility for the defence of Moravia to Lorraine. This was probably still his view in the conferences held at Wilanów on 15 July. With definite news of the siege of Vienna it became more puzzling to know how to act. Troops moving from the area round Warsaw, or from the western Polish provinces, towards Vienna by the shortest route would pass through Czestochowa to Tarnowskie through Silesia and so southwards. The rational plan for the King would have been to advance straight to Silesia, while the 'old' army came up on his left, first to cover Cracow, and then taking the road via Cieszyn (Teschen) to join him. It was rational, but impossible. With only the ghost of an army ready in the west by the end of July, the King had to go himself to Cracow in order to meet the forces riding towards the same point from Podolia and Galicia. They, and they alone, could provide the solid core of an army fit to advance against the Turks and to claim pride of place among the other forces marching to relieve Vienna. The question of prestige profoundly affected the King's dispositions: he could not afford to demean himself to the great dignitaries of Poland and Lithuania inside his own dominions, or to the Electors of the Empire who did not bear the title of King, or to the Habsburgs. Already his wife had seen fit to inform the court at Passau that her husband must be given the supreme command in the coming campaign.[17] Great personal ambition, and a severe consideration of political and military interests, were linked firmly together. Whatever happened to Vienna, it was first necessary to bring together a sufficiently large army before moving out of Poland.

The King waited at Cracow from 29 July until 10 August.[18] Pallavicini reports that troops came in almost daily. Field Hetman Sienawski arrived on 2 August, Crown Hetman Jablonowski on the 8th, the soldiers of both halted outside the city, and the King inspected them. Obviously very great efforts were made and a foreign eyewitness admitted the fact, testifying that 'everything which occurred in this period of preparation for the war was a real miracle, considering the state of this country where fulfilment rather lags behind intentions'. Against such praise must be set Sobieski's frank confession to Lorraine (on the 11th) that he would be leaving many troops behind, including the whole Lithuanian army and several thousand Cossacks. Nor did he allow any detailed specification of his force to be delivered to the Habsburg officials who would be responsible for quartering and provisioning the Polish army in Silesia and Moravia. The best calculation they could make put its size at 16,000 men, and this was somewhat higher than another estimate, of 13,000 or 14,000, given by Sobieski's secretary in a letter to Rome as late as 18 August.[19] But a Polish artillery officer states that Hetman Jablonowski's force was small when it left Cracow, and increased in the course of the march; while there is other evidence that large numbers only came up considerably later. A Moravian record mentions Polish contingents passing through a particular place on the road to Vienna every day between 1 and 26 September – some of them, therefore, after the defeat of the Turks outside the city.[20]

On 22 July the King had offered to send Sienawski forward independently of the main army, and on the strength of this Lorraine wrote directly to the Hetman requesting him to advance with all possible speed. The King next informed Lorraine that a vanguard was already on its way to him, which would be followed by those under the Field Hetman's command. But on the 10th he wrote that both contingents would wait near Olomouc for his own arrival – unless an emergency compelled Lorraine to ask them to move forward immediately. This delay occurred partly because the 'old' army did not get to Cracow until 2 August; partly (there is a suspiciously long interval between the 2nd and 10th) because the King was anxious not to lose touch with the Hetman by letting him move too far ahead. Polish military strength had not only to be sufficient; it was necessary for the King's control to be as complete as possible. The more difficult it was to raise new troops, the more important it became to keep a firm hold on the older troops and their commanders.

The problem of the itinerary to be followed concerned not only Sobieski and the Poles but the population and administrators of Silesia, Moravia and Austria. The passage of a sizeable army through these lands was bound to add to the troubles of a country-side already heavily taxed for the war. Some areas and towns, if they were lucky, might hope to escape actual contact with the advancing soldiers. On the other hand, the commissariats of this period had found it a matter of common experience that the supplies and communications of any one region could not bear the strain of excessive numbers passing through, and they preferred to spread them out widely, in order to gather forage and food from as many places as possible. Considerations of this kind at first disposed the King, partly advised by the Habsburg government at Breslau, to plan a threefold line of advance to the Danube. Sobieski reserved for himself a line of march through Opava (Troppau) to Brno, while the left wing went via Cieszyn (Teschen), and Crown Hetman Jablonowski was to take a wide sweep through Tarnowskie to the right, possibly as far west as Bohemia.[21] In the end Sobieski also went to Tarnowskie – the 'general rendezvous' –but the Crown Hetman and the main body of troops accompanied him through Moravia to Vienna. The route via Cieszyn was still assigned to Sienawski.

The administrative reasons for spreading out the Polish forces, which would also have given the Hetman an independent command, were less urgent than the King's need to lead his own troops. And he argued, as the authorities in Passau were arguing to Lorraine, that it was military madness to try to lift the siege of Vienna without employing the maximum force available. It turned out that the King's calculations, and theirs, were correct by the barest possible margin.

During the long halt at Cracow, other pieces of news were recorded by observers. Sobieski sent an envoy to negotiate with Thököly,[22] and his critics condemn this as obvious double-dealing; but the intention must have been to dissuade the Magyars from trying to raid into Poland during the King's

absence. Of greater popular interest was the celebration of St Laurence's day
(10 August) in the Cathedral. Amid a gathering of King, Queen, princes,
bishops, generals, palatines, soldiers and people, the nuncio published the
Pope's indulgence for all men going out to battle in this Holy War. After
hearing a powerful sermon on the same theme, the King moved down from
his throne to the altar steps for the benediction, and was blessed by the nuncio.
Pallavicini, writing afterwards to Innocent, recalled the singing, his sense of
the King's intense devotion, and the weeping of the Queen. The apostolic
brief was translated, and thousands of copies were printed and published.[23]
The general enthusiasm ran high, enhanced by reports of Polish feats of arms
under Lorraine and Lubomirski. It was time to go, and right to go, on the day
of Our Lady's Assumption the 15 August.

Sienawski had now hastened after his men, the forces under Jablonowski
were on their way to Tarnowskie. The King and Queen with their household,
and household troops, followed them up the Vistula valley and then turned
north again. It took no less than five days to cover this stretch of country.[24]
Tarnowskie is thirty miles from Czestochowa, and the King of Poland had
therefore spent twenty-five days in getting from one to the other. It must have
seemed an eternity to the Austrian ambassador who accompanied him. But
the King had at last collected his forces. A part of the 'old' troops first received
their marching orders in Podolia, others on the Moldavian frontier: they rode
250 miles to reach Cracow. Many of the 'new' men came an equal distance
from northern and central regions of the country. Only the Lithuanians and
the Cossacks defaulted completely. Nor could there be any doubt of the King's
energy, and of his determination to play the most conspicuous part possible
in a crisis which involved all his future prospects in Poland, and stirred up his
military ambition and his Christian fervour. As it happened, for the last time
in John Sobieski's lifetime his physique was equal to a grand occasion. He was
fifty-one years old in 1683, though already ailing too often, and far too fat.

On 19 August when the King was still some distance from Tarnowskie,
General Caraffa arrived from Lorraine's headquarters.[25] He brought news of
the greatest importance.

So far, information from Vienna emphasised that the relieving army must
not dawdle, but sounded hopeful enough to suggest that there was still time
to get such an army together. If there was not time, there was equally no point
in exposing too weak a force too far from Poland itself. And the contemporary
science of war tended to affirm that fortified cities with large garrisons did
not fall quickly. And conditions in Poland slowed down the King's advance.
This sequence of facts and calculations acted together like a drag on the
Polish military effort between mid-June and mid-August. The King had left
Warsaw later than he originally intended. He left Cracow later than he said he
would. He moved slowly even after leaving Cracow, and seemed increasingly
preoccupied by political and military arguments for keeping all his forces
together. This meant holding back the vanguard, and reducing the speed of his

lighter troops. Lorraine's plea, that Sienawski should go forward at once, met with a more and more guarded response. Hetman Jablonowski waited for the King. The King waited for the Queen, who appeared to dictate his speed by the pace of her own carriage. This could not go on indefinitely, and Caraffa came to clinch the view that it could not. He carried a letter from Lorraine of 15 August with copies of the first messages brought out of Vienna by Koltschitzky: the commandant Starhemberg was ill, Rimpler the chief engineer was dead, the garrison greatly weakened, the Turks were attaching their mines to one of the ravelins – 'I therefore beg your Majesty to come quickly, and in person with the foremost troops of your army, to assist us . . .' A similar appeal was addressed on two successive days to Hetman Jablonowski.[26]

Accompanied by Caraffa the King continued on his way to Tarnowskie. It was the rendezvous, and the first halt beyond the boundaries of old Poland. Final preparations were made, and a great review was held on the 22nd. One witness says that the Poles preferred to conceal from Caraffa their inadequate artillery and infantry by sending them on ahead.[27] Another, the enterprising reporter who sent an account to the Breslau newsheet, *Neu-Ankommender Kriegs-Curirer*, described the splendour of the scene with 50,000 men, 6,000 wagons and twenty-eight cannon on the field.[28] The first figure is incredible, the third sounds plausible. The King wrote once more to Lorraine and anticipated Caraffa's criticisms of the army, which they had inspected together, by giving his own view: it was not large enough, but the daily arrival of old and new troops, and their extraordinary spirit, now encouraged him to go forward. After one more day's march at the usual speed he himself proposed to advance with a picked body of fast troops.[29]

The King took an affectionate farewell of the Queen. She returned to Cracow to preside over the government of Poland, and this separation gave the King greater freedom of movement. It gave her that amazing series of letters, passionate and rhetorical, which he wrote in the course of his journey into Austria and Hungary.

The next few days were strenuous enough for the moving forces of men, and the districts through which they passed. The King spent the nights of the 22nd and 23rd in monastic houses. Crossing the Oder at Ratibor he was well entertained there by the Obersdorf family at the Emperor's expense.[30] His reception in Silesia satisfied the King, and provisioning for his army seems to have been adequate. The Habsburg administration gave the lightweight Polish coinage a limited legal currency, but naturally made every effort to keep the troops outside the towns; the quartermasters and commissaries were continually busy.[31] The Estates of nobility paid deferential attention to the King and the Polish grandees. At the same time the wheels of diplomacy went on turning. The King wrote to the Queen on the 23rd and 25th, to the Pope on the 23rd, to Lorraine on the 24th. News came in from Danzig, Paris, Lorraine's camp, and Cracow. With some 3,000 men the King definitely went ahead of the main army after the 24th, and on the next day hurried through Opava without loss of time. He went up into the hills along a steep and stony road. On the evening of the 25th, he was handed official messages of welcome from Leopold and his court. But King John describes these as 'impertinent' to his Marysienka; while at Olomouc the next night he was displeased equally by his lodgings and the character of the citizens. He slept under canvas for the first time on the 27th, and by the next evening reached a small town not far from Brno.

The news coming in from the south was bad. Lorraine was getting desperate about the situation in Vienna; correspondence with the garrison increased his fears. On the 21st he forwarded Starhemberg's letter of the 19th to the King and – the direct evidence has been lost – he must once again have appealed to Sienawski, who had advanced through Silesia and Moravia on Sobieski's left. There is no sure proof of the date when the King first read Starhemberg's letter but on the 25th he was highly alarmed by what he had learnt of Lorraine's new request to Sienawski, a request backed by Lubomirski. He did not want Lorraine to try to relieve the city before he arrived, nor did he want Lubomirski or his Field Hetman Sienawski to risk the terrible penalties of defeat by employing too small a force of men. Above all he did not want his personal prestige compromised. As he said: 'Precipitate action might cause disaster (which God forfend), or give to others the glory of forcing the enemy to retreat before I arrive, and therefore I am hurrying forward, having strictly commanded the Hetman to wait for me.[32] With this crucial problem on his mind, it is hardly surprising that the ceremonial harangues and the salvoes of municipal artillery at Olomouc did not appeal to him.

On the 27th he received a letter written by Lorraine two days earlier. Addressed to Sienawski, it contained a positive proposal for a meeting between the Austrian commander and the Hetman at Wolkersdorf (a long way down towards the Danube) on that very day, the 27th. In accordance with the King's previous instructions, this meeting could not and did not take place. Lorraine drew back to Korneuburg where there was enough to preoccupy him: guarding the area from which Thököly's men and the Turks had recently been driven, destroying the Vienna bridges which the Turks were trying to mend, and finishing the new bridge at Tulln.[33] The King moved on, hurrying but not to be hustled. He informed Lorraine on the 28th that he must wait for the troops behind him, while ordering Jablonowski to bring forward his cavalry and leave the infantry to follow. He received in audience one of the Liechtenstein family, proprietor of much of the neighbouring land. At Brno he dined with old Kolowrat, Lieutenant of Moravia. He admired the city, the citadel of the Spielberg above it, and the country-side round about which looked rich with the harvest – 'better land than the Ukraine', he wrote. He camped late that evening, signing his letters long after dusk. There was much to occupy his thoughts. A copy of Starhemberg's most recent appeal had arrived. So had Lubomirski in person, to give him first-hand impressions of the scene of war, and of the Habsburg leaders. But there was nothing from Poland. Had the

Queen reached Cracow? Where were those Cossacks and Lithuanians, after all the money spent on them? Or, looking south once more, why was the bridge at Tulln not ready yet? Should he lead his troops to Tulln, or Krems, or elsewhere? He now (on the 29th) asked for a conference with Lorraine as soon as possible.[34] Next day his troops began to cross the River Thaya, the Austrian frontier. Hilly country lay to the left where his men were trying to establish contact with Sienawski's detachments. Next day again they started at dawn, in clear cloudless weather, following a route south and westwards. Soon after noon Sienawski appeared on the road, and Lorraine shortly afterwards. The Duke, once a candidate for the Polish throne, and the King of Poland had met at last. They rode on to Ober-Hollabrun together where they found Waldeck, commander of the Franconian troops already camped on the other bank of the Danube, and various high-ranking officers. There were introductions, inspections, toasts and preliminary consultations. All the witnesses differ as to the details; all were aware that this was a significant occasion, and not only in the history of an Austrian village.

In 1683, so far, most men had discussed the great crisis of the day from a distance. Vienna was remote, beleaguered, and they pondered its probable fate in courts and townships between Madrid and Podolia. They continued to do so, but the meeting at Hollabrun signified that the Habsburg government was at length fusing together widely dispersed forces into a combined armament capable of relieving the city. When Sobieski and Lorraine and Waldeck met, it was as if the curtains had been pulled back, though only by an inch or two and for a moment, to disclose the possibility of an astonishing and decisive feat of arms. The Danube, the hills of the Wiener Wald, and the numbers of the enemy, had always appeared formidable obstacles to success. On closer inspection they still looked formidable, and yet it seemed possible to overcome and even to profit from them.

II

One other powerful force, from Saxony, had also been brought into the arena by this date.

Leopold's ministers, when the Sultan's army entered Hungary, sent Lamberg once more to John George in Dresden and to Frederick William in Berlin. They continued to think in terms of the defence of the Empire, but hoped that a satisfactory agreement with the greater German princes would free more Habsburg troops to deal with the Ottoman advance. A fresh negotiation began in Dresden, but was soon overshadowed by the Elector's dispute with his Estates. They refused to pay for his increasingly numerous standing army, while he insisted on larger grants of supply. Then the dreadful news from Vienna reached them, to be followed hot-foot by Lorraine's special envoy the Duke of Sachsen-Lauenburg, appealing for immediate aid.[35]

John George's military ardour was at once fired by the prospect of a catastrophe which his initiative might help to avert. He had in any case to face the threatening implications of a permanent Ottoman encampment within striking distance of the routes northwards from Moravia and Austria. But he also argued like his neighbours in Franconia:[36] it happened that at the moment he was maintaining numerous troops ready for action; that his own subjects objected strongly to the cost; and that the Turkish assault on Austria made their employment in the Empire unlikely because the Empire would have to acquiesce in a peace dictated by France. If, and the if was important, the Habsburg lands paid the costs, an expedition to Vienna looked like the reasonable temporary solution of a serious problem.[37] The crisis of 1683 in fact forced the Dresden government to use a tactic which was popular enough in the early history of German standing armies. In the next few years Saxon and Brandenburg and Hanoverian regiments, dispensable at home, would be hired out to fight for the Habsburgs in Hungary or for Venice in the Morea. These arrangements were often the result of the most exact and bitter bargaining; but John George proved on this occasion a somewhat careless politician.

He had taken his decision by 22 July without insisting on precise agreements about supply, or the command of his forces in the field. Sachsen-Lauenburg assured him that the Habsburg government was certain to satisfy him on the first point; the Elector vaguely felt that the second could cause little trouble because he himself was setting out at the head of his army. Lamberg wrote from Berlin to lay that he intended to come back immediately to Dresden, in order to complete detailed arrangements for the line of march through Bohemia, and the provisioning of the Saxon regiments. The Elector still had qualms that Frederick William of Brandenburg would secure more favourable terms from Leopold, and he therefore instructed his envoy Schutt to negotiate with the Habsburg statesmen at Passau. Schutt was to ask for the army's pay and supply on the march and during the campaign, for winter quarters, and also for a solution of current frontier disputes affecting forestlands claimed by both Bohemia and Saxon mining enterprises; if possible, Saxony wanted territorial concessions. It sounded grasping enough, but all these requests were robbed of their menace by John George's prior decision to go to Vienna.

This was the position on the last day of July, and the Elector left Dresden on 11th August.[38] The bustle in and about the city was tremendous. On 4th, 5th and 6th, some 7,000 infantry and 3,250 horse and dragoons were mustered on a great meadow by the banks of the Elbe, to be ceremonially reviewed by John George on 7 August. A first-class artillery officer and expert on fortifications, Caspar Klengel, selected artillery from the Dresden arsenal: 16 guns, 2 petards, 87 carts, 351 horses and 187 men were inspected on the 10th. The Elector's own household and staff, when the expedition set out, amounted to 344 persons. Meanwhile members of the Saxon Diet produced a final catalogue of their doubts, debts, and grievances, in a not so humble petition. Commissaries of the Saxon and Bohemian governments met in conference, they settled how fast the army should march and how often it should rest. The Saxons undertook to cross the Bohemian frontier on 13 August and the Austrians agreed in rather airy and imprecise terms to find the supplies which would be required in Bohemia.

The Saxon soldiers now began to move southwards. It was at once apparent that communications and commissariat were entirely inadequate in their own country. They must have put to one another the question, were conditions likely to improve across the border in Bohemia?

A bare recital of dates in the month of August, and of places passed, seems to record the steady progress of the expeditionary force.[39] It went over the heights to Teplice, and reached Lovosice by 16 August. Here it divided into two main bodies. Most of the cavalry moved up the Elbe valley, crossed to the right bank of the tributary Ultava (the Moldau) and then rode over the plains east of Prague, arriving in the uplands of southern Bohemia by the last day of the month. Meanwhile, the infantry and the Elector himself reached Prague on the 20th, followed the obvious southerly route to Tabor, turned south-east, and joined the cavalry in the neighbourhood of Nová Bystrice. They were now half-way between Prague and Vienna.

This record is deceptive. Only feverish negotiation, and hard riding by the negotiators, kept the army moving forward. On the day John George entered Bohemia, and on the next day when he rode to Teplice, a whole sequence of envoys reached his headquarters: the tireless Lamberg still shuttling between Brandenburg, Saxony and Passau; the Bohemian commissioners, who now announced that they were not empowered to provide supplies *gratis* to the Saxon troops; and a messenger from Schutt, to state that his discussions at Passau had not led to an agreement. Indeed the Habsburg ministers turned down every one of John George's demands: for winter quarters, supplies, the supreme command in the field, and territorial concessions of any kind. They simply continued to ask blandly for his help and of course, from their standpoint, they correctly assumed that the Elector would find it difficult to draw back. The Saxon counsellors conferred angrily at Teplice. The diary of one of the most influential, Bose, says that the case was argued for an immediate return to Dresden.[40] Lamberg intervened, pleaded, and finally secured a fresh statement of Saxon grievances with which he hurried off to Passau. The Elector said that he was determined not to advance beyond Prague until he received a satisfactory answer. The paper in Lamberg's hand repeated his original demands, but the envoy himself now saw that only one point was crucial: if the Habsburg ministers wanted the Saxon army, they must at least co-operate in finding the necessary food and forage; nor could the Saxons be expected to pay for these. The other demands could be evaded, as before, by sensible diplomatic inaction. The army moved on. The Elector delayed a few hours longer to enjoy the hunting and to admire the scenery.

What happened in Teplice happened in Prague. Schutt's message had been followed at a slower pace by a polite letter from Leopold, echoing the negative response of his councillors. The reply to the Saxon ultimatum carried by Lamberg had not yet come in. Once again the Elector sent off a messenger, Friessen, who was to state that the Elector proposed to advance no farther than two days' march beyond Prague unless he got a satisfactory answer. Prague, so the diarists report, was an enjoyable city, the entertainment given in the Duke of Sachsen-Lauenburg's palace was excellent; the Elector went sightseeing but, once again, he finally moved forward on 22 August without waiting for Leopold's reply.

He was still trying hard to find more money at home. He required his administration in Dresden to raise a loan of 200,000 thaler; they said, dryly, that it was out of the question. He required the Estates of Upper Lusatia to find him 30,000 thaler.[41] In both cases he wanted actual currency, his great need of the moment, not credit. Household economies at the Dresden court were also discussed; but there is no evidence that any of the suggestions provided extra money. The Saxon army simply continued to take from the rural population what it needed to keep moving. Payment was no doubt the exception rather than the rule, and no doubt the requisitioning of enough supplies for 10,000 men looked a hopeless business on the mountainous threshold of Bohemia round Teplice. But a week later in the central plain, just after the harvest, it was easier. For this reason, the threat to withdraw became less and less pointed; and John George knew that while the Elector of Brandenburg still held back, the Elector of Bavaria and the King of Poland were hurrying forward to take part in what might prove a glorious and exciting crusade. He and his officers were now near enough the Danube to smell battle.

Farther to the east, the cavalry continued to advance. The men and baggage of the infantry and artillery, with the Elector's staff, passed through Votice and got to Tabor on 27 August. At both towns, soothing assurances came in from the court at Passau. Leopold accepted the Saxon demand for the free consignment of supplies during the march through Habsburg territory to the theatre of war. He also offered supplies for the coming campaign, provided that these could ultimately be charged to the account of the Saxon government. He left John George in full command of his troops, though reserving his own ultimate authority and the possible claims of the King of Poland. In general terms he accepted the principle that the Saxons could claim winter quarters in Habsburg territory, if these should be judged necessary; but said not a word about an adjustment of the northern frontier in the Elector's favour. Bose, in his entry for 25 August, noted that 'the whole court expressed itself satisfied', and it seems as if the Habsburg assurances were just generous enough at a moment of crisis to silence John George's more exacting councillors. At Votice, also, another diarist recorded items of news beneath the notice of serious politicians: the 26th was a heavy thunderous day, four musketeers were court-martialled for plundering, and one was executed.[42]

Not long afterwards the two parts of the Saxon army began to knit together again. From Nová Bystrice Bose and Flemming were sent to the Emperor, now at Linz. The Saxons started crossing into Austria on the day that John Sobieski and Lorraine entered Ober-Hollabrun fifty miles east of them. They marched steadily forward, through Waidhofen which belonged to Lamberg's family, and through Horn which belonged to Count Hoya. The troops camped in the open, and the Elector quartered comfortably in the residences of these great landlords; from the windows of the palace at Horn it was possible to survey the whole encampment of the Saxon army on 2 September. On the 3rd the men rested, and then made their way to the Danube. They reached Krems on 6 September. The last few days had passed without incident, although there was considerable nervousness about the alleged marauding of the Poles, with whom the Saxons were coming into contact for the first time. For one night most of John George's regiments quartered on an island in the stream of the Danube. The Bavarians and Franconians were already over on the right bank of the river. The Poles were coming up on the left, farther downstream. The Saxons, in fact, now merged into the large and rapidly expanding army of relief, one of its best organised contingents.

III

Against this outstanding diplomatic success, the Emperor Leopold's advisers had to set the total failure of their approaches to Frederick William of Brandenburg. Certainly, the Habsburg interest had its champions in Berlin. The Elector was too good a politician to let Rébenac, the tireless French envoy, have everything his own way, and Lamberg's many visits served to remind Louis XIV that Frederick William never lost sight of the working alternative to his general policy (in these years) of partnership with France. If Fuchs and Meinders, industrious officials, were for the time being content to favour French interests and to accept modest French gifts of cash when offered,[43] Prince John George of Anhalt-Dessau was a very different proposition. Wealthy, aristocratic, with a princess of the house of Orange for his wife and normally resident in Berlin, he could afford to play the part of the Elector's life-long friend, unruffled by the Elector's famous tantrums; and throughout 1683 he acted as an enthusiastic supporter of the Habsburgs. Derfflinger, Austrian by birth, perhaps the Elector's favourite military commander, and the Electoral Prince Frederick, both stood by him. They all felt that Brandenburg ought to share in the common duty of states of the Empire, the defence of Emperor and Empire against aggressors. They urged, plausibly enough, that a Turkish thrust from Hungary towards Moravia and Silesia might come dangerously close to Brandenburg territory. They reminded the Elector of his claim by inheritance on some of the Silesian duchies. Yet they failed to assist Leopold at a time when their argument sounded strongest.

June and July 1683 were shocking months in the annals of the Hohenzollern court. It was learnt that Louis XIV had refused to ratify a draft agreement, by the terms of which French troops would have held the Brunswick princes in check while Brandenburg (with Denmark) invaded Swedish territory in north Germany.[44] The Elector's sister and daughter-in-law both died; the Elector himself was troubled by the stone and the gout, and fell seriously ill. The doctors despaired of him, but he gradually recovered. His mood of irritation with the King of France was such that Rébenac found, temporarily, that the critics of France at court were in the ascendant. In June the Elector welcomed, with considerable courtesy, another short visit by Lamberg. Anhalt was optimistic about the prospect of an alliance with the Habsburg court.[45]

On 7 July, shortly before he hurried away from Vienna, Leopold wrote to Lamberg at Dresden: the enemy was at the gates, and he must go at once to Berlin and ask for help. In consequence, from the moment of the envoy's arrival on 16 July, the Elector's household in Berlin and Potsdam became a centre of intense discussion and intrigue. Frederick William was at first too ill to see Lamberg, who asked for the dispatch of 6,000 men to Vienna and offered 200,000 thaler for them. Fuchs replied politely that neither figure was satisfactory. The Elector would require at least 300,000 thaler for 6,000 men, and in any case he was convinced that an expeditionary force of 12,000 was needed in so grand an emergency.[46] In his own mind, of course, the minister had to try and calculate whether a more or less substantial part of the army which had been intended for the campaign against Sweden, with the help of a French subsidy, could be transferred to Habsburg territory and maintained by Habsburg funds. He reminded Lamberg that the Elector expected the Emperor to come to terms with Louis XIV, but closed the discussion with two promising items of news. Anhalt was to go at once to Leopold's court. Derfflinger was to take charge of the military preparations.

On the 23rd, Anhalt left Berlin. Whatever the exact tenor of his instructions, he told Lamberg, he was determined to negotiate in the Emperor's favour. With an envoy so curiously insubordinate, the possibility of a misunderstanding was a very real one. To make matters worse Rébenac, writing an 28 July, was able to assure Louis XIV that 'the Prince will find his instructions quite different from what he thought they would be when he left.'[47] Indeed, the Elector's standpoint fluctuated. He lamented the weakness of the Christian states in the face of a violent Turkish attack; but he was swayed by the fact that later news from Vienna was less catastrophic than the first reports. Rébenac, in a long private interview, emphasised with eloquence and skill all the arguments against sending the Brandenburg troops too far afield; it soon became clear, for example, that the Brunswick troops would remain in north Germany. The Elector began again to recollect that French subsidies were punctually paid, to appreciate that his major interests were focused in this northern area between the Vistula and Rhine. Unless he squeezed very substantial concessions from the court at Passau, the case against helping the Emperor was not as weighty as the case for keeping him weak. Almost from hour to hour the Elector tacked and tacked, without in the end altering the general course of his diplomacy.

On 22 July he agreed to send a mere 1,200 men to aid Sobieski in accordance with old treaty obligations.[48] He sent a message to tell Anhalt that some 15,000 were assembling at Crossen on the Silesian border, but repeated to his envoy that a pacification in Germany must precede any military pact with Leopold. If old Derfflinger still felt hopeful of sharing the glories of a campaign against the Turks, Rébenac, steadily writing his dispatches to Louis XIV from Berlin, was confident that the Elector would stand firm in the French interest. Frederick William, he believed, had recovered his balance. The French envoy, not the Austrian soldier of fortune, was right.

Anhalt duly arrived at Passau with an impressive staff of servants and followers, and presented his proposals on Saturday, 7 August: peace must be made with France, the Elector offers 6,000 troops, he asks for their supply during the campaign, and lists a variety of financial demands which amount to a total of 500,000 thaler to be paid by Leopold.[49] An agreement could be worked out in three days, he concluded, a courier to Berlin needed five days more and at once the Elector's regiments would commence their march to the Danube. Königsegg, Stratmann and Zinzendorf, conferring together on the Sunday, did not share this rosy view of the immediate future. They found the Brandenburg demands unreasonable, requiring sums of money utterly beyond Leopold's capacity to pay. They disliked the suggestion that 'assignments' of the revenues of various principalities in the Empire should be made over to Brandenburg by the Emperor's fiat. They refused to admit the Elector's claim to the Silesian duchy of Jägerndorf, which he was now apparently willing to trade in return for a huge monetary compensation – 200,000 thaler, equal to the whole amount recently granted to Poland. Above all, in the Elector's proposals there was no hint that Brandenburg intended to join the Habsburg system of alliances in the Empire in order to resist France, even supposing that his troops took part in the war against the Sultan. And if those troops were forthcoming, they would surely arrive too late to help in the relief of Vienna: instead, they would arrive in time to demand winter-quarters on Habsburg territory. Having listed all these objections, Leopold's ministers solemnly decided to continue the discussions with Anhalt. It is possible that they realised the envoy's own determination to come to terms, and overestimated his influence at Berlin. They had in mind one further point. If Vienna fell to the Turks in September, an outright rejection of Frederick William's offer in August would have turned out unnecessary folly.

The second week of August in Passau, therefore, was partially taken up with conversations between Königsegg, Stratmann, and Anhalt. The debate can be reconstructed. One document, with comments added by Anhalt, shows Frederick William's demand for a settlement with France watered down to the plan of a personal interview between Leopold and the Elector, to take place in the following October at Regensburg to discuss such a settlement. The Brandenburg troops must join the Habsburg army before the end of the first week in September. The question of Jägerndorf, or of any financial equivalent for it, was to be left over until the close of the Turkish war. Anhalt then gave even more away. Certain it 'puncta foederis Caesareo-Brandenburgici' were drawn up.[50] In this extraordinary draft, the final article visualised a common effort to undo the 'reunions' of imperial territory to France, after the Turks had been repulsed with the aid of 12,000 Brandenburg soldiers. Not surprisingly, in Königsegg's lodging on Friday 13 August, the Austrian ministers reported to the Dutch and Swedish and Hanoverian representatives that they had been hard at work on a treaty with Frederick William.[51] On paper, at least, they had scored a real diplomatic triumph; and a courier set out for Berlin. Further progress in that quarter could hardly be expected within the next ten days.

IV

The ministers turned, perhaps wearily, to deal with another problem.

Their immediate and essential duty was to take all possible steps to rescue Vienna, but their fundamental responsibility remained the defence of Habsburg interests as a whole. And these interests still required, in their judgment, a stubborn championship of Leopold's position in Germany. When Louis XIV's ambassador, Verjus, made a new offer to the Estates of the Empire at Regensburg on 26 July, the statesmen at Passau had to consider their reply.

The French proposal, accompanied by the sharpest invective against the Austrian and Spanish Habsburgs and their allies – who had neglected to defend Europe against the Sultan in order to intrigue shamefully against Louis – was that both the King of France and the Empire should publicly recognise the status quo in the Rhineland for a period of thirty years, leaving undecided the legal problem of ultimate sovereignty in the territories which the French had occupied since 1679. The King would not ask for the compensation to which he was entitled; and the offer stood open until 31 August.[52] In other words, Louis and Louvois had determined not to intervene in the Empire for one more month; and during that month Turkish pressure, and the pressure of the German states friendly to France, and indeed of all those interests which genuinely believed that a settlement with France was the pre-condition of any effective action against the Ottoman power, were to squeeze from Leopold a significant gesture of surrender. In Regensburg the French knew that all the Rhineland Electors – Cologne, Mainz, Trier and the Palatine – were their allies, while the Brandenburg representative, Gottfried Jena,[53] never wavered from the Francophile line of policy unreservedly followed by Frederick William in the Diet. In fact, they could rely on the College of Electors. Were Leopold's ministers, expelled from Vienna, strong enough to resist Kara Mustafa, Louis XIV, and at least five of the Electors?

Stratmann and Königsegg were tough and intelligent statesmen. Their immediate aim was to collect forces for the relief of the city within two months. They had no use for concessions which did not strengthen the Emperor at once; resistance to France had been their great watchword in politics for years, their permanent assignment; and they were by now sceptical of these French time-limits which, so often renewed, had lost something of their original menace.[54] But they had to meet strong resistance from their friends. At Regensburg, Bavarian and Saxon diplomacy was less sympathetic to Leopold than in Vienna or Passau; and at Passau itself, a number of people close to the Emperor certainly wanted the French offer taken up without further delay. For them, it seemed obvious that there was no time to lose. On the other flank, the Dutch and Spanish envoys were justifiably alarmed, because if the French offer was indeed accepted, Louis XIV could not in future employ his armies in Germany, and would be likely to throw his whole weight against the Spanish Netherlands. As a result, these two diplomats weighed into the grand debate with all their skill.[55] They wanted the absolute rejection of the French proposal for a truce unless Louis explicitly agreed that it included lands in dispute outside the Empire – by which they meant Luxembourg* and the rest of the Spanish Netherlands. The Austrians, for their part, did not at first wish to rule out the chance of coming to terms with Louis if the worst should befall, and Vienna fell. The Dutchman, Brunincx, realised that they would then pay little or no attention to the interest of their allies in the north. This conflict made it difficult, in the first few weeks at Passau, to formulate a common policy; and the debate continued in the course of many discussions.

Early in August the Habsburg tactics were tentative, almost negative. Windischgrätz, the Imperial commissary at Regensburg, the 'mad Roland' who aroused the passionate dislike of Verjus and Gottfried Jena,[56] was instructed to brush aside the time-limit for the moment, and to inform the Diet of Leopold's intention to go himself to Regensburg in October in order to confer personally with the Electors and Princes on all matters of common interest. This was the project which had been raised in the parallel negotiations with Anhalt. Then more hopeful news reached the government from Vienna, and Waldeck also arrived at Passau, after arranging for the Franconian troops to follow him down the Danube.[57] It is clear that he gave powerful assistance to all those who meant to give nothing away to the French because they were confident that the Turks could also be repulsed. Another plea from the four Rhineland Electors, dated 21 August, was set aside in a firm reply from Leopold on the 23rd. His ministers had at length decided on their policy. They were *not* prepared to respond to the French offer before the time-limit expired on 31 August; and they were *not* prepared to say that it was acceptable provided that territories outside western Germany were included in the truce. This was much less negative than it may sound on a casual reading. Leopold had given

---

*Although Louis gave up his blockade of Luxembourg in April, 1682 (see pp. 52–3), it was obvious that he still hoped to win this great citadel by one method or another. Earlier in 1683 he made an 'offer' for it to the Spaniards, but here again his time-limit had run out by July.

nothing away to Louis XIV, and very little to the Spaniards and the Dutch, at a time when the pressure on him to do so was greatest.

On 24 August Waldeck wrote to William of Orange.[58] He was happy enough to report his own part in the strenuous discussions of the past week. The Emperor, he says, declared in conference that he would rather lose some of his lands than make a truce with Louis; but Waldeck believed that Louis was unlikely to 'insult' Leopold for the moment. His personal views on the Danubian theatre of war were simple and outspoken: the Habsburg government should never have left Vienna; the city would continue to hold out until it was relieved.

Anhalt's draft-treaty, when it reached Berlin, caused immense annoyance – and Rébenac was delighted. Frederick William replied at once, rebuked Anhalt for exceeding his instructions and recalled him. The Austrian ministers, by now in Linz, sadly concluded that they must write off their hopes of employing Derfflinger and 6,000 or 12,000 Brandenburg soldiers in the coming struggle for Vienna. They did however decide to pursue negotiations with Anhalt, who had himself determined to remain by the Danube and, if possible, take some share in the campaign ahead. He told the Austrians that he knew the Elector's temper: the last dispatch from Berlin was no doubt the product of insomnia and irritability; if the more militant clauses of the draft could be toned down, he hoped to convince the Elector of its value. On 1 September Stratmann and Königsegg still judged it worthwhile spending their valuable time discussing Habsburg relations with the Hohenzollern court. In retrospect their labour seems an unnecessary use of ink and energy. They had done what they could to mobilise the states of Europe; the troops had already marched out of Germany and Poland, already reached the Danube close to Vienna and the Ottoman besiegers. The months of diplomatic preparation in distant courts were over. Lorraine, Kara Mustafa and Sobieski, acting for the moment as soldiers rather than politicians, would have to shape the immediate future.

8

The Relief of Vienna

I

At this very time, during the second half of August, the courtiers at Passau were intensely excited. For some, the approaching confinement of the Empress was the immediate concern; the question whether she would give birth to a son or a daughter, even though overshadowed by a crisis in the grand antagonism of the Christian and Moslem worlds, had sufficient significance in this age of dynastic politics. For others, the movement of troops from Germany down the Danube whetted their excitement most. The Bavarians had already gone through Passau. On 21 August 6,000 Franconian infantry arrived, travelling by water; 2,000 cavalry were soon to follow by land. The military authorities were naturally anxious about the concentration of these forces in Lower Austria because they knew, in general terms, that the Saxons were already in Bohemia, that the Poles were in Silesia, while Lorraine himself was moving west. Less informed observers still hoped for the appearance of 15,000 Brandenburgers and 5,000 from the Brunswick lands, to make up a total of 100,000 troops for the relieving army. It was not only a matter of transport, food and other supplies, but of the collaboration of so many ruling princes which preoccupied the government. On this point, the Emperor himself felt the gravest doubts. He wanted to recover the personal prestige lost by his abrupt flight from Vienna, and to assert his Imperial status. On the other hand he also wanted to satisfy and pacify indispensable allies and, except in a few moments of daydreaming, did not visualise himself as the generalissimo which his father Ferdinand III had been. In effect, he enjoyed the proudest title on earth, while suffering from an acute sense of personal inferiority in many matters. A long series of discussions followed, in which most of the Habsburg ministers and the Spanish ambassador pressed strongly for Leopold's presence with the army. The nuncio disagreed: such a decision, he argued, could only irritate the other princes, who deserved credit for their determination to come to the rescue of

Vienna.[1] It would increase, not diminish, the dangers of useless quarrels over precedence. (The nuncio spoke as an expert: his correspondence is filled with the details of his ceaseless bickering at court to establish his own precedence over princes of the Empire and their representatives.) It was certainly true that an Emperor who arrived at camp with a retinue of thirty guards could only suffer by contrast with the panoply which the King of Poland and the Elector of Bavaria evidently intended to display. In fact, when the question of precedence did not affect the Catholic Church, Buonvisi blandly overlooked it. He thought that he had won the debate, when Leopold at length decided to move down the river to Linz.[2] This appeared to signify that the Emperor and the War Council simply proposed to get closer to the scene of action; but Leopold wanted to join the army, without having fully made up his mind to do so or determining exactly what part to try and play in the coming campaign. Because the Empress signified her willingness to accompany him he was able to temporise a little longer. The whole affair was one example, among thousands in the course of a long life, of his chronic difficulty in making a firm decision.

On 25 August from 8.30 in the morning until seven o'clock at night the government, including 'the four senior court officers, three chancellors, and two presidents* of the great offices of state, travelled down the Danube as far as Linz.[3] During the day Leopold wrote to Marco d'Aviano, who was himself coming over the Alps to the theatre of action, sent by Pope Innocent with the powers of a Papal Legate to bless and console the crusaders. Leopold, although anxious for yet more counsel, told Marco that he proposed to appear among the confederate princes and generals in order to stop quarrels between them. Then he reached Linz, and the court settled down again. Troops poured through from Germany, and he reviewed them. Max Emmanuel arrived by water, with a large staff which set the court-marshal a pretty problem in trying to accommodate their 600 horses. The old debate continued. Buonvisi urged his views once more, and apparently won over the Bishop of Vienna. Marco arrived on 2 September and also discussed the question with Leopold. Evidently it was understood between them that Marco, who left on the next day for Krems and Tulln, would advise the Emperor whether to proceed farther after he had sounded opinion at the military headquarters.

Momentarily Leopold seemed becalmed. On the 5th he made up his mind to go down the river again and join his army, although he had heard nothing from Marco. Then Prince George of Hanover arrived with his few followers, all that were spared from the powerful Brunswick forces in Lower Saxony. Then the Empress gave birth to a daughter, hastily christened Maria Anna Josepha Regina with the sponsorship of a single godfather, Max Emmanuel. Then a letter from Marco was delivered, and it said not a single word about the matter

---

*One of these was Herman of Baden, who went further down the river in order to confer with Lorraine and Sobieski, and was present at Ober-Hollabrun on 31 August.

uppermost in Leopold's mind. But he set off on the 8th. He left behind him the Empress and her household, and wrote once more begging for definite advice, at the same time admitting that he would wait for it.[4] In his own wavering fashion he was moving with the current of the Danube, and the course of circumstances; he hesitated to enforce the autocratic will vested in him, and yet not his own. He must go, and he must wait; while other and lesser figures participated and determined, he waited. This agonising, pathetic pause in the most dramatic moment of his whole reign, took place on the waters of the Danube somewhere near Dürnstein, on the great bend of the river there; below the bend is the little walled town; and on the height above the river stand the ancient ruins of a castle in which the Anglo-Norman King Richard, Coeur de Lion, was imprisoned in 1193. From here there is an immense panorama stretching miles downstream as far as the western edge of the Wiener Wald. No contemporary source says that anyone was sent up the ridge to observe signs of action in the landscape; but on board his boat Leopold remained from 9 to 12 September. He received a letter from Marco on the 11th, and replied at once. He received another, dated the 11th, on the 12th and again replied. Leopold throughout expresses a complete faith in the future: this crisis, thanks to God and all the saints, thanks to the Papal blessing and the Capuchin's presence in the army, will be surmounted. For the moment he repressed the alternative view, of the plague and the comet and the Turks as a part of a righteous judgment on himself and the sinfulness of man. But he still wanted to know whether the time had not come for the Emperor and hereditary ruler of these lands to negotiate personally with his allies and to show himself to his subjects. Marco said nothing; Leopold did nothing. The siege continued.

II

Starhemberg's letter from Vienna of 18 August was still serene and confident, reporting that the Turks had made little progress in the past week. This was no more than the truth even allowing for the fact that our principal Turkish source of information, which would have boasted of any Turkish gains, has an unfortunate gap from 14 to 17 August. However the Master of Ceremonies, on the 13th, gives two important items:[5] troops and commanders on the Danube islands were being brought round to reinforce the Janissaries and other units in the area in front of the Burg; while heavy rain, falling during the night, made the approaches temporarily unusable. His next entry, on the 18th, notes the Grand Vezir's urgent order to the commander at Neuhäusel to join the army at once.

The Austrians also mention the rain but they were much more preoccupied by the works then being carried out in the Burg and Löbel bastions. New trenches and walls were thrown up quickly, to give better protection to the defenders when and if the Turks reached these inner works. The pressure on the labour squads was intense. Large numbers were absent and ill. Starhemberg reprimanded the civilian authorities sharply for slackness, and insisted on a reorganisation of the burgher companies. Meanwhile all through the week, in front of the bastions, the moat was the scene of violent fighting every day. The soldiers, taking turn and turn about under different commanding officers – Souches, Württemberg, Serenyi and Scherffenberg – held on to the Burg-ravelin, to various block-houses to left and right of it, and to parts of the counterscarp even in this sector. Elsewhere they defended the counterscarp fairly easily. The Turks slowly dug down towards the floor of the moat, desperately trying to extend the area under their control. Trenches and tunnels required first to be dug, then to be strengthened and covered with timbers and sandbags. A few feet away from them their opponents were digging in the same way, using similar materials. Miners on both sides endeavoured to site their powder barrels undetected, and to countermine. After earth and masonry had been displaced by an explosion small groups of men, thirty, forty, or a hundred, went over to the assault, sometimes in daylight, sometimes at night with the darkness abruptly dispelled by flares here and there. On one occasion (the night of the 16th), an Austrian sortie led by Serenyi and Scherffenberg managed to set fire to the Turkish galleries projecting from the escarpment opposite the Löbel, and sufficient damage was done to hold up the enemy for ten or twelve days in this sector.[6] But foot by foot the Turks pressed forward; and on 18 August a much less effective sortie by the garrison troops, intended to push the Turks out of their corner of the ravelin, met with a decided repulse and resulted in the death of Colonel Dupigny, whose dragoons had been dismounted and now shared in the fighting. The consequences of the defeat might have been serious, and it was Starhemberg's good fortune that the Turks were not quick enough to profit from it.

Between 9 and 19 August 12,000 florins were paid out for work and materials needed on the fortifications, on the 13th nearly 1,000 florins were paid to the artillerymen, and on the 19th the troops got their fortnightly allotment of some 32,000 florins.[7] The first of these figures is exceptionally high, and is a fair indication of what was going on in the moat and on the bastions. On the 19th, as well, a small raiding party went out by the Carinthian-gate and was lucky enough to return with thirty-two oxen. The garrison also recovered that part of the ravelin which had been lost the day before.[8]

Indeed the administration in the city ticked on. The bitter and inch by inch struggle for ravelin and moat continued. The fears or hopes that something of a more spectacular kind would decide the issue were daily fed on not very substantial rumours and reports – like the rumour that the Turks were digging a tunnel right under the main wall into Leopold's wine-cellars, or the report that Turkish cavalry were overrunning all the countryside north of the Danube after Lorraine's regiments had marched away to the west.

On 25 August Starhemberg held an important conference with all his principal officers on the Löbel-bastion; immediately opposite the enemy had

been steadily making further progress in the last few days and was coming, as
far as he could judge, dangerously close. A major sortie was decided,

> and accordingly about four in the Afternoon Captain *Travers,* and Captain
> *Heneman* of the Regiment of *Souches* and Lieutenant *Simon* of the Regiment
> of *Beck,* were commanded out upon this Service; who passing through the
> Sallyports, were followed thither by Count *Sereni* and the Prince of *Wirtenberg*
> . . . And Count *Souches* having at the same time undertaken another Sally, not
> far from the same place, the Enemy was forced to give ground; and the Prince
> of *Wirtenberg* pursuing closely into their Trenches without the Counterscarp as
> far as one of their Batteries, upon which were planted three Pieces of Ordinance,
> it would have been very easie to have nailed up their Guns, if our men had
> been provided with Nails, but the Turks beginning to rally and to increase in
> number, they thought fit to retire into the Ditch, still firing upon the Enemy
> that followed them. In this Action were lost about two hundred Common
> Souldiers on our side.*

With that account may be compared the corresponding entry in a Turkish
version of the day's fighting:

> Before noon the Grand Vezir entered the trenches, and summoned to his
> headquarters Hussein pasha, Bekir pasha, the Aga of the Janissaries from
> Rodosto and the *kethuda beyi* Yusuf, as well as other commanders. He gave
> solemn warnings to them all, and ordered each one of them to do his utmost
> to bring the enterprise to a successful conclusion, expending life and property
> for the true faith. Then he returned to his own base outside the works. He
> granted the province of Eger to *kethuda* Ahmed pasha and the province of
> Maras to Omer pasha; he awarded them both insignia of the noblest rank.
> In the afternoon a mine was exploded in Ahmed pasha's sector on the left
> (that is, opposite the Löbel), and the flame of battle flickered for over half an
> hour. It seemed as if the struggle would never end, and the fighting continued
> with incredible bitterness. The commander of the volunteers was given insignia
> appropriate to his rank.[9]

Noticeably, the Turkish writer has played down this affair, but on those
occasions when the garrison had decidedly the worst of the encounter the
Austrian diarists have far less to say about it.

Two days later Starhemberg tried to repeat this tactic, and formidable assault
parties were thrown against the Turks in the moat, particularly in front of
the Burg-bastion. But although his men did a good deal of damage the Turks
were undeniably moving forward towards the main bastions at this stage, and
gradually more and more of the ravelin fell into their hands; the latter was by
now little more than a ruin, with heroic groups of Christian soldiers taking
turns to defend it as long as they could also hold the entrenchment which gave
access to it. That day and the next, a quantity of rockets were fired off from
the tower of St Stephen's at nightfall, in an attempt to warn Lorraine of the
growing urgency of the crisis at hand. The volunteer Michaelovitz prepared
to set out with one more dispatch to the world outside the city. The Turks

---

*From the English version 'printed for William Nott in the Pall Mall, and George
Wells Bookseller in St Paul's Church-yard, 1684'.[10]

welcomed those rockets as a sign of the garrison's distress. 'May the almighty Lord of Heaven obliterate the infidels utterly from the face of the earth.'[11]

At last the Turks closed in on the ravelin and, as they did so, began to concentrate their attack on the two bastions. On 2 September after slight rainfall, one powerful mine brought down a part of the wall of the Burg-bastion, and during the same night the post of fifty men under Captain Heisterman (of Starhemberg's regiment) on the ravelin suffered terrible losses when the enemy set fire to the timbers around them. But although Heisterman had orders to retire if it proved necessary, he held on until he was relieved at two o'clock on the next day. Then, and then only, Starhemberg finally gave up the ravelin. For both sides it was the beginning of the end, and they knew it.

The defence, underestimating considerably the Turkish working-parties in the moat, was surprised by the suddenness of the next major attack. At two o'clock in the afternoon of the 4th, after a showery morning of relative calm, the great blow fell.[12] Colonel Hoffman relates that a violent explosion shook the house in which he was just then resting. Like everyone else he rushed towards the Burg-bastion where Souches, taking his turn to command the post, had placed his men on guard behind the foremost works. The mine had torn a large hole in the wall to the left of the tip of the bastion – Starhemberg's precautions having apparently forced the Turks to place their powder at some distance from the most vulnerable point of all – and Hoffman now saw the tops of the Turkish flags and standards coming into view through the breach as the troops climbed up to the assault. Thirty feet of the defences were down, cries of 'Allah! Allah! Allah!' mingled with the fire from batteries on the counterscarp directed at the wall and bastions immediately opposite them; and for the defence this was a moment of anguish and desperation. But it soon rallied. Some units concentrated on the steady employment of their muskets, others heroically managed to stop the gap with planks and sacks. They wheeled forward the ready-made 'chevaux de frise', made of these materials; they were reinforced by troops who were in any case preparing to relieve the guard at that time. They were not dismayed by the continual storm of bombs, stones, arrows, which continued to come at them from the counterscarp, nor by the very great number of the attackers who put to good use the multitude of tunnels and passages in the Turkish works to get from the approaches and down into the moat at alarming speed. The onslaught lasted two hours, Starhemberg lost 200 men, the enemy many more. Kara Mustafa had failed, when the day ended, to make good a footing on the bastion; but his opponents, rightly, were never more alarmed for the safety of the city. They could no longer hope to hold out indefinitely by their own efforts. This had been argued before. It was now incontrovertible, even by the boldest.

At one o'clock in the morning of 6 September, Kuniz in great agitation hurried off a letter to his government. He wrote that the Turks now believed on the testimony of 'the servant of an Armenian doctor' – whom they had captured – that Starhemberg's position was desperate. The garrison contained no more than 5,000 effective fighting men, they were told. The citizens and the military command were quarrelling. If the assault of the 4th had been pressed a little further and a little longer, the municipality would have offered to surrender.[13] This news vastly encouraged the Grand Vezir, who determined to continue mining and cannonading with all his strength. Kuniz, in the Ottoman camp, was correspondingly depressed.

The Turks then turned to the Löbel.* Certainly, Souches had here taken immense pains to prepare for an attack. Forewarned by events on the Burg-bastion barricades were set up at all points, and careful arrangements made to avoid confusion; the duties of each of the guards were laid down in detail. But exactly at noon on the 8th two mines went off; the tip of the bastion and a part of the left-hand wall crumbled at once, leaving only a small portion of the masonry intact. (It was not large enough to give shelter to the defenders.) Up came the Turks, while different parties of the garrison fired at close range from the barricades on top of the bastion, as well as from the positions which they still held in the moat. The assault lasted a full hour, but possibly the extreme heat of the day helped to blunt its fierceness. In the end, the Turks retreated. The Habsburg officers took in hand a partial repair of the gaps in the wall; where these improvisations were weakest, fires were lit and kept burning to ward off the next onrush, and to impede the miners. As it was, the motive behind the tactics of Kara Mustafa and his advisers gradually became clearer. They had substantially weakened the Burg-bastion, then weakened the Löbel; they next began to advance their works across the moat on both sides of the ruined ravelin to the curtain-wall between the bastions, in order to mine it. The defenders had now to reckon that five mines were being attached to this section of their own works, while there were evident preparations to weaken the bastions still further. The stage was to be set for a general storm of the city on a grand and irresistible scale.

Moreover the garrison was tiring. Hoffman calculated that Starhemberg had only 4,000 fit men at his disposal by now.[14] The commander dared not accept the suggestion that the casemates of the Löbel should be opened, so that a sortie could be made against the Turkish workmen only thirty or forty paces distant, as they prepared the charges at the base of the curtain-wall. Instead, during the next few days he redoubled the defences at the higher level, and even fortified the houses behind them. It was here that the troops were quartered in order to be ready for immediate action in every emergency, although they were tired and desperate men by now, complaining bitterly. Starhemberg did his best to avoid trouble at this crucial moment by a general re-allocation of commands and duties. But much more depended on the ability of the besiegers to keep up their pressure, and to make it overwhelming. Fortunately for those exhausted men in the houses behind the Löbel and in the Burg, they could not do so.

---

*On the left-hand side of illustration VI. The Burg-bastion is on the right.

No less harassed were the civilians.[15] The death-rate due to dysentery and other fevers crept up steadily during August, partly because food cost more and was harder to find; the official pegging of prices was increasingly disregarded. The municipality issued scores of instructions and orders, especially to the bakers, and tried to arrange for the fair distribution of bread which in any case became less and less edible, but found itself hampered by insistent requisitioning for the soldiers of the garrison. Donkey and cat meat took the place of veal. Yet one finds few notices of outright shortage. Instead there was great suffering just short of starvation, so that mostly older men and women died off. The overall sense of strain tightened sharply when September began, and Starhemberg's grip on the civil population grew harsher as his position grew weaker.

Between 30 August and 4 September a fresh sequence of edicts attempted to mobilise more people for guard and labour duties. It was officially stated that such persons might be required to replace soldiers, when the soldiers were too tired or too few. Between 7 and 10 September Lieutenant-Colonel Balfour carried out a house-to-house inspection in order to muster further manpower: shirkers, and householders who concealed them, were alike threatened with the death penalty. Three more companies of unwilling conscripts were at length assembled on the Burgplatz, and immediately sent to work on the defences. Starhemberg also complained to the city council about burgher officers who failed to appear for duty on the watches to which they and their men had been assigned. Then on the 9th, burgomaster Liebenberg, ill and useless for many weeks past, finally died. On the very next day his incompetent nominee, who had been titular commander of all the civilian companies, was dismissed and replaced by a professional officer. He, a Major Rosstaucher, at once set about drawing up new and stringent regulations to enforce better discipline.

All this while, from the top of St Stephen's tower the landscape around Vienna was under eager observation. Lorraine's cavalry had reappeared opposite the city, fought an engagement with both Turks and Magyars, and then vanished again to the west. The Turks were also sending out large foraging parties which in due course came back. And they seemed to be redistributing their forces. Some moved in from the countryside to the suburb of St Marx, while others crossed over the Canal from Leopoldstadt and camped much closer to the Grand Vezir's headquarters. From the tower, too, the garrison sent up its rockets at night to signal the safe arrival of Seradly or Michaelovitz. Away across the river the Bisamberg responded, while in the darkness between 7 and 8 September other rockets were seen rising from the direction of the Kahlenberg,[16] on the Vienna side of the Danube – a first, breathtaking sign that an army of liberation had approached the heights of the Wiener Wald.

III

On 15 August after the safe arrival of Gregorovitz and Koltschitzki, Lorraine at last had in his hands authoritative Viennese dispatches of the 4th, 8th and 12th of the month. He now knew more clearly the condition and prospects of the garrison. But Thököly's marauders were still giving trouble in Moravia; and the irritating silence of the Passau government still vetoed a decisive move to the west. He reluctantly kept his station by the Morava, after sending forward the Grana and Baden foot-regiments under the Prince of Croy, with orders to prepare for the construction of a bridge at Tulln. Then Starhemberg's message of the 18th, and his postscript of the 19th, reached him: the Turks had finally entered the moat in force. Next day, on the 21st, Lorraine set off with all his cavalry behind him.[17]

Angern – Wolkersdorf – Stockerau:* the road goes due east and west across the country, some twenty miles north of Vienna at its nearest point. From Stockerau, Lorraine himself went on ahead to examine the position opposite Tulln. The preparations for making a bridge here were well advanced; and the bridgehead on the other side of the river, the town of Tulln itself, had been reinforced by the few infantrymen he could muster.[18] He returned to the camp at Stockerau and on the following morning, 24 August, detached a few troops to guard the plain farther north and east. The remaining regiments got ready to continue on their course to the west, when news suddenly came in that the enemy had appeared, not many miles distant; villages around the Bisamberg were on fire. Indeed, the Turks beaten at Pressburg a few weeks earlier were now moving forward again, out of Hungary and through the Little Carpathians, then riding west along the left bank of the Danube. With them came a sprinkle of Thököly's Magyars, while volunteers from the main Turkish forces had crossed the river below Vienna to join them. Lorraine at once turned his men about. The enemy horse came in sight. Confused fighting began at two o'clock in the afternoon and the Turks were at first successful on both flanks, breaking through to the second line of Habsburg companies. But 'our main body advanced in good order' and its opponents retreated. The Magyars hurried back to the Morava, while other groups were observed trying to get away across the channels of the Danube. The boats (by which they had come) were miles downstream, few others could be found, so that possibly more men were drowned that day than were killed in the fighting beforehand. Such was the obscure, uncertain course of events sometimes labelled 'the affair of Stammersdorf', but the Turks evidently failed to interrupt the allied concentration north of the Danube. They tried next to rebuild the bridges leading across the river from Leopoldstadt, dismantled earlier by Lorraine. The water-level had fallen since then, so that the old timber foundations were accessible. Teams of Wallachian and Moldavian labourers duly arrived, and by

*For these, see the maps on pp. xiv–xvii and p. 163.

the morning of 30 August a third of the main bridge was restored. Next day Lorraine struck. His own regiment advanced, and with the help of a battery swept the Turks out, making the bridge unusable.

Most of Lorraine's troops were still at Stockerau, when he himself at last rode off to greet the King of Poland.

It was clear to all observers that the meeting of John Sobieski, Lorraine and Waldeck at Ober-Hollabrun, on 31 August, ended one phase of this campaign against the Turks and opened another. Leopold having forbidden Lorraine to move unaided against Kara Mustafa, it had been possible to concentrate simply on getting the Polish King and the German Electors into Austria. It was now necessary to choose a plan for the actual relief of Vienna, and to carry it out at once. The course of events at the end of August more or less settled the main issue. The Saxons and Poles were both present in force, some 35,000 men strong in Austria and Moravia, with 18,000 Franconians and Bavarians camped on the right bank of the Danube opposite Krems. The repulse of Thököly left Lorraine free to employ most of his 10,000 for the relief of Vienna. Even the difficult problem of transport across the Danube was nearly solved. Since those desperate days early in July, when the Lower Austrian Estates considered a proposal to destroy the bridge at Stein in order to keep the Tartars out of Krems, this crossing had proved its use to the troops and supplies coming down from the Empire. Moreover, two Turkish assaults on Klosterneuburg on 22 and 23 August failed ignominiously; it was therefore safe to proceed with the construction of another bridge at Tulln, half-way between Stein and Vienna. This plan was discussed at various times and by different authorities, ever since the Turks first settled down to the siege of Vienna. The Dutch engineer Peter Rulant reported in mid-August that the materials were ready, but that labour was scarce.[19] Lorraine was insistent. Finally the military commander in Krems, Leslie, placed the business in the hands of a boastful but competent officer, Tobias Haslingen. By the end of the month the concentration of a massive relieving force south of the Danube, made possible by using the bridges both at Stein and Tulln, to be followed by the passage of this army through the Wiener Wald (along one route or another), was Lorraine's immediate purpose. Sobieski had already agreed to the plan in outline.[20]

It is not easy at this distance of time to thread one's way through a confused series of meetings, held during the next few days in order to settle outstanding questions.[21] After a final banquet in Sobieski's company on 31 August – 'there was hardly a man there, but you could tell he'd been drinking,' wrote Le Bègue – Lorraine returned to his camp at Korneuburg, and Waldeck to the neighbouring village of Stockerau. On 1 September rain began to fall, and fell through the day and night following; the advance of troops and the parley of generals were both hindered. A meeting at the north end of the Tulln bridge, arranged for the purpose of a private discussion between Waldeck and Lorraine, was put off. John Sobieski, who had firmly determined to keep Leopold away from the army in order to claim the supreme command, still debated whether he ought not at least to go to Krems for a personal interview with the Emperor. In fact he waited, and met Lorraine once again on the 2nd. On this occasion Michaelovitz was presented to him; the stout-hearted messenger, surviving his perilous journey from Vienna, had already delivered to Lorraine the letters written by Starhemberg and Caplirs six days earlier. The need for urgency was heavily underlined; but, apart from the weather, there is little doubt that the Habsburg generals and Waldeck were still groping for an answer to the problem of the command. If the Emperor expected to preside over the consultations of his allies, let alone to accompany the army on its march to Vienna, the chances of an effective partnership with Sobieski would be sharply reduced. The King of Poland insisted, to a certain extent he was bound to insist, on securing the prestige of leadership for himself. At the same time the Saxon Elector, and no doubt General Degenfeld (representing Elector Max Emmanuel) were determined to preserve the independent command of their own troops.

On 3 September John George left Horn, in order to meet his allies by attending the conference which he was told would take place at Krems. Halfway he had warning that the other leaders had changed their plans and were conferring in Count Hardegg's castle at Stetteldorf, where the ground finally drops away into the waterlogged plain through which the Danube flows. He discovered, when he arrived, that one important meeting had already taken place while a second was still going on: the first, between Lorraine and Waldeck and the Bavarian Degenfeld, and the other a larger gathering with Sobieski, Herman of Baden and various generals present. It seems that Lorraine, Waldeck and Degenfeld had framed a set of questions and answers 'to be deliberated' by the whole conference. The King of Poland made no difficulty in agreeing to the main proposals; nor, when it came to his turn to speak, did the Elector of Saxony. The new Tulln bridges were assigned to Lorraine's and Sobieski's troops, the bridge at Stein to the Saxons. They were all to cross the Danube not later than 6 or 7 September, the whole army assembling in and around Tulln. The combined force would then cross the Wiener Wald in the area between the Danube and the River Wien; and this decision finally scotched the plan favoured by Herman of Baden, of a detour round the hills in order to attack the Ottoman army from the south, possibly cutting off its line of retreat into Hungary. But the great men at Stetteldorf touched in guarded terms on the most delicate problem of all. 'If his Imperial Majesty does not appear,' it was concluded, 'the supreme command will rest with his Majesty the King of Poland, each prince retaining command of his own troops.'[22] The formula satisfied everybody, but Lorraine and Herman of Baden must both have realised that it was essential to keep Leopold at a safe distance. The Emperor, by his presence, would not compose discords; he would excite them. It must be assumed that they briefed Marco d'Aviano accordingly, when he reached Tulln a few days later.

After the conference John George moved west again to the village of Hadersdorf where he spent the next two nights. His regiments overtook him and reached Krems. On 5 September some of them were camped on an island in the Danube. They crossed the river, and covered part of the way along the south bank by the evening of the 6th, following behind the Bavarians and other troops of the Empire. At Tulln itself activity was intense. Haslingen relates, no doubt in exaggerated terms, how he had negotiated for a supply of money with the Estates of both Lower and Upper Austria, spent it freely on materials and equipment at the industrial centre of Steyr, and then succeeded in building two pontoon bridges at Tulln. Finally, with a labour force of 600 peasants and 1,000 musketeers, he hacked a way through the undergrowth of the flats between Stetteldorf and the river, so that troops could march down to the bridges without loss of time.[23] The vanguard of the Poles appeared. Sobieski himself expressed admiration for what had been done, although he was preoccupied by the continuous repairs needed, which held up the wagons containing his supplies – a point of the greatest importance, because forage was very short in the ravaged country south of the Danube.[24] He, like any spectator of the present day, was somewhat awed by the pace and weight of the main Danube current.

The concentration of troops on the level plain outside Tulln required three full days. The Bavarians, Franconians and Saxons took up positions nearest the Wiener Wald. The Habsburg troops drew up behind them; the Poles swung right after crossing the bridges and camped in the rear.[25] In the town Marco d'Aviano bravely stoked up the enthusiasm for battle, and another council of war (on 8 September) discussed current problems, above all the dispositions for the march and for battle. A copy of an 'ordre de bataille' apparently drafted by John Sobieski has been recorded.[26] If genuine (and it certainly contains some of the ideas expressed by the King in his correspondence) it must belong to an early phase in the negotiations. This document makes the distribution of troops in the camp at Tulln the basis of the order for battle. The Saxons, Bavarians and contingents from the Empire were to form the left wing marching closest to the Danube, the Habsburg soldiers the 'corps de bataille' in the centre, and to the Poles – coming up from their place in the rear of the camp – was assigned the place of honour on the right. It also stated that the infantry should move first in order to ease the progress of cavalry through heavily wooded hills, and then retire behind the horsemen when level ground in the neighbourhood of Vienna was reached. Guns were to be equally distributed between the different contingents, Habsburg, Imperial, and Polish; while German infantry units stiffened the Polish wing in return for the transposition of some mounted Polish troops to the left. One can only conclude that the council of generals, probably when Lorraine insisted, altered these arrangements in one fundamental particular; nor did the King of Poland leave on record any protest against the change. The Habsburg infantry, and part of their cavalry, were transferred to the left wing, with the Saxons placed next to them, while the Bavarians and troops of the Empire were posted to the centre. As before, the Poles remained on the right.

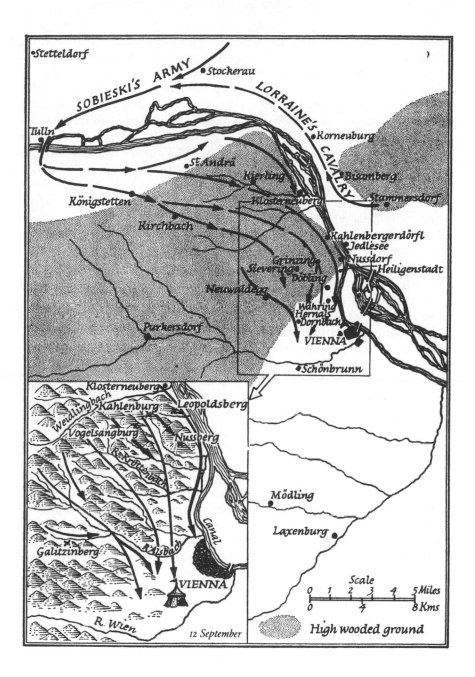

Stetteldorf

SOBIESKI'S ARMY

Stockerau

LORRAINE'S CAVALRY

Tulln

Korneuburg

St Andrä

Kierling

Bisanberg

Königstetten

Klosterneuburg

Stammersdorf

Kirchbach

Kahlenbergerdörfl

Jedlesee

Nussdorf

Grinzing

Sievering

Döbling

Heiligenstadt

Neuwaldegg

Währing

Hernals

Dornbach

Purkersdorf

VIENNA

Schönbrunn

Klosterneuberg

Leopoldsberg

Weidlingbach

Kahlenburg

Vogelsangburg

Nussberg

R. Krottenbach

Mödling

Canal

Galitzinberg

R. Alsbach

Laxenburg

VIENNA

R. Wien

12 September

Scale

0 1 2 3 4 5 Miles
0   4   8 Kms

High wooded ground

The routes to be followed across the Wiener Wald must also have been discussed, but no existing papers refer to the matter at this stage.

Meanwhile popular interest was focused on the enthralling spectacle of noble and princely volunteers from many parts of Europe congregating in this little Austrian town: like Prince George of Hanover-Calenberg, princes from Pfalz-Neuburg and Hesse-Kassel, and the English Lord Lansdowne. The Elector Max Emmanuel arrived to take command of his troops. He also claimed that his status in the constitution of the Empire gave him the right to lead the contingents from the Bavarian and Franconian Circles; in practice he was willing, on this point, to defer to Waldeck. Questions of precedence no doubt mattered intensely to individual rulers and generals, but it was the whole concourse of great men and large bodies of troops which impressed everyone, and in particular the King of Poland, who felt proud and pleased to act the part of generalissimo over them all.[27]

Lorraine had already sent 600 dragoons under Colonel Heisler to Klosterneuburg, and General Mercy now took other mounted troops to reconnoitre the Wiener Wald itself.[28] While the army was still assembling at Tulln, several units began to move out of the camp. The main advance began on 9 September and by the end of the first day had reached the villages of St Andrä* and Königstetten, three miles apart, where the plain ends and the hills begin to rise up sharply; they were the two obvious points of departure for routes through much more difficult, thickly-wooded country. Lorraine meanwhile received news of the most recent Turkish failure to capture the Burg-bastion, and Mercy reached him again after a strenuous traverse across the Wald, having met with little in the way of Turkish or Tartar opposition. Lorraine's staff now complained that Sobieski, previously so anxious to hurry on at all costs, held back; but the King may well have been reluctant to advance without the baggage (and troops) still in transit across the Danube. In any case Polish forces reached Königstetten by the evening of the 9th. That evening, officers spoke to foresters with a detailed knowledge of the ground ahead, the command sifted intelligence from various sources, and made its dispositions for the next morning.[29]

On the 10th, Lorraine at St Andrä split his forces. Some cavalry (including Lubomirski's Poles) were sent round the northern edge of the hills, close to the Danube; others, including probably most of the German infantry, took the road across the hills. Both converged on Klosterneuburg. Sobieski's cavalry, with his infantry well in the rear, began to climb up towards the villages of Kirling and Kirchbach. The intention was to make a rendezvous in the valley of the Weidlingbach,[30] which lies beyond Klosterneuburg beneath the topmost ridge of the Wiener Wald, but the slopes were excessively steep, and particularly the haulage of artillery carriages and carts proved an arduous, heart-breaking business. The foremost troops on the left did indeed spend the

---

*For St Andrä, see Illustration XI and, for the hills, streams and villages mentioned here, the map p. 163.

next night on the Vienna side of Klosterneuburg, but others bivouacked on heights west of the little town, while the Poles were farther behind.[31] They were still sufficiently in touch with forces in the centre, and the centre with those of the left, on sheltered ground which enemy forces did not venture to dispute. Sobieski moved ahead of his men, and conferred with Lorraine in full view of the great ridge which the army would have to climb.[32] The suggestion that this could be attempted at once was turned down; but plans were made for the day following, 11 September.

During the night Lorraine, tireless in his tours of inspection, had second thoughts. At 2 a.m. he sent forward reinforcements to Heisler, and an attack was launched on the Turkish outposts which guarded the ridge from the ruined Camuldensian monastery at the top of St Joseph's Berg (now called the Kahlenberg) and the Chapel of St Leopold on the Leopoldsberg, the two most northerly heights of the Wiener Wald. The Turks were successfully thrown out, and pushed back down the other side of the ridge. Rockets or flares shot up into the night to cheer the inhabitants of Vienna, five miles distant.

At dawn the troops began to move again, and the arrangement of the whole force becomes gradually clearer to us; even though, at the time, heavy rain and a storm must have obscured the view and depressed the spirit of everyone present. Heisler's dragoons were already on the northern end of the ridge. Below them, on their left, were Habsburg and Polish cavalry moving alongside the Danube, pushing round the last shoulder of the hills fronting the river. Behind the dragoons were regiments of Habsburg infantry under Herman of Baden, and the Saxon infantry, followed by Saxon troops of horse commanded by the Elector himself. In the centre marched the Bavarians under Max Emmanuel, together with the Franconians under Waldeck. The foremost of all these contingents had reached the ridge by 11 a.m., holding it from the Leopoldsberg on the left to the Vogelsangberg on the right, with the Kahlenberg in the centre. Farther right still, regiments of Habsburg cavalry and dragoons, Bavarian and Franconian cavalry, were climbing up from the Weidlingbach and soon they too reached the top.

The Poles faced a much longer ordeal on the 11th. At the start they were farther behind, but they made progress, crossed the Weidlingbach, and by nightfall an indeterminate proportion of their cavalry was up on the high ground, fanning well out to the south. They were being followed by part of their infantry, but other units advanced very slowly; and a Polish artillery officer admits that more and more of his equipment had to be abandoned in the course of the day. In any case, his unit was still at the foot of the ridge when night fell. If there were more accounts like this, it is almost certain that we should have a picture of numerous contingents, German as well as Polish, moving many hours behind the foremost troops, leaving their carts and guns in the rear, climbing desperately up and forward during the hours of darkness, and then groping past positions which were already packed with other companies and squadrons.

Much earlier in the day, Father Marco had climbed the heights and written a letter to Leopold 'dal monte a veduta di Vienna', praising the good order of the men and the harmony of the generals, the stout action of the city's beleaguered garrison and the providence of God. In front of him Christian volunteers were already skirmishing down the slopes, and brushing with parties of Janissaries who hastily started to dig entrenchments at various points.[33]

Marco's harmonious generals and princes now inspected the great panorama to the south. Some of them had travelled hundreds of miles to see it, with the city in the middle-distance, surrounded by Turkish siegeworks and camps, the Danube on their left and the greater wooded hills to their right, with everything somewhat dimmed by the smoke rising from the guns, mines, and campfires of a siege in its final stages. Their principal concern was the ground between them and the walls of Vienna, and John Sobieski for one was grievously disappointed. Misled (as he thought) by maps previously submitted to him by Habsburg commanders who should have known better, he had expected the contours to fall away smoothly to the plain in which the city stood. Instead he saw precipices, ravines, dense woodland on steep slopes, and farther ridges in the immediate foreground, with the more level terrain far in the distance. He felt tempted to conclude that the whole direction of the army's march in the last few days involved an error of judgment: either a long detour to the south was now advisable or, at the least, a slow advance inch by inch 'à la Spinola' would be necessary from the Kahlenberg, a tactic requiring time and caution. His French engineer, Dupont, supported and possibly inspired these arguments.[34] In conference with the other generals, including Lorraine, the first of these ideas was firmly overruled; a full-scale attack from the ridge of the Wiener Wald was approved, but another council was called for the following morning, and it seems probable that a final decision about the timing of this attack was deferred. Sobieski also secured from Lorraine the transfer of four Habsburg infantry regiments to the right wing in order to give support to the Polish cavalry. Undoubtedly his nervousness was counterbalanced by a firm conviction that the Grand Vezir was a poor commander. He noted that the Turks had been foolish in not trying to defend the routes across the Wiener Wald, and even more so in not fortifying their encampments round Vienna. This was also Lorraine's opinion. During the hours of darkness the King composed a long letter to his Queen, floridly outlining the situation, his hopes, and his fears; he gives the hour as three a.m. and only stopped writing when the time came to go and meet the other commanders again.[35]

IV

What had Kara Mustafa been doing? He made many mistakes in 1683, but the fundamental miscalculation was the span of time and the amount of effort needed to capture Vienna itself. He underestimated the tenacity of the defence. Therefore he concentrated all his efforts on the siege after the first month; therefore he neglected to take measures which would have safeguarded the besieging army. He took too little interest in the no-man's-land of the Wiener Wald. He could have tried harder to occupy Klosterneuburg. He could have sent more Turkish cavalry, as well as the Tartars, to patrol the plain round Tulln, and it is possibly an oblique admission of this error that one Turkish writer of the period invariably abuses the Tartar Khan. He relates a story that the Khan was close enough to Tulln to observe the crossing of the Danube by Polish troops, and was advised to attack them. He refused, alleging that he had never been given sufficient support or encouragement by Kara Mustafa who always insulted him: he would not move to save this despicable general.[36] In addition, the Ottoman command had not seriously attempted to stiffen its observation-posts on the ridge of the Wiener Wald, and only at the last moment were instructions given for ditches to be dug, and guns set in position, at selected points in the area between the eastern slopes of the hills and the encampments – with all their baggage and supplies – of the Turkish troops.

The Grand Vezir's serious consideration of dangers threatening from behind the Wiener Wald dates back to 4 September. On that day a captured prisoner seems to have given him detailed, if exaggerated, accounts of the relieving army; the Poles and Germans combined were said to number 80,000 foot and 40,000 cavalry. Kara Mustafa at once ordered old Ibrahim of Buda, the one man who had boldly criticised the whole plan of campaign two months earlier, to bring all his troops from Györ to Vienna immediately.[37] Four days later another prisoner was taken, who knew that Lorraine's and Sobieski's forces had crossed the river at Tulln, and were advancing towards the hillcountry with 200 pieces of artillery.[38] The Pasha of Karahisar was sent westwards to get confirmation of this. Ibrahim arrived with 8,000 men and large supplies. The same evening and on the following morning (8 and 9 September) councils of war were held. Some commanders argued that the whole armament of the Turkish force should be employed to oppose Lorraine's advance. The Grand Vezir disagreed, and determined to maintain full pressure on the city. On the 9th it was finally decided to adopt this second course. The Turks had very little experience in dealing with a difficult military problem familiar to western soldiers: the command of a force caught between a powerful garrison and a powerful relieving army. Probably no Christian general of this decade would have neglected to fortify the outer lines of a great camp from which an army was besieging a city.

Significantly evidence for the whereabouts of the positions west of Vienna, which were in fact fortified or entrenched by the Turks, is very uncertain. Something was certainly done to strengthen Nussdorf, a ruined village in the area farthest north, close to the Danube and underneath the Leopoldsberg. Other accounts refer to a redoubt constructed at Währing two miles south-west, the 'Türkenschanz' of which the alleged site survives to this day; but the Turks did not, apparently, attempt to defend it seriously.[39] At the other end of the whole terrain, on the ridges above the left bank of the Wien, they strengthened a number of points with ditches and guns. Between Währing and the Wien, they hoped to make good use of the walls and buildings of vineyards on the lower slopes of the hills; behind these the ground was left open, presumably to give greater freedom of movement to the cavalry. In all, about sixty guns were withdrawn from the siegeworks and some 6,000 infantry. They employed in the field 22,000 horsemen,[40] so that the relieving army was infinitely superior in manpower. The total Turkish force employed in the battle numbered perhaps 28,500 men a total increased but not strengthened by an indeterminate quantity of Wallachian, Moldavian and Tartar auxiliaries. The left and centre of Lorraine's army alone numbered over 40,000 and the right wing under Sobieski's immediate command was probably 20,000 strong. Lorraine and Sobieski together employed up to twice as many fieldpieces as the Turkish commanders.

There are signs that Kara Mustafa, between 9 and 12 September, altered his dispositions in a way which later enfeebled his power of resistance. By the 9th, enough information had been gathered from prisoners and from the Tartars to make preparations to deal with their opponents a matter of the utmost urgency. After a council of war in the morning, the Grand Vezir and other commanders toured and inspected the whole area west of the city in the afternoon; and they conferred with the Tartar Khan. The cavalry was divided into a vanguard under Kara Mehmed of Diyarbakir (5,400) and a main body under Ibrahim of Buda (23,000), and allotted the task of resisting Lorraine and Sobieski. The Grand Vezir was to stand firm in his headquarters at St Ulrich while troops under the command of Abaza Sari Hussein guarded both banks of the Wien. In this way the Grand Vezir's camp was regarded as the core of the Turkish defence, with powerful forces protecting it on each side. On the 10th and 11th these preparations were intensified but fresh information showed that the immediate threat was bound to come from the north, from the area of the Kahlenberg and Leopoldsberg; units were then brought over from the other side of the Canal, while the great majority of Ibrahim's troops moved into position behind the vanguard which was now in Nussdorf and Heiligenstadt (on the road between Nussdorf and Vienna).[41] Accordingly, to meet the threat from the Kahlenberg there was a general shift of weight to the Turkish right, facing Lorraine. This probably weakened their defences elsewhere.

Few men can have slept soundly that Saturday night the 11th of September, whether on the hills, camped on the plain, or in the city. The particular preoccupation of the Christian leaders was with their artillery, which it took so much longer to move across the Wiener Wald than any other part of the army. Marco, writing earlier in the day, noted how they were waiting for it, and one Polish officer admits the delay.[42] At last some pieces reached the ridge; and long before dawn on Sunday 12 September General Leslie was putting in hand the construction of a battery on the forward edge of the descent from the Leopoldsberg.[43] An officer in charge there noticed that the Turks were preparing to mount an attack from the Nussberg (a hill immediately north of Nussdorf) on the half-finished works; he sent forward two battalions which were soon engaged. The Turks also occupied some of the higher ground immediately to their left, from which they threatened to advance, so that Lorraine had to send down more troops. Other Turkish forces pushed from Nussdorf up the valley between the two heights; Lorraine responded by setting the whole of his left wing in motion at about 5 a.m. In effect, the Turks had forced a decision on their opponents by the time Sobieski was making his way to Lorraine for the conference between them, agreed to the day before;[44] a major encounter could not possibly be delayed. At last the hour was reached when the Christian army, to use the emphatic language of a contemporary Turkish writer, became a flood of black pitch coming down the mountain, consuming everything it touched.[45]

This great battle, for most of those who took part, was a confused series of separate encounters occurring within a wide area. Only occasionally did Sobieski and Lorraine, and to a far lesser degree Kara Mustafa, manage to impose a coherent tactical pattern on the fighting. As one man remarked: 'there were places where the ground looked even, but on getting nearer we found very deep ravines, and vineyards surrounded by lofty walls'; and another: we fought 'from ridge to valley, and from valley to ridge.'[46] Troops constantly disappeared from view. The number of formal lines varied. Horse and foot got entangled. Units were moved across, on the sudden initiative of a single commander, to support others when these found themselves in difficulties.[47] Certainly, all the serious fighting before noon was on the Christian left and Turkish right. More and more troops were thrown into the struggle for the Nussberg by both sides. Habsburg and Saxon dragoons under Heister, which had been coming round the shoulder of the Leopoldsberg, entered the village of Kahlenbergerdörfl, opening up a new line of approach to the Nussberg and Nussdorf. Then the Turks pushed back the Grana foot regiment, which was already in the outskirts of Nussdorf. More Saxon troops, both foot and horse, were ordered into the fray. Then, at last, Leslie managed to get a part of his artillery on to the Nussberg hill. At eight o'clock the Turks were still defending strongly the battered buildings of the village below it, making use of every scrap of stonework; but their predicament was a serious one. In the course of the next hour, Lorraine organised a devastating attack. Heister's men arrived from the Kahlenbergerdörfl. Habsburg and Saxon dragoons dismounted to fight on foot. Finally infantry under Herman of Baden's command entered the ruined village, and drove the Turks southwards. It was the first positive step forward in the final advance along the shore of the Canal towards Vienna, three miles distant.

Thereafter, in this sector the troops pressed steadily on from the valley in which Nussdorf stands into Heiligenstadt, another mile ahead. They tied up an ever-increasing proportion of Ibrahim's available force. They made

successful use of their artillery, causing great alarm in the enemy ranks. Nor
did the Turks manage to seal off these troops from the regiments coming down
and across the slopes farther inland – although for a short while they nearly
managed to do so, until Lorraine closed an ugly gap – so that Heiligenstadt
was occupied without much difficulty. Farther inland still Bavarians and
Franconians continued to fan downwards, so that by noon Lorraine had
established a front line which extended from Heiligenstadt to Grinzing, and
Grinzing to the village of Sievering. Owing to a failure of nerve or lack of
control in their command, the Turks had been unable to restrain themselves
from fighting too many isolated and unsuccessful encounters on the slopes
and in the gullies. Their shortage of manpower was aggravated before they
withdrew to the more level ground, on which they might have attacked to
better advantage.

These proceedings were watched with intense anxiety from vantage-points
like the tower of St Stephen's, in Vienna itself. Men observed the dense rows
of infantry coming down from the ridge, disappearing and reappearing as the
ground dipped and flattened. The guns would be pushed on ahead, firing at
intervals; and then the troops closed up on them, moving forward thirty or
forty paces at a time, a tactic repeated over and over again.[48] At least in the
centre, the tempo of the advance was determined more by the terrain than by
Turkish opposition.

All reports agree that, on this day of blistering sunshine, there was a pause
in the fighting at noon. It was a pause to recover breath, but the allied
commanders were also determined not to weaken their position by pressing
too far forward on their left before the right wing had begun to put pressure
on the Ottoman defence. Concealed by the folding of the ground, and the
thickness of woods, the pace of the Polish advance was difficult to estimate; it
certainly appeared somewhat slow. But no one underestimated the importance
of these troops, who were expected to come down the Alsbach, a tributary
stream descending to the houses at Dornbach and ultimately to Hernals: a line
of march which would bring the attack much closer to the main Turkish camp
and to the Grand Vezir's headquarters.

Some historians have blamed the Poles for their sluggishness, but it would
be more helpful if evidence were found which explained why they were
sluggish. Many Polish detachments were well behind the regiments of the
left and centre already on the previous day, and can only have reached the
upper ridges late in the evening, hungry and tired; there are no records which
show how complete their preparations were during the night of 11th September.
Even in the case of the German regiments put at John Sobieski's disposal, it
is known that they were in position on the Galitzinberg – well forward, and
on the extreme right – by the time serious fighting began in this area, after
midday; but it is not known whether they were already in position in the early
hours of morning.[49] Another possibility is that, when the council of war ended
on the 11th Sobieski was by no means clear that the attack would begin at dawn,

and therefore did not give positive instructions to his officers to make ready for action. The Turkish raids above Nussdorf, in conjunction with Lorraine's purposeful itch to try and relieve Vienna without delay, altered the whole situation. But it took the King of Poland most of the morning, while fierce fighting continued on his left, to advance his right wing. He was already past his prime as an instinctive war-leader, a slow and very corpulent man who now lacked the energy to dominate a crisis on the battlefield; nor were the discipline and promptness of his aristocratic cavalry generals very marked, in spite of their many other military virtues.

Moreover, although it was a relatively simple matter to occupy the higher ground on both sides of the Alsbach, the descent of large numbers of men into the valley proved more arduous.[50] Even then the greatest difficulty of all remained, to get them out of this narrow avenue of approach and reorganise them as a battle-formation, strong enough to meet a massive Turkish attack; the Turks were bound to try and interrupt and to crush the whole unwieldly manoeuvre. By one o'clock the Polish vanguard had reached Dornbach, where the woods and the slopes die away. They became visible to the forces anxiously waiting far away on their left. Shouts of joy and relief from the Germans saluted them, and dismayed the enemy. The heights on both sides of the Alsbach were in firm and friendly hands. From those on the left, the King himself directed operations, and he was in touch with the Franconian units and their leaders to his left. On the right Hetman Jablonowski commanded the Poles, some German infantry held the Galitzinberg, and a certain amount of support from artillery was assured. Fortunately the scattered Tartar forces still farther south were never a serious nuisance in this quarter. The future depended on the heroism and energy of the Polish centre under General Katski as it emerged from the narrower part of the Alsbach valley.

First of all select troops of volunteer hussars advanced. After a momentary success the Turks pushed them back, and then the conflict swayed uncertainly to and fro. It cannot be stated with any certainty whether the final result was determined by the steady refusal of these Poles on the lower ground to give up the costly struggle, or by the efforts of German foot soldiers coming down from the Galitzinberg, or by the extra forces which Sobieski threw in (aided by reinforcements of Austrian and Bavarian cavalry) from the heights on the left. After a fearful tussle the Turks gave way; their horsemen fled, and took shelter with the Turkish infantry and guns on a defensive position farther back. Sobieski now began to deploy his whole force on more level ground, having swung them slightly round so that they faced south-east. They were arranged in two lines, the intervals in the first being covered by contingents in the second. As before, Habsburg and Bavarian cavalry stood behind them on their immediate left. There were more Polish horsemen and dragoons on the right.

This achievement altered the whole face of the battle. The Polish wing of the army had caught up with the left and centre. It was a strong position, won after a hard-fought day. The great question, now, was whether to stop or to launch a further attack. Undoubtedly Lorraine himself wanted to press forward; and there is probably something in the famous story that when one experienced general, the Saxon commander Goltz, was asked for his opinion, he replied: 'I am an old man, and I want comfortable quarters in Vienna tonight.' Waldeck agreed. Sobieski agreed. They must have all based their hopes on signs of disorder and exhaustion in the enemy troops facing them. On one wing, the relieving army was two miles away from the walls of Vienna at their nearest point. On the other, it was a little more than two miles to Kara Mustafa's headquarters in St Ulrich.

Preparations to mount an overwhelming attack were made along the whole front. At 3.20, in the fiercest heat of the afternoon the action began again on the left. The Turkish position here ran along the Vienna side of the Krottenbach (a stream reaching the Canal near Heiligenstadt) but soon turned to the south-west, where it faced first the centre of the Christian army, and then the Poles. The Turk's resistance was ineffectual, and they soon began to withdraw rapidly to the left wing of Kara Mustafa's defence. Some of the Habsburg troops at once made straight towards the nearest siegeworks of the city, others swung to the right. The same thing happened on the central part of the front: the Saxons, and then the troops of the Empire, pushed forward again – and swung to the right. The Poles had meanwhile thrown everything they had into their attack on the main armament of the Turks. For a short while the battle was doubtful; but the thrust of the Bavarian troops (under Degenfeld and Max Emmanuel himself), and then of other troops coming up from the more northerly sectors, weakened the flank of the Turkish position; the Poles finally plunged forward with their cavalry to sweep southwards. Here, other Turkish units made an obstinate stand;[51] they had their backs to the River Wien, and when they finally gave way Kara Mustafa ran a real risk of being cut off by swift cavalry movements in his rear from any possible line of retreat. Meanwhile the bodyguards of the Grand Vezir resisted desperately when the Poles began to enter his great encampment from the west. On its northern side, Janissaries and other household troops were still fighting hard; the Franconians under Waldeck, and on his initiative, seem to have given Sobieski useful support in this final phase of the struggle. The total collapse of the Turks began, and when their soldiers still in the galleries and trenches in front of the Hofburg were instructed to come to the rescue of those in the camp, they fled. Kara Mustafa himself then retreated in perilous and disorderly haste, though he succeeded in taking with him the great Moslem standard, the Flag of the Prophet so vainly displayed on this bitter occasion, and the major part of his stock of money. Many other Turkish leaders and contingents had already left the battlefield several hours before; and so ended one of the most resounding of all Christian victories, and Ottoman defeats. By five-thirty the battle was over. Vienna was saved. The plundering began.

An Irish officer summarised the events of the day in his own terse way:[52] 'If the victory be not so complete as we promised ourselves it should, it proceeded only from the cowardice of our enemies, whom from morning till night we drove before us, beating them from post to post, without their having the courage to look us in the face, and that through several defiles, which had they any reasonable courage we could never have forced. The combat held longest where the King of Poland was, but that only added to his glory, he having beaten them with the loss of their cannon and their men; they have left us their whole camp in general, with their tents, bag and baggage, and time will tell us more particulars.'

9

The Consequences of Victory

I

Naturally on this memorable day the Christian leaders were men of the sword, not of the pen. Only Marco d'Aviano, while the battle still went on, wrote to the Emperor with news that the Turks were fighting at a disadvantage. Leopold's craft had moved downstream, and was somewhere between Krems and Tulln when he replied in hopeful but anxious terms. By nightfall he knew better. As for John Sobieski, he did not write to his wife until the evening of Monday the 13th, from one of Kara Mustafa's finest apartments in the ruined Turkish encampment.[1] For him, all was momentarily triumph and glory; because the Poles on the right wing had faced the brunt of the Turk's final attack, because they had arrived first in the great camp with its amazing impedimenta, he himself claimed the victory. And if the Grand Vezir's ostrich was dead, he wrote, and his parrakeet flown away, the Queen of Poland still could not say to her consort – like a Tartar princess rebuking her man who came back from the wars empty-handed – 'you have brought me nothing home', because here were jewels and treasure galore, rich furnishings and captured standards, left behind by the great defeated multitude of 150,000 (or was it 300,000?) Turks. Sobieski did not deny, at the same time, that the main treasury of the enemy had been withdrawn before the retreat began, nor that Polish looters were quickly reducing the value of the Turkish stores. They wantonly exploded kegs of powder, for instance. But great heat in a land of vineyards after bitter fighting, he thought, was bound to demoralise a gallant soldiery. The King himself was intoxicated by the immense success of his achievement.[2] 'We came, we saw, and God conquered,' he wrote to Innocent XI on the same day,[3] but there was no doubt that Sobieski was His instrument and popular acclaim strengthened the conviction. Earlier on this 13 September the King, with a number of the German princes and commanders, had examined the Turkish siegeworks and then entered Vienna itself.[4] They went first to the Loretto chapel of the Augustinian church, before attending a banquet given by Starhemberg; and over the table the talk flowed proud and bombastic. Sobieski and the others present declared roundly that, with good fellowship between them, they would drive the Turk deep into Hungary that same autumn. Later, in St Stephen's, the crowds pressed in upon the hero who returned his gratitude in his prayers. Had not the holy Marco seen a dove poised above the warriors on the field of battle?

The Habsburg authorities were perplexed by the assertiveness of their ally. Their own troops had reached the walls of Vienna first, but he made himself master of the Turkish camp and monopolised its spoils. Further, it was a right surely due to the Emperor Leopold, now approaching down the Danube, to take precedence and set foot in his own capital city before other princes presumed to do so. Sobieski, by showing himself in Vienna before Leopold, aggravated the sense of shame caused by the Habsburg court's too rapid desertion of the city in July. He embarrassed its servants by this public entry which they dared not deny him, and by the citizens' welcome which they apparently tried to curtail. From his own point of view, Sobieski was sensible enough in insisting on ceremonial successes of this kind. He had many enemies, above all in Poland, and could not afford to lose any opportunity of impressing on his fellow countrymen, both in the army and at home, the greatness of their elected ruler.*

The news of victory began to travel, slowly by latterday standards, from the battlefield out across western Europe.[5] It seems probably that beacons on the hilltops flashed in triumph as far as Linz on the night of the 13th, but cautious diplomats at court preferred to keep the couriers waiting until a captain of the Souches regiment arrived with authentic intelligence for the Countess Souches at Linz from her husband in Vienna. There, already before the fighting ended, Sobieski sent off his French engineer Dupont hurrying towards Cracow, and Pallavicini tells us that the Queen was appropriately praying in the Cathedral when the messenger arrived at ten-thirty in the morning of 16th September to be followed some while later by the bearer of the King's great dispatch from the Grand Vezir's headquarters. Sobieski also sent to Italy his secretary Talenti, who carried with him what was believed to be the most precious of all the captured Turkish regalia, the veritable Flag of the Prophet Mahomet, as well as grandiloquent messages addressed to the Pope and the Doge. The Flag was displayed in city after city south of the Alps until it reached Rome. After a few weeks plain men were disappointed to learn from scholars that the King of Poland's offering to the Pope was, after all, no more than an Ottoman standard of lesser importance. Talenti's journey was universally the occasion for the closing of shops, for fireworks and demonstrations of delight

---

*Sobieski's flair for publicity is one of his most interesting traits. He describes his letter of 13 September to the Queen as a 'gazette' – 'and I would ask you to use it as such'. On other occasions he states what passages were to be suppressed before publication.

and thanksgiving. After leaving Venice the good news preceded him, so that the waiting crowds were ready with their welcome when he entered Rome on 25 September. Meanwhile, from Vienna the Prince of Neuburg sent the good tidings to his old father at Neuburg on the Danube. John George of Anhalt wrote to the Elector of Brandenburg (who was hunting in the country many miles from Berlin), and Francis Taafe to his brother in England, while one amazing horseman galloped so fast to give the news to Ernest Augustus at Hanover that he fell dead at his journey's end, as his epitaph relates.[6] The full tide of formal congratulations later flowed back to the Emperor, to Sobieski and other commanders in the battle. From the western lands they came pre-eminently to Lorraine, whose secretary copied them into a stout volume for his archives where they remain to this day, in the prose and verse of many languages.

That Monday, 13 September, was by no means all sunshine. Lorraine himself was not present at Starhemberg's banquet, after a difference of opinion with Sobieski which grew wider as the hours passed.[7] Lorraine had pressed for the speediest possible pursuit of the demoralised Turkish forces. The King, when they conferred in the morning, at first declared that this was out of the question. His own men were exhausted; they had marched or ridden much farther than their colleagues on the day before; a pause was essential. Lorraine persisted, and it was at last agreed that the army would move again in the course of the afternoon. Lorraine spent the next few hours in making preparations, while Sobieski made his entry into the city. He returned too late to his quarters, and once more refused to budge. But on Tuesday the 14th it was the Habsburg commander's turn to be caught at a disadvantage. The Emperor had reached Vienna, and it was necessary to receive and escort him, to repeat the whole ceremonial of inspections, solemn entries, presentations, banquets and thanksgiving in Vienna, while Sobieski outside the walls loudly protested that his advance was now held up by the unwillingness of his allies to move. There were other grievances on both sides. Not only did the Germans believe that the Poles had seized most of the spoil in the enemy camp; they knew that the Poles were pillaging and damaging useful Turkish stores of munitions and foodstuffs. But some of the Poles were themselves in difficulties, and wanted bread from the town; the Habsburg officers stiffly refused to help them.[8]

On the same day a meeting between the Emperor and the King of Poland took place and caused further momentary unpleasantness, in spite of careful discussion by their subordinates about the procedure to be followed. Leopold wished to salute his ally, but could not dream of surrendering his claim to precedence in his own territory. John Sobieski, for his part, determined to insist on the most public testimony to his status which the world could afford: the Emperor's punctilio towards him at a personal interview. Leopold and his staff rode up towards the Polish troops near Schwechat east of the city. Sobieski, surrounded with a body of guards who carried no standards, rode to meet him. The two men faced one another on horseback: there could be no question of either claiming precedence by being on the other's right, which was the crux of the ceremonial problem. The King remained uncovered for just as long as the Emperor, and no longer. They conversed in Latin for a few minutes. Leopold expressed gratitude, and Sobieski praised Lorraine and the Habsburg soldiers. So far the honours of a difficult occasion were even, although Sobieski's nerves were very much on edge; he was thoroughly agitated when he tried to present his son Jacob to Leopold, and Leopold failed to acknowledge the introduction. Abashed, Sobieski did not accompany the Emperor during an inspection of the Polish troops immediately afterwards. Leopold, who described the day in a letter to Marco, sounds bland and satisfied. Jacob, in his childish but informative diary, simply suggests that the Emperor was preoccupied in controlling his horse.[9] A good deal has been made of this contretemps by later German and Polish writers. We may doubt whether it affected the future course of events in the slightest.[10] The alliance between the two men held firm, although the short period after its greatest triumph was the moment of maximum friction.

Of greater practical importance was the abrupt departure of Elector John George for Saxony.[11] Neither then nor later did he disclose his reasoning very clearly, but he took a prompt and startling decision. On 15 September his troops began their long return journey to Saxony. The Elector simply informed Leopold, in a short letter from Klosterneuburg, that he had to go at once. The battered condition of one of his regiments, the unkind treatment of Protestants in the Austrian lands, the undefended state of his dominion while his army was absent – with Brandenburg troops not very far distant from Dresden – were the obvious explanations of the Saxon retreat from Vienna at this early date, to be offered by both contemporaries and later historians. As the Venetian envoy at Linz remarked, they were 'feeble'. More probably, John George just felt himself being elbowed out of the credit due to him in the forty-eight hours after his regiments' splendid performance in the battle; nor did they get a reasonable share of the spoils. Sobieski was the grand monopoliser, Lorraine could not be denied a leading influence in the councils of war, while the Elector of Bavaria stood on much more intimate terms with the Habsburg court and its members. John George, in this highly competitive company, was the most colourless and the least effective.

A more resolute leader also took his leave. Waldeck wanted to call a halt to any further campaigning against the Turks.[12] In any case, he said, his Franconian troops could not advance beyond Vienna without the consent of the Franconian princes. Then he fell ill and retired to Klosterneuburg. When he recovered, he expressed himself still more strongly. For him the eastern crisis was over, but the defences of the Empire and the Netherlands were never in more desperate need of Leopold's help. The Turks had vanished over the horizon, thoroughly beaten, while he now knew that Louis XIV's regiments ravaged Hainault and threatened the Rhineland. William of Orange, in his letters to Waldeck, begged him to work for the transfer of German military forces from the east to the west. Waldeck therefore went back to Linz in order to support Borgomanero; for the Spanish ambassador stuck to his old arguments on this matter of the priority between east and west with undiminished fire and emphasis.

Outside the walls of Vienna, other discords began to cut deeply.[13] A number of conferences were held on the Thursday, Friday and Saturday, and Lorraine gradually realised that Max Emmanuel, encouraged by some of Leopold's ministers, was asking for an independent command. He wanted to lead an expedition of his own against the vital Turkish citadel at Neuhäusel. Lorraine, furious and dismayed, threatened to resign and the plan was dropped. Max Emmanuel spoke of going back to Munich at once. He, too, fell ill and it was not to be clear for some time whether he would permit his troops to be used in Hungary. They moved over to the north side of the Danube. Indeed there seemed no end to the discontents of the princes and generals. Leopold promoted Starhemberg to the rank of Field-Marshal on 15 September, an obvious reward for the defender of the city during the long siege. The Duke of Sachsen-Lauenburg at once protested against what he thought was an affront to his own status, had his baggage assembled, and left the army. Caplirs, Leslie, Salm, Aeneas Caprara (who said that Starhemberg had been only a volunteer when he was a colonel) – they all grumbled. Meanwhile, enormous numbers of the troops were as sick with dysentery as Max Emmanuel, Waldeck and (less seriously) Lorraine; possibly half the fighting men were affected. The devastation of wide areas by the Turks who had stripped the country south of the Danube, lack of transport across the river at any point below Tulln, and the inevitable shortage of food in Vienna by the last day of the siege, made the feeding of men and horses a hopeless task for the Habsburg commissariat. One argument alone was strong enough, and was seen to be strong enough, to push a majority of the confederates forward again: the utter disarray of the Turks, as reported by deserters, prisoners, and the Habsburg commanders at Györ and Komárom. It was too obvious an opportunity to miss. On 17 September the Poles led the way, advancing down the right bank of the river. Two days later, Leopold left Vienna for Linz once more.

At times fearful of undoing the effects of victory by risking another encounter at the fag-end of a campaign, more often aggressive and enthusiastic, Sobieski at first wanted a direct pursuit of the enemy. The awful bareness of the countryside – 'it is like an Arabian desert', he told his wife – soon led him to agree with Lorraine that this was an impossible strategy. The army must first find supplies by quartering on ground not held earlier by the Turks; which meant, at least past Pressburg, getting on to the Schütt across the river.[14] It was once again a question of bridge-building. Lack of bridges over the Danube ruled out an alternative, which he also considered, the speedy withdrawal of his whole force back to Poland.

Le Bègue relates that, already on 7 September Lorraine gave orders for the pontoon-boats at Tulln to be moved downstream to Vienna as soon as the relief of the city was assured; the order was repeated on the 13th.[15] Unfortunately, he adds, the boatmen had been dismissed for want of money to pay them. It also seems likely that Polish troops were still coming up through Moravia towards the Tulln bridgehead. At any rate a serious delay occurred. The movement of supplies across the river was held up, and the whole army pinned to the south bank until 23 September. Engineers finally reconstructed the bridge at a point just below Pressburg and the troops, including the Poles' unwieldy baggage-train, began to cross to the Schütt. The boats were then moved downstream once more to Komárom.

A week later, on 2 October, Sobieski and Lorraine conferred. Wet weather had set in and they learnt that the ground around the enemy stronghold of Neuhäusel was already too waterlogged to make an attack worth while. They decided to advance towards Párkány, on the north side of the Danube which protected a bridge crossing the river from Esztergom on the opposite bank. For the Turks, of course, this bridge linked Neuhäusel with Buda, and enabled them to put pressure on Thököly and his Magyars. It would be a valuable prize.

II

Kara Mustafa – with his right eye in bandages – reached the outskirts of Györ two days after the battle, preceded by Turkish forces which had certainly left Vienna before its final phase began, and without his authority to do so. He and his followers now crossed the River Rába but fierce fighting at once broke out between troops which wished to continue their flight eastwards and others, still obedient to orders, whom he sent to hold them back – as a Christian captive concealed in the neighbouring vineyards, our old friend Luigi Marsigli, observed with malicious pleasure. The revolt was crushed, but we have only a few scraps of evidence for the next few days, and these show the Grand Vezir, bitter and desperate, pondering the whole bewildering situation in which he found himself.[16] Did a defeat on the scale of his reported losses at Vienna destroy his standing at court? Could he rely on the loyalty shown by Sultan Mehmed IV, for the last twenty-five years, to the Grand Vezirs governing in his name? The great empire was intact, the Sultan still ruled in Ottoman Hungary. If there was treachery – as there had been – let there be retribution and punishment. Then, if the next campaign ended with credit, no one would doubt the goodness of God and the irresistible strength of His servant the Ottoman Sultan, or of His servant's blameless servant Kara Mustafa.

The principal scapegoat, the leader of those disloyal incompetents responsible for the defeat at Vienna, was easy to choose. The Grand Vezir at once had Ibrahim of Buda, and certain other senior commanders, executed in the camp outside Györ. But the old man's offence was really a double one. Not only had he opposed the whole policy of Kara Mustafa since the beginning of the year, above all the strategy of the march out of Hungary into Austria. His personal connections were dangerous, because his wife was a sister of the Sultan; so that if the politicians at Belgrade or Adrianople ever pressed for a serious analysis of the conduct of the recent campaign, the Grand Vezir could hardly doubt that Ibrahim would inspire his fiercest critics. Moreover, it was intolerable and demoralising to have an important commander on the actual theatre of war who was able to say: 'I told you so.' After the blood-bath Kara Mustafa composed an eloquent apologia, explaining what he had done and why, and sent it to Belgrade.

He spent three more days trying to reorganise and reanimate his sadly shrunken force. But while we know that many Poles and Germans were short of supplies, sick or exhausted after 12 September, there is little firm evidence about the condition of the Ottoman army. Messages which Prince Apafi* sent to Lorraine and Sobieski suggest that it was deplorable.[17] In consequence the Grand Vezir decided that he could not risk losing control by staying any longer among his desperate men, who surrounded him. It was simply too dangerous. He withdrew at once to Buda.

On 6 October the Poles were already close to Párkány.[18] The German cavalry stood farther back while the infantry, under Starhemberg, were still coming through the Schütt. The commanders at first agreed that the troops in front should pause for a day, but Sobieski abruptly changed his mind and ordered an attack. Something went wrong, the Poles were routed by their opponents while Ottoman reinforcements came quickly across the bridge from Esztergom. Sobieski, his son Jacob and other high-ranking commanders were all in danger of death or capture, and their retreat was disorderly. Everything changed next day when the infantry arrived, and some 16,700 German troops and 8,000 (or 10,000) Poles confronted possibly 16,000 of the Sultan's men. Sobieski was never a more loyal ally of Lorraine and Leopold than on this occasion. Conversely, both Thököly and the Tartars preferred to keep their distance from the Turkish commanders. The Sultan's men, outnumbered, dashed out from Párkány attacking wildly. The Christians, in good order, soon closed in and after an hour's fighting drove them back to the river bank. A battery was brought up to fire on the bridge, and its central section collapsed. Some Turks tried to get across it, others to float down and across the stream by clinging to odd bits of timber. The greatest massacre of the year began, the most shocking and pitiable carnage which eye-witnesses tell us they had ever seen. There was a veritable bridge of death, the broken section of the structure gradually filling up with corpses, over whom others tried to clamber to the pontoons on the Esztergom side; more and more men were drowned. Others escaped along the north bank of the Danube to Pest. Some got over the river to Esztergom. Others were captured. Nine thousand, it was believed, were dead.

---

*The Prince of Transylvania had left Vienna, with the Grand Vezir's consent, well before the final battle.

Kara Mustafa was quickly losing his power, while still retaining authority. He hastily left Buda for Belgrade the day (or two days) after the battle, after pronouncing the deposition of the Khan of the Tartars. Speech with the Sultan face to face, it must have seemed, was his best chance for the future. But the Sultan, probably for reasons unconnected with the events in Hungary, had just left Belgrade for Adrianople; so that while the Grand Vezir, arrived in Belgrade, asserted himself and gave orders as usual, in Adrianople his enemies at court were unopposed while trying to destroy his credit with the Sultan.

The Austrian pontoon boats had been moving gradually down the Danube channels, to replace the ruined timberwork of the Ottoman bridge at Párkány. Several Polish officers still opposed the idea of further fighting, but Sobieski and Lorraine together favoured one more venture, an assault on Esztergom in their year of triumph. A Brandenburg contingent of 1,200 appeared on the scene (their belated entry in the season's warfare), followed by Max Emmanuel with his Bavarians, to make the Christian armament look even stronger.[19] The bridge was ready by 19 October, the troops in Párkány crossed the Danube and a siege of Esztergom began. The Turks had little desire to fight, the town was taken and the high ground of its citadel encircled. The Ottoman commander soon capitulated on terms which allowed him to leave with his troops. This archepiscopal seat and city, and grand Ottoman stronghold, had been recovered for the Christian interest. Kara Mustafa predictably responded by ordering the execution of those officers (including Janissaries) who had quitted Esztergom. But their senior, the Aga of the Janissaries, was already on the road to Belgrade.

News of the fresh disaster soon travelled further. We have no reliable account of what followed in Adrianople, of the dialogue between attendant office-holders and courtiers and the Sultan, but their alarm can be understood from the words of the French ambassador, writing from Istanbul. 'I have just learnt that the Imperialists have taken Esztergom, that desertion, terror, disorder and agitation against the Grand Vezir and the Sultan himself increase every day.'[20] Against the Sultan! It was time for a change of government! On this occasion Ottoman government responded with speed and effect. Messengers rode back to Belgrade. They made their plans with the Aga of the Janissaries, and on 25 December presented themselves before the Grand Vezir. They bid him, in accordance with the Sultan's command, hand over the symbols of his high authority, his seal, the Prophet's holy standard and the key of the Kaaba at Mecca. He obeyed or was compelled to obey, and asked: 'Am I to die?' 'Yes, it must be so,' they said. 'As God pleases,' he replied. Then the executioner came forward with his cord. The Grand Vezir Kara Mustafa was dead, but for the Christian world it was Christmas day.[21]

These events, the capture of Esztergom and the death of the Grand Vezir, were like milestones in the development of Habsburg international policy. What had seemed a possibility after the relief of Vienna, a campaign or a series of campaigns aimed at the reconquest of Turkish Hungary, was quickly transformed by these victories into an obligation to fight offensively on this front, an obligation which Leopold's government could no longer lightly set aside in order to defend the Rhineland, as in earlier years. It led to a new tactic of appeasement in the west, and a new militancy in the east, which step by step altered the overall balance of Habsburg policy. For this reason the year 1683 was an epoch in the history of Europe.

III

Not only did the Habsburg and Polish armies gain a decisive victory in Hungary in October. The working partnership of the two governments improved, in spite of many difficulties which led to interminable correspondence and argument.[18] Friction with John Sobieski had been profoundly disturbing to the Habsburg ministers from the day after Vienna was relieved. The unequal distribution of the Turkish spoils, the interview with Leopold, Sobieski's undeviating emphasis on the tokens of personal prestige, the military problem of what to do next and how to do it, the shortage of essential supplies for the forces, were all important enough; but nothing caused more nervousness than Sobieski's attitude towards Thököly. The Poles were not obliged by the treaty with Leopold to co-operate in the conquest of Hungary, and it was arguable that Polish interests were best served by bolstering up Thököly against both the Turks and the Habsburgs. Away over the mountains in Cracow, circles round the Queen cherished the empty dream that, with or without Thököly's help, the Magyars would consider making her son Jacob a hereditary Prince in Hungary.[19] The King himself at first adopted the tactics of appeasement preferred by Herman of Baden and his friends in the first half of 1683; although there were now no signs that Baden's party at Linz was strong enough to support Sobieski on this point. Instead Leopold's ambassador Zierowski, who accompanied the King on the march into Hungary, was repeatedly instructed to see that the Polish negotiations with Thököly were thwarted. Lorraine backed up Zierowski. Buonvisi warned the King from Linz that his policy amounted to a silly and dangerous intrigue; and he begged the Pope to intervene. Innocent XI composed a solemn admonition. Pallavicini, in Cracow, even tried to convince Polish senators that the original wording of the treaty of alliance designated the Turks 'and the Rebels' as the common enemies.

This battery of criticism by no means overwhelmed Sobieski. He took the very reasonable view that, for the Poles, Thököly was worth winning over, and believed quite wrongly that this was practical politics. He even regretted the hasty departure of John George of Saxony from the theatre of war: the man best placed to urge the cause of the Hungarian Protestants on Leopold. After the capture of Esztergom, Thököly's envoys at length came to the King's headquarters and presented his demands.[20] They were no less extravagant than in the early months of the year. Further conferences, in which Lorraine also took part, soon showed that the Malcontent Magyars and the Austrians – in their new, victorious mood and understandably anxious not to alienate the loyal Magyars like Esterházy – would never agree. Sobieski's patience began to wear thin while he also waged a different war against critics on another front, his own subjects. Many in the army, ever since 12 September, wanted to go home. Others, in Poland itself, felt angrily that the recent victories gave the Sobieskis too much power; and the phantom of hereditary authority vested in a single family roused their jealousies once more. The King retorted in angry and eloquent letters, addressed to the Queen but written for a wider audience, that he intended to keep the troops in Hungary in order to spare Poland expense and (he admitted) devastation, and to be in the best possible position to start the next campaign early in 1684. The war, he wrote, and the successful continuation of the war, was the opportunity of a thousand years.[21] Such a chance might never occur again in the whole future history of his beloved country. The problem of Thököly soon became entwined with the problem of winter quarters in Hungary.[22] Sobieski's error of judgment was profound. He believed that Thököly would not or could not object if the Polish troops spent the coming months in the areas which Thököly still claimed to control. On this assumption, he negotiated with Lorraine an agreement about the distribution of quarters in Upper Hungary between his own and the Habsburg regiments. Their march began in mid-November. In fact, every castle and town was barred against the Poles by the Malcontents. Violence was tried on both sides. Men lost their tempers, and then they lost their lives. The anarchy was complete and this part of Sobieski's policy was in ruins. The consequences were two: most of the Polish army, as well as the King himself, moved over the border back into Poland; and he was forced to rally wholeheartedly to the Habsburg alliance.

The ministers at Linz meanwhile reviewed and partially revised their policy towards the Magyars. By January a commission had been set up in Pressburg, authorised to grant an amnesty to individual Magyars guilty of recognising the rule of Thököly or the Turks in 1683, who now declared – to the commission's satisfaction – their loyalty to Leopold. As might be expected, there were difficulties. Habsburg officials had sequestrated a large number of the domains belonging to such persons in order to raise supplies for the troops, and it was not always easy to find alternative quarters. Moreover some respectable precedents allowed the Hungarian Palatine to take for his own use, even to acquire permanently, the property of rebels. Paul Esterházy's personal losses had been immense, he claimed redress, and the government had to try and pacify him. The commission did its best.[23] While firmly excluding Thököly and his immediate supporters, it granted pardons to magnates like Draskovich and Batthyány. The temper of the country became a little more friendly to the Habsburg interest; Sobieski could take some of the credit for the change. At least the campaign of 1684 was not to be prejudiced by too much direct disaffection in Hungary.

IV

A much broader issue had been raised. After the relief of Vienna, tens of thousands of men were drawing away again from the arena of their decisive encounter, a small strip of ground in central Europe. Franconians and Bavarians moved back into Germany. Winter-quarters were being assigned to Habsburg troops in Bohemia and Hungary, the Poles marched east and then north. The Turks were in retreat and the Grand Vezir dismissed his Tartar, Transylvanian, Moldavian and Wallachian auxiliaries to their own distant homesteads. Only the Lithuanians still belatedly drifted through Poland to Moravia and Hungary on their way to the wars. In this new context, statesmen once more tried to assess future prospects and wondered whether the shock of defeat would conceivably loosen the whole structure of the Ottoman empire. The help occasionally given by Serban Cantacuzene, Prince of Wallachia, to Kuniz during the siege had been a promising sign, although the Prince withdrew eastwards after the battle of 12 September. Prince Apafi of Transylvania was also careful to keep in touch with the Christian commanders from near Buda. The crushing defeat of the Turks at Párkány and Esztergom, it might be thought, was bound to encourage these rulers to watch for an opportunity to change sides if the Ottoman power came any closer to a total collapse.

On 22 October an important conference met at Linz, with Kuniz and Caprara both present.[24] The Emperor had already decided to send Zierowski to Moscow, but now they considered whether to appeal for support to the Danubian princes and the Shah of Persia as well as to the Czars of Muscovy. A Transylvanian Catholic of great experience in Balkan politics, Count Czáky, was commissioned to go through Poland to Wallachia in order to negotiate secretly with Cantacuzene. Meanwhile Pallavicini reported from Cracow to Rome that Sobieski wanted to send the Cossacks into action. The King recalled that the recovery of Kamenets in Podolia, not long since, had been his great and necessary ambition. He knew that Petriceicu, once a Hospodar of Moldavia and then deposed by the Turks, hoped to regain the government of his country. He feared that the Tartars would raid into Polish territory on their way home from Hungary. It followed that this was an opportunity to use both Petriceicu and the Cossacks to stop and shatter them. Even the Austrians, from recent bitter experience, had an interest in the grand strategy of an attack on the Tartars hundreds of miles to the east. By the end of October the nuncio was enthusiastically describing the value of a recent promise from Rome of additional funds.[25] Sobieski could now hasten the recruitment of Cossack bands, waiting eagerly for cash and equipment in the area beyond Lvov.

In December, therefore, fighting began again in Bessarabia and Moldavia. Petriceicu and the Cossack leaders won a notable victory near the mouth of the Dniester, of which lurid details were soon published in Cracow.[26] The

King had hopes of a heavy Polish thrust in the near future north and east of the Carpathians, and then into the Principalities. But he looked even farther afield and visualised a threefold advance on the grand scale. While the Poles and Cossacks fought in the east, and the Habsburg army in the centre, the Venetians would intervene in Greece and possibly the Dardanelles. This had been an old project discussed by mission priests in the Balkans, and by the papal nuncios at various European courts. An invitation to Venice figured in the debates and correspondence which preceded the alliance between Leopold and Sobieski in 1682–3. Now at last it formed a basis for serious negotiations, which led step by step to the Holy League concluded at Linz in March 1684. Venice agreed to join the existing offensive pact of King and Emperor against the Sultan. It was another major victory.

Certain groups of politicians in Venice were always critical of the cautiously yielding attitude which those in office, with greater responsibilities and a clearer view of the Republic's weakness, had adopted towards the Ottoman power after the loss of Crete in 1669.[27] These critics wanted to recover the island and they pointed out that the Sultan's government, if it ever overcame the Emperor and forced him to make peace, would unhesitatingly turn to deal with a much weaker opponent. The danger was all the greater because of the influential interest, at Vienna, which so obviously wished to come to terms with the Sultan in order to deal with Louis XIV. However the Venetian administration continued to watch and wait during the critical summer months of 1683. Restless irregular forces in Dalmatia, who raided into Turkish territory and invited reprisals, added to the uncertainties of the crisis. Venice acquiesced tamely when Istanbul demanded lavish compensation. Then the wonderful news from Vienna, following close on false rumours which anticipated the truth, reached the city. Talenti, Sobieski's secretary, arrived with his trophies of victory bound for Rome.[28] It is possible, though not proven, that he had already been instructed to invite the Venetians to join in a grandiose attack on the infidel. When he returned from Rome, the project of an expanded Holy League under the aegis of the Pope had already taken a clearer shape in some minds; while by this time Leopold had made informal approaches to Contarini, the Venetian ambassador in Linz.[29]

News of the victory at Esztergom strengthened the militants in Venice but others still argued that no move should be made unless the Balkan peoples first rose in revolt against the Ottoman government. The course of events in Germany and Flanders, with its effect on court politics at Linz, continued to worry them. Contarini, a good patriot, was in the best position to size up this last problem, and he pushed steadily in favour of an offensive alliance with the Emperor. Early in December Königsegg formally proposed such an alliance, suggesting that both Muscovy and Persia would join in the war against a common enemy. Leopold's envoy in Venice worked hard at his end of the negotiation. The Venetians at length settled their current disputes with Innocent XI over ecclesiastical jurisdiction and privilege; their envoy at

Rome, and the nuncio in Venice, entered vigorously into detailed discussions. Marco d'Aviano also spoke up for the good cause; Venetia, after all, was his own country. In December and January the interests which championed the League gradually wore down their opponents, in the complex of interlocking committees which were an essential feature of the Venetian constitution; they resolved the problems caused by the changing membership of these bodies, due to fresh elections at short intervals. Contarini was empowered to negotiate at Linz. Here a Polish plenipotentiary had also arrived, and the papal nuncio managed to reconcile their differences. Both Sobieski and Leopold's ministers were very anxious to commit the Republic to a direct assault on the Dardanelles, and they wanted a clause in the treaty specifying the size of the Venetian force, in men and ships, to be mounted against the Turks. There were also difficulties over the King of Hungary's ancient claim to sovereignty in Dalmatia, which Venice naturally wished to recover and to rule. Contarini and Buonvisi evaded these demands. The Poles and the Austrians did not press them and the agreement was completed on 5 March 1684, almost exactly twelve months after the ratification of the original treaty between the Emperor and Poland. The great victories of the year, therefore, had in this way led to the organisation of a combined attack on the Ottoman empire from Poland, Hungary and the Mediterranean. Never before, in the two previous centuries, did the three Christian states most directly concerned agree so positively on a common enterprise; and they soon began to tap the military resources of many of the German princes. Without much exaggeration, the war of 1683–1699 against the Sultan can be called the last of the crusades.

The attempt to bring Muscovy into this crusade was a failure. The effect of the warfare in the Ukraine between Sultan and Czar in the years before 1681 had been plain enough to all intelligent observers; it diverted Ottoman forces from the west.[30] The willingness and ability of the Poles to fight the Turks also depended on Russo-Polish amity, and if Leopold could help to maintain the peace between them, so much the better for the whole Christian alliance. Unfortunately, long before Zierowski reached the Russian frontier a conference between the Russians and Poles had broken down.[31] Positive co-operation was out of the question. Nonetheless the envoy completed his journey to Moscow, accompanied by a staff which included not only professional. diplomats but also a Jesuit, Johann Schmidt, Zierowski's almoner. Schmidt represented a different facet of Habsburg policy. The Jesuits working in Lithuania had appealed to Rome for assistance; they wanted to do something for the handful of Catholics who lived in Moscow and they wanted – if conditions allowed – to proselytise. In June 1684 a much more influential Jesuit joined Zierowski and Schmidt, Father Carlo Vota, a negotiator of great subtlety who won over the dominant Muscovite statesman of the day, Galitzin. As a result, although the political discussions led nowhere Zierowski left behind in Moscow a mission which was also a missionary centre. Its chief responsibility was the tiny Catholic population in the city but its expenses were met by the Habsburg

The following Lines are Engraven in the *Roman Language*
I N
Letters of Gold,
UPON THE
𝕲𝖆𝖙𝖊𝖘 of VIENNA:
In Honour of thofe Illuftrious Hero's, and in perpetual Memory of
the late Famous Victory obtained over the *TURKS*,
before the Walls of *Vienna*.

 Y the Sanctity and Liberality of Pope *INNOCENT*
the XI.

By the Counfel and Induftry of the Auguft Emper-
our *Leopold* I.

By the Happy Succefs and Expedition of *JOHN*
the III. King of *Poland*.

By the Induftry of ——— Duke Elector of *Bavaria*.

By the Fidelity and Valour of *John George* the 3d.
Duke Elector of *Saxony*.

By the Vigilance of *CHARLES* Duke of *Lorrain* in the Field:
By the Conftancy and Courage of *Ernestus*, Count *Staremberg*, within the Walls.
In fine, by the United Strength
Of the Fighting Empire, and Praying Priefthood.
By the admirable Concord of all in the beft Caufe.
VVith the Help of *JESUS CHRIST*,
Without the Help of the Moft Chriftian ⎱
Againft the Moft Antichriftian ⎰ *MONARCH.*
VIENNA ftands Freed.
The *Turkifh* Power Totters.
Rebellion Falls.
The Gates of *Strigonium* open.
Happy *AUSTRIA* (for which GOD always doth Wonders againft
the *Turks* and *French*) Arifes from her Afhes, and (after
Devaftation) TRIUMPHS.
You therefore, that are Euemies, Fear GOD, Fighting for *Leopold*.
You that are Subjects, love *Leopold*, Fighting for GOD.
You that are Rebells, expect the utmoft Ruine.
You that are Loyal, hope for a perfect VICTORY.
For though the powers of the Ayr, Earth and Hell be moved, at laft
The Chriftian Caufe will Triumph.

LONDON, Printed by *J. M.* for *W. Davis*, MDCLXXXIV.

government.[32] Just conceivably this venture, one of the humbler results of the victory at Vienna, could have had far-reaching effects – had not Catholic enthusiasts hoped to spread Catholic influence into Russia ever since the sixteenth century? But they sadly miscalculated, and the Russians of Peter the Great's generation soon showed that they could more easily be made to learn technological skills from the Protestant peoples of northern Europe than religion from Rome.

It so happened that in 1683 the Catholic Bishop of Naxivan* in Persia, the Dominican Sebastian Knabb, was in Poland.[33] He carried a brief from Innocent XI to Shah Suleiman, dated 12 June, begging for help against the Turks in that hour of crisis. After 12 September both Sobieski and Leopold wished him to take their own letters, containing an appeal to the Shah to profit from the Sultan's recent disaster by joining them in a combined attack. Knabb next appears in Moscow[34] and finally found his way overland to the Shah's court. The European Catholics in Persia were well aware that Christian envoys had not the slightest chance of persuading Suleiman to declare war on the Turks.[35] The Holy Alliance never won his support, just as nothing came of a vague hope that the Abyssinians might be induced to mount an assault on the Sultan's authority in Egypt. But these fantasies were a feature in politics at this particular date.

Sobieski likewise suggested to Innocent that Dutch and English sea-captains might be encouraged to sail under the Papal flag, and to attack Turkish ports and ships.[36] Innocent firmly disapproved; but he put to Louis XIV's ambassador in Rome a variant of this proposal, an idea which he had himself aired on many earlier occasions. He asked that the King of France, the Most Christian, should send his great fleet to assail the common enemy.[37] The King declined.

V

Louis XIV certainly wished to impress the Sultan with his naval power. This had been one motive for the dispatch of Admiral Du Quesne into the Aegean in 1681 and 1682. At the same time he distinguished very clearly reasons of state, which forbade him to sacrifice his interests in western Europe by helping Leopold against the Turks in 1683, from the commercial and ideological considerations which justified a fierce assault on the corsairs of the western Mediterranean. This assault was *his* crusade, an enterprise which satisfied the French king and his subjects that they also fought boldly for the Christian cause; but the Moslem strongholds of Tunis or Algiers were remote, peripheral, and to attack them was not to weaken the Sultan.

---

*Nakhichevan, now in Azerbaijan, lies 60 miles SE of Mount Ararat.

Ever since 1680 Du Quesne's ships of war had been in action against the corsairs.[38] In 1682 he bombarded Algiers, and in June 1683 appeared there for the second time. On this occasion, in spite of the great strength of the French, resistance was very determined and culminated in a brutal execution of the French consul in the town. Louis' dispatch of 25 July had instructed Du Quesne to insist on the complete humiliation of the enemy. Another dispatch, of 10 August, witheringly reproached the Admiral for his failure to take the place, and pressed for a relentless bombardment with an exceptionally heavy, new type of mortar by which the French set great store; technically it was a more striking novelty than anything that either the attack or the defence at Vienna, in this very month, had to show. For another four weeks the fate of Algiers was in doubt, before the French finally withdrew. Louis continued to hope for a resounding victory over the infidel, just when the crisis in Vienna was coming to its climax. At the same moment, in the middle of August, he decided to send his troops into the Spanish Netherlands. It seemed certain that no one could help Grana, the Viceroy at Brussels, and Leopold was manifestly unable to do so. If the Spaniards collapsed in Flanders, their ambassador in Passau or Linz would in turn find it impossible to maintain the interest at Leopold's court which still opposed a settlement in the Empire and the Netherlands on Louis' terms. But simultaneously Louis would impress Europe as the victor at Algiers, the redeemer of all those Christian captives and slaves in north Africa.

He had other more personal factors to take into account in this crowded period.[39] At the end of July the Queen of France died suddenly, the lady whom the King esteemed (as he admitted) because she never said 'No' to him in the whole course of her life. Louis had at once to settle with someone of far greater will-power, Mme de Maintenon, whose influence over him had been growing in the previous few years. She was perfectly capable of saying 'No' if the monarch asked for an irregular union. Discreet references in Mme de Maintenon's correspondence in the months of August, September and October 1683, show that she and the King were then struggling to decide their future relationship; it was the extraordinary affair 'sur l'article de Louis et Françoise'. On 12 August (the day the Turks entered the counterscarp of Vienna), she begged her confidante Mme de Brianon, 'to pray constantly for the King – he needs grace more than ever, in order to behave in a manner contrary to his inclinations and habits'. The battle, for so it may be called, was fought out at Fontainebleau; early in September Louis injured an arm, and abandoned an earlier plan to take the court to Touraine for the autumn. The decision in favour of a secret marriage was reached by mid-September, and the ceremony probably took place in the second week of October. One other major domestic alteration occurred at the same moment. On 6 September Colbert died and it became necessary to choose between the candidates who competed busily for the various offices which he had held.

There is no proven connection between Louis' personal problem and

French foreign policy in the summer and autumn of 1683, but the autocrat in Fontainebleau was surely too preoccupied to consider seriously the arguments for a spectacular intervention in the Empire, for making a positive offer to send troops at once to the Danube in return for concessions. For some years he had used Turkish pressure on the Habsburgs as a powerful lever to squeeze such concessions from Leopold. The siege screwed up that pressure to a maximum and he continued unhesitatingly to use it in August 1683. The dispatches from his ambassador in Passau suggested – at least, until the end of the month – that Vienna was unlikely to surrender; while a long series of reports from French envoys at Istanbul had usually deprecated the military efficiency of the Ottoman army. It was justifiable, on the basis of this evidence, to weaken Leopold's powers of resistance by refusing to help him, and to rebuff the Pope who called for the collaboration of all Christian states in the hour of supreme danger. It was expedient to bully the Regensburg Diet by making one more offer – which stood open for forty days, and no longer[40] – for a settlement in the Empire. But to go further, and to send troops into the Empire to enforce such a settlement, would have profoundly disturbed the French clergy and nobility when they were already worried by a serious dispute with the Pope. In 1682 Innocent had roundly condemned Louis' ecclesiastical policy and, less directly, the fundamental statement of principle embodied in the Gallican Articles of that year.

The Church in France, the Catholic laity and the King therefore combined to support measures which effectively demonstrated their Christian zeal. The fleet's actions in the Mediterranean was one such measure; and hostility to the Protestants was another. The quartering of soldiers on Huguenot families, as a set act of policy, began in May 1681. In July 1683 Protestants in the Vivarais and Dauphiné appeared in arms, and troops were sent to deal with them.

French hostility to Leopold was tempered by these considerations, making an outright alliance with the Sultan unthinkable during the crisis. If Mme de Maintenon could not directly influence the policy of Louis or Louvois, it is significant that the papal nuncio in Paris, Ranuzzi, gave her a number of valuable presents during August for which she expressed great gratitude to the Pope. An absolute breach with Rome would have disgusted her whole circle of friends and dependents. For instance, we can listen to the redoubtable voice of Bossuet on this theme, as he preached the funeral oration for Maria Theresa at St Denis on 1 September.[41] 'The very name and shadow of dissension,' he declared, 'was abhorrent to the Queen, as to all pious souls. Let there be no mistake: the Holy See can never forget France, or France be unmindful of what is due to the Holy See, which must be honoured in the lawful manner and with profound submission.' And in more than one splendid passage he went on to warn his audience of the horrors of the Turkish invasion of Hungary and Austria, begging them to recall the great exploits in Crete and on the Rába (in 1664), when 'Louis revived in the infidels' breasts the opinion they had of old, of the prowess of French arms ever fatal to their tyranny, and by peerless deeds became Austria's bulwark after being her dread.' On the day that Bossuet was speaking, French troops under Marshal d'Humières entered the Spanish Netherlands without a declaration of war.[42]

The right policy, then, was not to attack the Empire while the Turks stood outside Vienna, but to use Turkish pressure on the states of the Empire in order to squeeze a power – Spain – which those states were far too preoccupied to help, while at the same time the principalities of north Germany were distracted by the continuing Baltic crisis, in turn partly maintained by French diplomacy.[43] Louis, Louvois and Colbert de Croissy had indeed judged the situation to a nicety. Although Grana published a violent manifesto of defiance, he lacked the force to offer an effective resistance. D'Humières took Courtrai first, and then Dixmude; his colleague Créqui bombarded the town of Luxembourg while parts of Hainault and Flanders were later ravaged in a thorough and brutal fashion. The Spaniards found themselves powerless. Above all their obvious champion William of Orange, strongly opposed by many of his countrymen, was less able to help them than at any earlier or later period in his long career.

One of the many reasons for William's weakness was the failure of his assistant, Waldeck, to win the real support of Leopold's government.[44]

Having argued unsuccessfully at Vienna that Lorraine's army ought not to advance into Hungary, Waldeck had retraced his steps to Linz. There he tried to persuade both the Habsburg counsellors and Max Emmanuel (on his way back to Bavaria) to prepare for speedy action in the Empire. On 17 November the Elector joined the 'Association' of states which had earlier bound themselves to defend – in principle – the Westphalian and Nymegen treaties. On 18 November Waldeck was present at a conference of Habsburg ministers which agreed that Leopold's representative should join with envoys at The Hague early in 1684, in order to consider a common policy for dealing with the emergency in Flanders and other areas threatened by France.[45] A little later the Emperor formally appointed Waldeck as one of his own spokesmen at this conference. Waldeck, much embarrassed, feared that the honour would compromise him in the view of unfriendly critics; but possibly Leopold's advisers deliberately wished to place on his shoulders the responsibility for a policy which they themselves did not intend to carry very far. By the end of 1683 he was on his way back to The Hague where William anxiously awaited him.

The Habsburg government, partly because the situation in eastern Europe increasingly compelled it to seize the opportunity to try to reconquer Hungary and even to encourage rebellion in the Balkans, formed a much more detached view of the whole situation in the west than did Waldeck, William, or Grana. When Borgomanero asked for help, in a personal conference with Leopold at the close of the year, threatening that without it Spain would come to terms with Louis XIV, the Emperor pointedly asked what force the Spaniards intended to put into the field to save themselves.[46] Nor was the court at Linz pleased by Madrid's formal declaration of war in December, which made a passive policy more difficult to sustain. Leopold's advisers appreciated, as William or Waldeck did not, that neither Brandenburg nor Saxony had any intention of opposing Louis XIV on Spanish territories, a point confirmed by Lamberg in the spring of 1684 after one more journey to Dresden and Berlin. They also knew well enough that the Hanoverian and Brunswick rulers were by this date unable to consider joining in a war against France. The combined forces of Ernest Augustus and George William, kept ready for action against the Danes and Brandenburgers at great cost throughout the winter, certainly made them formidable. But they were encircled by enemies; and Ernest Augustus had hinted to Leopold, already in July 1683, that his policy was changing, that he saw the need for an accommodation with Louis.[47] By December he pressed more insistently for a peaceful settlement with France in the Empire, and he dared not contemplate joining William of Orange and Spain. When the time came to send a Hanoverian representative to The Hague conference, his instructions were so drawn that they restrained him from agreeing to any positive commitment.

The conference duly met and talked while William continued to battle with his enemies in Holland.[48] He hoped that a promise by other powers to help Spain would satisfy them. But they knew well enough that reports from Dutch ambassadors abroad all testified to the weakness or the unpopularity of the Spaniards. Equally, foreign observers at The Hague soon realised that tension in the United Provinces jeopardised any chance of effective intervention by the Dutch in the dispute between Louis XIV and the King of Spain. While Waldeck began enlarging the magazines at Maestricht, of which he was governor, and William tried to assemble sufficient troops in Gelderland, the Estates of Groningen and Friesland actually called home their own soldiers.[49] The Amsterdam municipality remained intransigent and the conference of William's allies gradually petered out, after spending many hours on detailed plans for the defence of various frontiers. On 18 May Louis began the siege of Luxembourg, a powerful fortress but inadequately garrisoned. Vauban was never more skilful in his approaches, so that the swift progress of the siege left Grana and William little to hope for. As a last, desperate move Waldeck set out on another mission to Germany.[50] He reckoned on the good will of Max Emmanuel, and quite unaccountably thought that Ernest Augustus still intended to intervene. Above all he wished to convince the Habsburg court that the whole future of the Empire was in the balance.

A year earlier, Waldeck might have persuaded Leopold's ministers that after a resounding victory in Hungary they ought to throw their forces into action against France. But was such action still the paramount necessity?

Louis XIV had since then committed a sizeable part of his own armament to a campaign in Flanders and Luxembourg, revealing more clearly than ever before that in this area the potential allies of the Austrian Habsburgs were weak and divided. Yet the defence of the Empire, and the possible recovery of Strasbourg with Alsace, depended on the deployment of forces which would have to come either from Holland and north Germany or from Bavaria and Austria. The Dutch, Spaniards and north Germans, it seemed, were unable to protect even the territory between the lower Rhine and the Meuse, while the Austrians and Bavarians were tempted by the prospect of easier successes down the Danube. A crushing series of defeats had proved the vulnerability of the Turks. As a result, and always assuming that Louis XIV did not ask for more than Strasbourg (which he already held) and Luxembourg, the old interest represented at the Habsburg court by Herman of Baden and Borgomanero continued to grow weaker. Lorraine after his victories at Vienna and Esztergom, and Max Emmanuel, both drew closer to Buonvisi and Innocent XI. Leopold listened to Marco d'Aviano* who wanted a religious crusade, he listened less to Waldeck and Herman of Baden. During the winter of 1683–4 there were only some 10,000 Habsburg troops quartered in the Empire, and no attempt was made to transfer more regiments to the western theatre.[51] The government negotiated for the entry of Venice into the League against the Sultan, and prepared for the next campaign in Hungary. Leopold personally overrode objections expressed by Herman of Baden, while Lorraine presided over important military conferences on 8 and 24 February. At these, the question of strategy was thoroughly considered and plans were made on the assumption that the Turkish war would last for several years, with Habsburg forces gradually advancing down the Danube and Drava valleys. Buonvisi, for his part, tried manfully to diminish the gaping deficits of Habsburg finance by arranging for the taxing of the Church in the Habsburg lands, and distributing funds supplied by the Pope from clerical taxation elsewhere; and both Pope and nuncio pressed more urgently than ever for a settlement with France. Their appeal accorded, at last, with a sober analysis of European politics.

If Louis XIV had died suddenly, if the siege of Luxembourg had been the scene of a surprising military reverse which disconcerted the French, it is possible that the German and Habsburg courts would have altered their course. But Max Emmanuel simply told Waldeck that – although his troops had been kept in readiness for a march to the western frontiers in case of emergency during the past few months, although he had refused to sanction their departure down the Danube to Hungary – his final word depended on the instructions of the Habsburg government to its own regiments. Leopold in turn stated that he could do nothing without a firm promise of support from William of Orange and other princes.[52] It was an impasse. Luxembourg fell on 7 June, the Dutch Estates-General came rapidly to terms with Louis, while William with Grana and the Spanish government had to acknowledge their own complete repulse. Louis XIV's long-standing offer to negotiate a

---

*Innocent also sent Marco on a special mission to Munich to persuade Max Emmanuel that the war against the Sultan deserved priority over everything else.

settlement, on the basis of a formula which by-passed the question of ultimate sovereignty in the lands of the Empire annexed by him between 1679 and 1681, and also in Luxembourg, but recognised his right to occupy them for many years to come, was at last accepted by Leopold. The bargaining at Regensburg, which finally fixed the duration of the 'truce' for a period of twenty years, ended on 24 August 1684.

The decision to give way to Louis was clinched by unfavourable news from Hungary, where the siege of Buda had been going badly. This was indeed the significant point, that there could be no thought of withdrawing from the Turkish war. The capture of Buda, for Leopold and the majority of his ministers, now took precedence over the recovery of Strasbourg, Freiburg or Luxembourg as the most immediately practical, desirable objective for their arms and diplomacy. After many months of elaborate sparring on the western front, it was clearer than ever before that the victories of 1683 along the Danube had made a fundamental contribution to future Habsburg statecraft, committing it to the long sequence of campaigns against the Ottoman Sultan which ended only with the treaty of Karlowitz in 1699. If Louis XIV gained time, and strengthened further that marvellously complete system of defences which saved France in the wars of the great coalitions against it between 1688 and 1714, Emperor Leopold and his successors won a new Hungarian empire.

VI

The advance down the Danube, one of the major developments of seventeenth century history, anticipated by a few years the expansion of Russian power under Czar Peter. The Austrian Habsburgs no less than Russia and the Great Britain of Queen Anne, were to draw abreast of the French monarchy or at least to counter-balance it by their victories in the field. With Lorraine still in command Buda was taken in 1686, and Max Emmanuel triumphed at Belgrade in 1688. Year by year Habsburg forces tightened their hold on Transylvania and the plains of Hungary. But the first of all these victories, the relief of Vienna, had been won at the heaviest possible cost to the inhabitants of the city itself, so that against the background of empire-building on the grand scale it seems prudent – if we are to draw an honest picture of men and events in a period no less complex than any other – to take a final glance at the city of Vienna, the citizens, and the landscape surrounding them, in the years after the siege.

Statistics of any use are hard to come by. It was believed, in 1689, that half a million people had died in Austria as a result of the Turkish invasion, a figure which seems incredible; but there can be little doubt, first, that the plague years of 1679 and 1680 already created serious gaps in the working population of the whole area – in Vienna alone the loss was not less than 50,000 – and second, that before society had properly recovered from this earlier disaster the events of 1683 dealt another crushing blow to the population of most towns and villages in Lower Austria south of the Danube. On this occasion, the civilians in Vienna certainly suffered fewer losses than in 1679–80, or than the inhabitants of the surrounding district in 1683. But depopulation in the Wiener Wald was so great that its historian has spoken of 'a new wave of colonisation'[53] which continued for the next twenty-five years, gradually making good the enormous losses. He has also discovered, from an inspection of parish registers, that possibly a fifth of the immigrants came from outside Lower Austria, above all from Styria and Bavaria. A minor misfortune for the Viennese was these strangers' ignorance of the skills needed for work in their ravaged vineyards. Much worse, the plague of 1713 again decimated the population. The government, in greater need of high taxes than ever before during its long and expensive wars, was bombarded with pleas for exemption from them; villages had too many ruined houses, and estates too few labourers, to pay what the old assessments required. The whole process of recovery was painfully slow. Lower Austria ranks with the Rhenish Palatinate as one of the areas most devastated by the ravaging of armies in this period.

Immediately after the siege, certain matters were urgent. The Turks might return and the allied army dissolve into its separate parts while the rival rulers adjusted, or failed to adjust, their mutual jealousies. The remains of the Turkish camp had to be dismantled, and all stores of value moved into the city. It was even more important to level the Turkish siege-works, so that they could not be used a second time. The engineers Suttinger and Anguissola first made accurate drawings of them,[54] and then sufficient labour was mobilised to fill in the galleries and clear the glacis in a manner which satisfied the military authorities. Once again the city council was asked to find 1,000 workmen, with each house responsible for producing a man or his pay. Another 870 artisans from the civilian companies now being disbanded, as well as some of the infantry, had to join them. Once again, after protests, the Estates of Lower Austria brought in forced labour from the countryside. Meanwhile Turkish prisoners cleaned up the streets of the city. One repair, essential on all counts, was taken in hand during the winter: the bridges over the Canal and the Danube were rebuilt. The ability of a disrupted economy to create employment remained very low for a number of years, and public works of this type probably met a real need. The lack of accommodation and foodstuffs in September 1683 had prevented the permanent return of the government to Vienna; Leopold passed the five nights of his short stay in the Stallburg because his quarters in the Hofburg were too damaged; but the court's long absence at Linz, until August 1684, no doubt robbed the Viennese of their most rewarding customer. A civic deputation, headed by Hocke the syndic, handed in a petition to Leopold at Linz in June which described. the general condition of Vienna as truly desperate.[55] The economic tightness was such that every privileged person or institution tried hard to evade common liabilities. Taxes were not paid, the rights of the guilds were not observed by the unprivileged. The friction was intense.

In fact the halcyon moment had ended, although the Emperor slowly offered promotions of title to men who had acquitted themselves well during the siege. City councillors became 'imperial' councillors. Individuals in the War Council and the Treasury (like Belchamps, who handled finance so competently throughout the crisis), were advanced to the status of 'Freiherren'. A large number of officers rose in rank. Gratuities in cash were given, or at least promised; and Starhemberg saw to it that all the regiments which had served in the garrison were paid something extra on 21 September 1683. The Vienna municipality gave presents to the colonels and commanders who had defended them against the Turk. They then gave smaller rewards to some of their own number. The treasurer and the syndic, for example, did not refuse a modest 300 florins each. With merit in the past duly rewarded, everyone now had to take stock of a new set of problems, doing what they could for themselves or for others. Bishop Kollonics gathered together hundreds of children, waifs and strays left behind in the Turkish camp, and housed them in Leopoldstadt. In the same district, the sponsors of a scheme for starting up an academy for the education of young noblemen looked sadly at the ruins of a building which they had just secured for the purpose in 1682, and began to search for new quarters. This academy later became an important school for military engineers, under the direction of Anguissola the mapmaker of 1683. In Leopoldstadt also, the irrepressible Koltschitzki obtained a tax-free house from the city fathers. According to legend, it was he who now persuaded the Viennese to take pleasure in a new drink. Soon after the siege individual Greeks and Serbs certainly started to open coffee-houses in the town – but Koltschitzki has somehow taken most of the credit.[56]

It is not easy to give details about the return to more normal conditions in Vienna, and for a very simple reason. Those men who thought it worth while to keep journals during the crisis, or to write its memorable history soon afterwards, saw no point in continuing with their work after the Turks had fled. There was no European public for the merely municipal history of Vienna after 12 September 1683. Instead, readers everywhere wished eagerly to discover what had happened within the walls during the two months when the city was cut off from the Christian world outside, how the army of relief had been got together, and what were the exploits of the Poles, Saxons, and Bavarians respectively in the winning of this glorious victory. The honour of states, regiments and commanders was in debate. Printing presses were soon at work to profit from the universal curiosity, individual (though sometimes anonymous) writers endeavouring to defend or enhance this or that reputation. At first, Koltschitzki's publicity seemed the most intense. His tale of dangerous journeys in disguise, more and more fancifully embroidered, stole the limelight in various languages. Then other and better descriptions of the whole siege appeared.[57] Reuss, a tax-officer who had served as an adjutant to Starhemberg in the commander's dealings with the city-council, was anticipated by Leopold's official 'Historiographer', John Peter Vaelckeren, providentially trapped in the city by the advancing Turks for the benefit of later historians. The publisher John Ghelen, a civilian volunteer during the siege, issued a *Relazione compendiosa ma veredica* of 'everything that happened' at Vienna in the months just past. The syndic, Hocke, reluctant to let the achievements of the city fathers be unfairly forgotten, because most other accounts emphasised the military history of the siege, published his own 'Short Description' in 1685. But every one of these authors ended his tale a few days after the flight of the Turks; while the informative foreign diplomats accredited to Leopold, who might have told us much more about Vienna in the winter that followed, remained at Linz with the court for another year.

So, gradually, the event receded into the past, with men's view of it determined at first by a cloud of pamphlets and broadsheets, and then by the myth-making of later generations. These knew well enough what prodigious violence had once been done in a region which was quiet and orderly during most decades of the eighteenth century, although Magyar rebels again ravaged the Wiener Wald in 1704. The military authorities built a defensive wall round the suburbs; they continued to keep the glacis outside the old wall fairly clear, and the bastions and outworks in a state of repair sufficient to remind the citizens, increasingly hemmed in by them, of the ever-memorable siege-year 1683. Beyond the glacis, Vienna grew. In size and in the magnificence of its best buildings, it at last became worthy of the expanded Habsburg empire, which had partly sprung from that bitter fighting across the ground where now the traffic roars in the Ring and in the suburbs.

Notes and References
Index

ABBREVIATIONS

Acta   *Acta regis Joannis III ad res anno 1683*, ed. F. Kluczycki *(Acta historica res gestas Poloniae illustrantia 1507–1795,* vol. vi), Cracow, 1883.

A.ö.G.   *Archiv für österreichische Geschichte* (including *Archiv für Kunde Österreichischer Geschichts-Quellen*).

Bojani   F. Bojani, *Innocent XI. Sa correspondance avec ses nonces,* vol. iii, Roulers, 1912.

B.L.   British Library.

Hammer   J. Hammer, *Geschichte des osmanischen Reiches,* vol. vi, Pest, 1830.

H. H. S.   Haus-, Hof- und Staatsarchiv, Vienna.

Hocke   N. Hocke, *Kurtze Beschreibung . . . Wienn von 7 Julii bis 12 Septembris* (Vienna, 1685).

K.J.   'Das Kriegsjahr 1683 nach Acten und anderen authentischen Quellen', *Mitteilungen des K. K. Kriegs-Archivs,* Vienna, 1883.

Klopp   O. Klopp, *Das Jahr 1683 und der folgende grosse Türkenkrieg bis zum Frieden von Carlowitz 1699,* Graz, 1882.

Kreutel   *Kara Mustafa vor Wien. Das türkische Tagebuch der Belagerung Wiens 1683, verfasst vom Zeremonienmeister der Hohen Pforte,* ed. R. F. Kreutel, Graz, 1955.

M.I.ö.G.   *Mitteilungen des österreichischen Instituts für Geschichtsforschung.*

M.M.   Necati Salim, 'Die zweite Belagerung Wiens im Jahre 1683', *Militärwissenschaftliche Mitteilungen,* vol. lxiv, Vienna, 1933.

Newald   J. Newald, *Beiträge zur Geschichte der Belagerung von Wien durch die Türken, im Jahre 1683,* Vienna, 1883–4.

N.Q.   'Neue Quellen zur Geschichte des Türkenjahres 1683 aus dem Lothringischen Hausarchiv', ed. F. Stöller, *M.I.ö.G.* Ergänzungs-Bd. xiii, Vienna, 1933.

Renner   V. Renner, *Wien im Jahre 1683,* Vienna 1883.

U. und A.   *Urkunden und Aktenstücke zur Geschichte des Kurfürsten Friedrich Wilhelm von Brandenburg,* Berlin, 1864–1930.

BIBLIOGRAPHICAL NOTE

The great modern bibliography of the second (as of the first) siege of Vienna, which supersedes all previous lists of the kind, is W. Sturminger, *Bibliographie und Ikonographie der Türkenbelagerungen Wiens 1529 und 1683 (Veröffentlichungen der Kommissiom für neuere Geschichte Österreichs,* vol. xli), Graz, 1955. It lists 2,547 published items on the siege of 1683.

It is noticeable that the second centenary of 1683 produced a very large number of publications, both of the primary sources and of critical studies, and therefore the best introduction to the whole subject may perhaps be found in two reviews of that time: K. Uhlirz, 'Die neueste Literatur über des Jahres 1683', pp. 325–49, in *M.I.ö.G.,* v (1884), and F. Maresch, 'Das Jahr 1683', pp. 179–216, in *Historisches Jahrbuch. Görres-Gesellschaft,* v. (1884). Fifty years later there was a good but less copious harvest. Among the works which appeared in 1933, R. Lorentz, *Türkenjahr 1683* (a revised edition was published in 1944) gives a good general account of the siege, and the notes and bibliography refer to the researches which have been carried out since 1883. Its subtitle, *Das Reich im Kampf um den Ostraum,* gives a fair idea of the author's leading theme.

The third century of the siege was celebrated in many places, from New York via Vienna and Warsaw to Istanbul. There was a modest output of new studies, and of new primary sources. A general survey of these will be found in W. Leitsch and M. D.

Peyfuss, 'Drei hundert Jahre seit dem Entsatz von Wien 1683' in *Jahrbuch für Geschichte Osteuropas*, 32 (1984).

The most comprehensive account of the whole topic is Thomas M. Barker, *Double Eagle and Crescent. Vienna's second Turkish siege and its historical setting* (Albany, New York, 1967).

Chapter 1: The Origins of the Ottoman Attack.

1 Hammer, p. 382; Klopp, pp. 120–2.

2 *M.M.*, p. 664. The date is not certain: any day between 6 and 12 October is possible. Contemporary writers by no means agree on many points of detail.

3 G. Benaglia, *Relatione del viaggio fatto à Constantinopoli, e ritorno in Germania* (Bologna, 1684), pp. 136–50.

4 Caprara's dispatch, 14 April, 1683. H.H.S., Turcica, 1. fz. 152.

5 Benaglia, pp. 180–1; E. Browne, A *Brief Account of Some Travels* (ed. London, 1685), pp. 3, 25.

6 *M.M.*, p. 667.

7 O. Brunner, 'Eine osmanische Quelle zur Geschichte der Belagerung Wiens im Jahre 1683', in *Mitt. des Vereines für Geschichte der Stadt Wien*, v (1925), pp. 37–41.

8 *Narrative of Travels in Europe, Asia and Africa* (London, 1834–50), especially vol. i (part 2), pp. 54–7, 100 ff, and vol. ii., pp. 60–2; A. Pallis, *In the Days of the Janissaries* (London, 1951).

9 H. A. R. Gibb and H. Bowen, *Islamic Society and the West* (London, 1950–7), i. 37.

10 B. Miller, *The Palace School of Muhammad the Conqueror* (Harvard, 1941), 172 ff.

11 F. W. Hasluck, *Christianity and Islam under the Sultans* (Oxford, 1929), ii. 419–22, 611.

12 G. F. Abbott, *Under the Turk in Constantinople . . . 1674–1681* (London, 1920), 227 ff, 284.

13 Gibb and Bowen, ii. 258.

14 N. Jorga, *Geschichte des osmanischen Reiches* (Gotha, 1911), iv. 62–70.

15 Hammer, p. 322.

16 In 1659, the local Ottoman headquarters were moved from Timisoara to Jenö, somewhat closer to Transylvanian territory (L. Fekete, *Die Siyāqat-Schrift in der türkischen Finanzverwaltung* (Budapest, 1955), i. 699). Oradea, captured in 1660, strengthened the Turkish position farther north.

17 *Literaturdenkmäler aus Ungarns Türkenzeit*, ed. Babinger (Berlin, 1927), pp. 15–19.

18 The traveller Jean Chardin reported of Caffa (Feodosiya) in 1672: 'During the forty days that I stayed there, I saw come in and go out above 400 sail of ships, not counting little vessels that keep close to the shore.' *Travels* (ed. London, 1685), p. 69.

19 L. Makkai, *Histoire de Transylvanie* (Paris, 1946), pp. 237–47; *Österreichische Staatsverträge. Siebenbürgen*, ed. R. Gooss (Vienna, 1911), pp. 806–45.

20 *Encyclopaedia of Islam*, art. 'Kara Mustafa Pasha'.

21 Abbott, p. 194.

22 This was the view of foreign diplomats at Istanbul (Barozzi and Berchet, *Le Relazioni . . . Turchia*, ii (1872), pp. 207, 235, and K. Koehler, *Die orientalische Politik Ludwigs XIV* (Leipzig, 1907), p. 75), shared by Hammer, p. 337. It still amounts to no more than a guess.

23 S. Buxhoeveden, A *Cavalier in Muscovy* (London, 1938), p. 249.

24 Hammer, pp. 341, 726–9; Jorga, iv. 154.

25 Gooss, *Siebenbürgen*, pp. 858–63.

26 Cf. G. Tolnai, 'Le comte Michel Teleki', in *Nouvelle Revue de Hongrie*, xxxiii (1940), pp. 304-10.

27 O. Redlich, *Geschichte Österreichs* (Gotha, 1921), pp. 292-8.

28 E. Hurmuzaki, *Fragmente zur Geschichte der Rumänen* (Bucharest, 1889), iii. 325-6; *Monumenta Comitialia Regni Transylvaniae* (Budapest, 1894), xvii. 184.

29 Koehler, pp. 95, 97, 123.

30 G. Fantuzzi, *Notizie degli scrittori bolognesi*, iii (Bologna, 1783), pp. 101-7; and the *Insegnamenti del vivere del conte Alberto Caprara a Massimo suo nipote* (Bologna, 1672).

31 Hammer, p. 731-2.

32 Hammer, p. 378.

33 *Monumenta Comitialia Regni Transylvaniae*, xvii. 38.

34 Cf. R. F. Kreutel, *Im Reiche des goldenen Apfels* (Graz, 1957).

35 Klopp, pp. 533, 539-40.

36 In 1682 or 1683, also, the Turkish geographer Ebubekr, who had earlier completed a Turkish version of Blaeu's *Atlas Major*, from the copy of this work presented to the Sultan by the Dutch ambassador in 1668, was ordered to compose an account of Hungary and Germany. F. Taeschner, 'Zur Geschichte des Djihānnumā', *Mitt. des Seminars für örientalische Sprachen*, xxix, pt. 2 (Berlin, 1926), pp. 99-111.

37 Caprara's dispatch from Buda, 19th February, 1682. H.H.S., Turcica, i. fz. 151.

38 It was taken by Caprara's servant, G. B. da Fabris, who was instructed to gather all possible information in the course of his journey through Hungary.

39 Letters from Benaglia to Caprara of 11 and 13 July refer to their difficulty in finding a courier to go from Istanbul to Vienna. H. H. S., Turcica, i. fz. 152.

40 Klopp, p. 539. Cf. p. 111 below.

41 Hurmuzaki, *Documente privitoré la istoria românilor*, v, pt. I (Bucharest, 1885), pp. 100-1.

42 F. Babinger, 'Qara Mustafa Paschas Essegger Sendschreiben an den Markgrafen Herman von Baden', in *Archiv Orientální*, iv (1932), 23-33.

43 'Diarium, was sich vom 7. Juny anno 1683 . . . bey der türkischen armee zugetragen', *A.ö.G.* iv (1850), p. 498.

44 For the Khan see F. Kraelitz-Greifenhorst, 'Aufforderungs-und Kontributions-schreiben des Tartaren-Hans Murad Giraj vom Jahre 1683 an Wiener-Neustadt' *Mitt. zur osmanischen Geschichte*, i (1921-2), pp. 223-31.

45 The Turkish authorities for this conference differ on many points, and the account given above is no more than plausible. *M.M.*, pp. 667, 693; Hammer, pp. 392-3; cf. E. Lovarini, *La schiavitù del generale Marsigli sotto i Tartari e i Turchi* (Bologna, 1931), pp. 69, 103.

46 Caprara to Leopold, 20th October, 1682. Vienna, Kriegsarchiv, Feldakten, fz. 162.

47 Benaglia, p. 168.

48 'Relatione particolare . . . del Conte Alberto Caprara Anno 1682 e 1683'. H.H.S. Böhm MS. 758, f.91.

Chapter 2: Leopold I and the City of Vienna

1 *Privatbriefe K. Leopold I . . . 1662-1673* (ed. Pribram, 1903-4); H. Srbik, *Wien und Versailles 1692-1697* (Munich, 1944), pp. 25-8, and references given there.

2 Cf. T. Fellner and H. Kretschmayr, *Die österreichische Zentralverwaltung* (Vienna,

1907); H. F. Schwarz, *The Imperial Privy Council in the Seventeenth Century* (Harvard, 1943).

3 Wurm, *Die Jörger von Tollet* (Linz, 1955), pp. 167, 198–205.

4 M. Vachon, 'La France et l'Autriche au siège de Vienne en 1683', *La Nouvelle Revue*, xxiii (1883), pp. 775–7.

5 B. Kucyznski, *Stratmann* (Würzburg, 1934). He was still the Neuburg vicechancellor while representing Leopold at Nymegen. Ibid., p. 34.

6 P. Wentzcke, *Feldherr des Kaisers. Leben und Taten Herzog Karls V. von Lothringen* (Leipzig, 1943).

7 *Acta*, pp. 330–1. The translation has been abbreviated.

8 Wentzcke, p. 168.

9 M. Immich, *Papst Innocenz XI* (Berlin, 1900).

10 Bojani, pp. 345 ff, 592 ff; A. M. Trivellini, *Il Cardinale Francesco Buonvisi a Vienna 1675–1689* (Florence, 1948).

11 Cf. the curious poem, in which the author prophesies a judgment on sinners, *Über den grossen und entsetzlichen den 16/26 Decemb. anno 1680 zu Regensburg erschienenen Comet*. B.L. Cat.: 8610.bb.41.

12 M. Héyret, *P. Marcus von Aviano* (1937–46), especially vol. iv. 1–50.

13 *Corrispondenza epistolare tra Leopold Imperatore I. ed il P. Marco d'Aviano*, ed. O. Klopp (Graz, 1888).

14 M. Dreger, *Baugeschichte der K. K. Hofburg* (Vienna, 1914), 89 ff. The three towers of the old Burg are clearly seen in illustration VI.

15 H. Kühnel, *Der Leopoldinische Trakt der Wiener Hofburg* (Vienna, 1960).

16 R. Feuchtmüller, *Das niederösterreichische Landhaus 1530–1850* (Vienna, 1949), pp. 12–29.

17 A. F. Pribram, 'Die niederösterreichischen Stände und die Krone in der Zeit Kaiser Leopold I', *M.I.ö.G.*, xiv (1889), pp. 589–652.

18 F. Walter, *Wien*, ii (1941), p. 211

19 *Geschichte der Stadt Wien* (Alterthurnsverein zu Wien), iv (1911), pp. 218–65.

20 A. Camesina, 'Wiens Bedrängnis im Jahre 1683', *Berichte und Mitt. des Alterthumsvereines zu Wien*, vol. viii (1865), Supplement, pp. 153–5.

21 *Geschichte der Stadt Wien*, iv. 182–5. Whatever may be said against the 'Stadt Guardia', one of its pikemen from 1670 onwards was Daniel Suttinger, whose models and maps of the city were outstandingly good.

22 Newald, i.1 ff.

23 T. Mayer, *Der auswärtige Handel des Herzogtums Österreich im Mittelalter* (Innsbruck, 1909).

24 H. Voltelini, 'Die Wiener Stadt-und Stadtgerichtsordnung Ferdinands I von 1526', *Mitt. des Vereines für Geschichte der Stadt Wien*, ix–x (1929–30), pp. 105–29.

25 Renner, pp. 133–40, 349–57; *Geschichte der Stadt Wien*, iv. 411 ff.

26 A. T. Leitich, *Vienna Gloriosa* (Vienna, 1947), pp. 98–9.

27 Quoted in *Geschichte der Stadt Wien*, iv. 389.

Chapter 3: The Defence of Habsburg Interests in Europe

1 P. Dirr, *Zur Geschichte der Reichskriegsverfassung . . .* (Munich, 1901), p. 25.

2 *Österreichische Staatsverträge. Niederland*, ed. H. Srbik (Vienna, 1912), p. 199.

3 R. Fester, *Die armierten Stände und die Reichskriegsverfassung 1681–1697* (Frankfurt, 1886), p. 41.

4 M. Strich, *Das Kurhaus Bayern im Zeitalter Ludwigs XIV* . . . (Munich, 1933), ii. 291.

5 Srbik, *Wien und Versailles,* p. 14; P. Vidal de la Blache and L. Gallois, *Le Bassin de la Sarre* (Paris, 1918), p. 21.

6 W. Platzhoff, 'Ludwig XIV, das Kaisertum und die europäische Krisis von 1683', *Historische Zeitung,* cxxi (1920), pp. 377–412; but cf. Strich, ii. 299.

7 Wentzcke, *Feldherr des Kaisers,* p. 184.

8 T. Srbik, *Niederland,* p. 200.

9 B. Gebhardt, *Handbuch der deutschen Geschichte* (ed. 1955), ii. 33–4.

10 *U. und A.,* xiv, 905 ff.

11 Ibid. p. 1026.

12 Ibid. pp. 1043, 1052.

13 Strich, ii. 148.

14 Ibid. ii. 35 ff., 293, 303.

15 *U. und A.,* xiv. 915.

16 B. Auerbach, *La diplomatie française et la cour de Saxe 1648–1680* (Paris, 1888), pp. 480–4.

17 W. Thenius, *Die Anfänge des stehenden Heerwesens in Kursachsen* . . . (Leipzig, 1912), p. 7.

18 Auerbach, p. 485.

19 G. Schnath, *Geschichte Hannovers . . . 1674–1714* (Hildesheim, 1931), i. 171–80.

20 P. L. Muller, *Wilhelm III von Oranien und Georg Friedrich Waldeck* (The Hague, 1873, 1882), i. 154–82.

21 Cf. p. 78 above.

22 K. Koehler, *Die orientalische Politik Ludwigs XIV,* p. 74 ff.

23 Srbik, p. 211.

24 Koehler, pp. 88, 97, 102, 123.

25 A. Sorel, *Receuil des Instructions Données . . . Autriche* (Paris, 1884), pp. 95–6.

26 Renner, pp. 107, 468; Newald, i. 3–19.

27 This schedule had been slightly adjusted by this date, so that the Bohemian lands paid a little less than two-thirds of the total, and the Austrian duchies correspondingly more.

28 *M.I.ö.G.,* xiv. 602–18

29 Newald, i. 5.

30 Newald, i. 10–11.

31 Bojani, pp. 603–17, 616–17; Renner, pp. 104–5.

32 Renner, pp. 91–8; A. Wrede, *Geschichte der K. und K. Wehrmacht* (Vienna, 1898–1905), ii. 152 and iii. 540.

33 Wrede, i. 163, 187, 232, 256, 529; iii. 182. The old regiments stationed round Philippsburg had little difficulty in recruiting more men, who were then diverted to the new regiments. Fresh troops were also raised in Bohemia and Silesia; very few were raised in the Austrian duchies.

34 He was Prince Eugene of Savoy's elder brother. The news of his death on 7 July 1683 no doubt clinched Eugene's decision to leave Paris, and seek preferment at the Emperor's court: after all, his brother's colonelcy was now vacant. M. Braubach, *Geschichte und Abenteuer. Gestalten um den Prinzen Eugen* (Munich, 1950), pp. 22–3, 97–9.

35 Wrede, iii. 646.

36 G. A. Kittler, 'Georg Rimpler . . . im Türkenkrieg 1683,' *Zt. für die Geschichte des Oberrheins*, xcix. (1951), pp. 174–5.

37 It is impossible, on the evidence available, to decide whether the defences of Györ had been substantially modernised by June, 1683. Kittler (in *M.I.o.G.* lxiv (1956), pp. 32–3) gives a reproduction from V. M. Coronelli, *Atlante Veneto* which, he suggests, is a plan of Györ showing the work carried out by Rimpler in 16811–3; it illustrates a most complex design of bastions, ravelins, lunettes and the like. The claim is possible, but doubtful.

38 A newsletter writer, in touch with the Secretary of State in London, expected this tour to begin on 1st February (while General Rabatta was to go likewise to view the more southerly frontier zone). But Baden only left Vienna on 28 March, 'with many Ingenieurs, and little Money', B.M. Additional MS. 41838, f. 105.

39 *Autobiografia di Luigi Ferdinando Marsili*, ed. E. Lovarini (Bologna, 1930) p. 39; E. Lovarini, *La schiavitù del generale Marsigli*, pp. ii, 59 ff.

40 See p. 46 above.

41 A. Winkler, *Die Zisterzienser am Neusiedlersee* (Mödling, 1923), pp. 85–89, gives additional reasons for friction between the Draskovich family and the Habsburg government.

42 *K.J.* 1 ff.

43 *N.Q.*, pp. 12–13.

44 Newald, i. 32–3, and chap. ii *passim*; Renner, pp. 157–67.

45 Kittler, *art. cit.*, p. 179.

46 A. Schachinger, 'Das kaiserliche Waldamt . . . 1683', in *Jb. für Landeskunde von Niederösterreich*, N.S., xxix (1948), 170–3.

47 Renner, pp. 161–3.

48 B.M. Additional MS. 41838, fos. 34–6, 53, 77–81.

49 Newald, i. 41–3, 264–8.

50 *A.ö.G.*, xxxvii (1867), pp. 371–2. I have somewhat simplified and abbreviated the original.

51 F. Maresch, 'Das Jahr 1683', *Historisches Jahrbuch*, v (1884), pp. 183–91.

52 Maresch, pp. 1911; Bojani, pp. 601–2.

53 On the other hand, Innocent XI soon showed his readiness to authorise the taxation of ecclesiastical property in the Habsburg lands to meet the emergency, and to allow the Emperor to make use of state-revenues which had been handed over to the church for various purposes. Bojani, pp. 608–32.

54 *U. und A.*, xiv. 1049 ff.

55 M. Doeberl, *Entwickelungsgeschichte Bayerns* (Munich, 1928), ii.108–9.

56 S. Riezler, *Geschichte Baierns* (Gotha, 1913), vii. 272.

57 Schnath, *Geschichte Hannovers*, i. 189–92.

58 Cf. A. Lossky, *Louis XIV, William III, and the Baltic Crisis of 1683* (Berkeley, 1954).

59 Renner, pp. 169–82.

60 It was a part of the settlement of the Sopron Diet in 1681 that the great office of the Lord Palatine, the supreme dignitary chosen by the Estates, should be restored. Paul Esterházy (1631–1705) had been appointed.

61 Bojani, pp. 157, 569; *Acta historica res gestas Poloniae illustrantia*, vii (ed. K. Waliszewski, 1884), pp. 249, 255, 573, 579; *Acta*, pp. 2–3; Newald, i. 63–76.

62 O. Forst de Battaglia, *Jan Sobieski* (Einsiedeln, 1946), 157 ff.

63 The French envoy in Poland, de Vitry, although also present at Jawarów and

Stryy, was kept completely in the dark. Louis XIV was better informed from other sources. *Acta Historica*, vii. 240, 275, 277; S. Rubinstein, *Les relations entre la France et la Pologne de 1680 à 1683* (Paris, 1913), pp. 102–17.

64 Bojani, 633 ff.; *Acta*, pp. 18–87, 47–9.

65 Bojani, 588 ff.

66 Bojani, 619 ff.

67 *Acta*, p. 13.

68 *Acta*, pp. 22–3, 93, 156–9. The sums of money given here are in terms of Austrian currency. Cf. pp. 91–3 above.

69 *Acta*, pp. 32–43, 105–10.

70 See above, note to p. 106 on p. 34.

71 *Acta*, p. 124.

72 *Acta*, p. 141; Bojani, p. 673.

73 Bojani, pp. 636–7, 653–5, 682; *Acta*, p. 68.

74 *Acta*, pp. 80–6.

75 Moreover, the news of the conclusion of this latter treaty – in which he was nominated protector and guarantor by both signatories – stirred Innocent XI into playing a much more active part in rallying support for the threatened powers. See his letters of 12 May in A. Sauer, *Rom und Wien im Jahre 1683* (Vienna, 1883), pp. 3–6.

Chapter 4: The Threat to Vienna

1   *K.J.*, pp. 13–18

2   *K.J.*, pp. 14, 31.

3   Newald, i. 88.

4   See p. 59 above.

5   *N.J.*, p. 11; *K.J.*, pp. 25–8; Newald, i. 88.

6   *K.J.*, pp. 28–32; *N.J.*, pp. 11–13, 55–60; Bojani, pp. 669–71.

7   *N.Q.*, pp. 14, 60.

8   *K.J.*, p. 36.

9   *N.Q.*, pp. 14–15, 61–7.

10 H. H. S. Lothringisches Hausarchiv, MS. 50, fos. 227–34.

11 *N.Q.*, pp. 62–3.

12 Le Bègue even believed that Rimpler was 'feigning illness'. MS. 50, f. 234.

13 *K.J.*, 48 ff.; *N.Q.*, pp. 15, 70.

14 *N.Q.*, pp. 71–5, 15-17; *K.J.*, p. 52.

15 He refers to 'tre guadi che esigono defesa particolare'. Lovarini *La schiavitù*, pp. 11–14, 60–2; L. F. Marsigli,' *L'état militaire de l'empire ottoman* (The Hague, 1732), ii. 49–50.

16 *N.Q.*, pp. 17–19, 75–7.

17 Newald, i. 90, 94 and ii. 18–19; *N.Q.*, pp. 19–20, 77–8.

18 *Flucht und Zuflucht. Das Tagebuch des Priesters Balthasar Kleinschroth aus dem Türkenjahr 1683*, ed. P. H. Watzl (Graz, 1956), pp. 17–32.

19 *Codex Austriacus* (Vienna, 1704), i. 394–6 and ii. 360-i.

20 The title page of *Auff/auff Ihr Christen!* has the date 8 July 1683. The book was apparently printed in Vienna by John Gehlen, although the author was in Graz.

21 Newald, ii. 20–2.

22 For events from 7 July onwards, see L. Baur. 'Berichte des hessendarmstädtischen

Gesandten Justus Eberhard Passer an die Landgräfin Elizabeth Dorothea . . . von 1680 bis 1683,' *A.ö.G.*, xxxvii (1867), pp. 385–409; F. Mencik, ' Ein Tagebuch während der Belagerung von Wien im Jahre 1683', A.6.G., lxxxvi; J. P. Valcaren (Vaelckeren), *A relation or diary of the siege of Vienna* (London, 1684), of which the original version is the Latin *Vienna a Turcis obsessa . . . sive Diarium obsidionis Viennensis* (Vienna, 1683) and other contemporary journals.

23 Newald, ii. 96–107.

24 It was a point of some importance that he added, temporarily, to that section of the War Council left in Vienna all the senior officers in the garrison, and also George Rimpler, Baden's trusted engineer.

25 For Caplirs, see J. A. Helfert, *Der Chef der Wiener Stadtvertheidigung, 1683, gegen die Türken* (Prague, 1883).

26 Newald i. 107–11 and ii. 35–53.

27 Maurer, *Cardinal Leopold Graf Kollonitsch* (Innsbruck, 1887), pp. 140–57.

28 Hocke, pp. 14–18.

29 For Lorraine's withdrawal across the Danube, see also pp. 113–4 below.

30 Bojani, p. 689; *A.ö.G.*, lxxxvi. 213.

31 Newald, i. 97 and ii. 26–7; F. Porsch, 'Gregor Schinnerers Erlebnisberichte über den Türkeneinfall des J. 1683', *Unsere Heimat*, xxvi (1955), pp. 1609; Helfert, pp. 20–1.

32 *A.ö.G.*, xxxvii 386.

33 *Acta*, pp. 166–8.

34 *Acta*, pp. 172, 177–9, 199.

35 W. Pillich, 'Die Flüchtigung der Schatzkammer, des Archives und der Hofbibliothek aus Wien in Jahre 1683', *Mitt. des österreichischen Staatsarchivs*, x. (1957), pp. 136–47.

36 *Flucht und Zuflucht*, 55.

37 J. Zahn, 'Das Jahr 1683 in der Steiermark', *Mitt. des historischen Vereines für Steiertnark*, xxxi. (1883), pp. 67–117. Fürstenfeld is 30 miles east from Graz.

Chapter 5: The Siege

1 Kreutel, *Kara Mustafa vor Wien*, 24 ff.

2 Kreutel, *Im Reiche des goldenen Apfels*, pp. 53, 216-17.

3 See pp. 34–5 above.

4 Kreutel, 30 ff.

5 At this very date one of the pioneer works on the Turkish language compiled in western Europe, the *Thesaurus Linguarum Orientalium* of Mesgnien Meninski, was being printed (1680–7) in Rossau. Kreutel, *Im Reiche des Goldenen Apfels*, p. 212.

6 One eye-witness commented later: 'Everyone knows that an encampment, set by a good general, is also an order-of-battle; but the Turks' camp, following their ancient practice, was simply a confused mass of tents and baggage, ranged in a semi-circle.' Hence (he says) the camp was more vulnerable than the city. Marsigli, *L'état militaire de l'empire ottoman*, pp. 75, 120.

7 G. Jacob, 'Türkische Urkunden', *Der Islam*, vii. (1917), pp. 269–87.

8 Kreutel, p. 32.

9 In the past, the municipality had always had the right (or duty) to man the Dominican (or Burghers') Bastion.

10 The principal guide, quoting a vast array of older sources, to events inside the city

during the siege, is A. Camesina, *Wiens Bedrängnis im Jahre 1683*, supplemented by Renner, chaps. iii. and iv., and by Newald, i. chap. ii.

11 *N.Q.*, pp. 20–2; Kreutel, pp. 36–40; Hammer, p. 401; J. G. W. Reuss, *Wahrhaffte und grundliche Relation . . . Wien* (Vienna, 1683), pp. 13–4.

12 L. A[nguissola], *Assedio di Vienna . . . 1683* (Modena, 1684), 81.

13 An *okka* is a little under 3 lbs. in weight. *M.M.*, pp. 675, 693.

14 'Relation du siege de Vienne par un officier de la garnison', *N.Q.*, pp. 128–38. The officer in question was probably Adjutant-Colonel Hoffman, whom we have already met in the course of negotiations with Thököly. See p. 67 above.

15 *K.J.*, pp. 146–8.

16 Camesina, pp. 19–70, with corrections in Newald, *passim*.

17 *K.J.*, pp. 143–5; Newald, i. 114–15. The Turks had exact information about the size of the garrison and knew the names of the regiments which composed it. *Mitt. des Vereines für Geschichte der Stadt Wien*, v. 40.

18 Renner, 341 ff.

19 *N.Q.*, p. 131.

20 Camesina, p. 31; Kreutel, pp. 42, 58.

21 A third member of the family died of wounds a few days later. Valcaren, p. 52.

Chapter 6: Outisde the City

1 V. Kraus, 'Herzogenburg und Umgebung während der Türkennoth', *Blätter für Geschichte von Niederösterreich*, ii. (1866), pp. 186–200.

2 *Hanns Tschánys Ungrische Chronik 1670–1714*, ed. I. Páur (Pest, 1858), 69 ff.

3 H. Kunnert, 'Das Burgenland im Türkenkrieg, *1683*', *Burgenländische Heimatblätter* (1922), pp. 157–67. The Castelli dragoons held Wiener-Neustadt; a summons from the Tartars that the townsmen should buy their safety, at a price of 1,500 'Lion' piastres and 60 horses, was disregarded.

4 K. Holter, 'Türkische Urkunden für Bruck an der Leitha aus dem Jahre 1683', in *Unsere Heimat*, ix. (1936), pp. 268–79.

5 Kleinschroth, *Flucht und Zuflucht*, pp. 206–9, 222, 234.

6 Franconian troops also did a great deal of damage on the Sinzendorf lands two months later, on their way to Vienna. M. Kroissmayr, 'Geschichte der Herrschaft Walpersdorf', *Jb. für Landeskunde von Niederösterreich*, iii. (1904), pp. 159–226.

7 Cf. *Unsere Heimat*, xxvi. 160–9.

8 *N.Q.*, pp. 21–8; 80–93; *K.J.*, pp. 160; *Acta*, pp. 175, 178.

9 Newald, ii. 94.

10 *K.J.*, p. 81; *Acta*, pp. 181–5.

11 *Acta*, pp. 180, 192, 201–2; Newald, i. 124–5.

12 Thaly, *Késmárki Thököly Imre Naplói* (Budapest, 1868–73), ii. 5–9, 38–40, 60. See the map, p. 132 above.

13 Kreutel, pp. 147–8; *M.M.*, pp. 677–9.

14 *K.J.*, pp. 82–92; *Acta*, pp. 202–10.

15 *K.J.*, pp. 88–92; *Acta*, pp. 267–8.

16 Newald, i. 175–6; *Acta*, p. 275.

17 For this mission see p. 126 below.

18 *N.Q.*, pp. 26, 28.

19 Renner, pp. 404–7. Some particulars about these places can be gleaned from

J. M. Korabinsky, *Geographisches-Historisches und Produkten Lexikon von Ungarn* (Pressburg, 1786).

20 *N.Q.*, p. 87.

21 W. Sturminger, 'Die Kundschaften zur Zeit der zweiten Türkenbelagerung Wiens im Jahre 1681', *Festschrift zur Feier des 200-jährigen Bestandes des Haus-, Hof- und Staatsarchivs*, ii. (1951), pp. 349-69.

22 Hocke, p. 53; *K.J.*, pp. 165-6; Newald. i. 135; Kreutel, p. 47.

23 *K.J.*, p. 176; Newald, i. 141-2; Hocke, p. 91.

24 Maurer, *Kollonitsch*, p. 158.

25 *N.Q.*, pp. 27, 91.

26 Duncker, 'Drei Berichte aus der belagerten Wien, 1683', in *Mitt. des K.K. Kriegs-Archivs*, 1893, pp. 265-72. For Koltschitzki see K. Teply, 'Die Einführung des Kaffees in Wien', *Forschung und Beiträge zu Wiener Stadtgeschichte*, 6 (1980).

27 See pp. 38, 102 above.

28 *Acta*, pp. 218-3; Klopp, pp. 233-5. Cf. *True Copy of a Letter from Count Starhemberg to the Duke of Lorraine . . . 18th August, 1683* (London, 1683).

29 Klopp, pp. 239-41.

30 Sturminger, *art. cit.*, p. 361.

31 Bojani, 694 ff.

32 *A.ö.G.*, lxxxvi. 219-39.

33 Newald, ii. 53-62.

34 The instructions to his commanding officer for the campaign 'in Hungary' are dated as early as 21 July. C. Staudinger, *Das K. Bayerische II Infanterie-Regiment 'Kronprinz' 1682-1882* (Munich, 1882-7), i. Appendix 8.

35 G. Rauchbar, *Leben und Thaten des Fürsten Georg Friedrich von Waldeck* (Arolsen, 1870-2), ii. 247-50; P. Hassel and Vitzthum v. Eckstädt, *Zur Geschichte des Türkenkrieges im Jahre 1683* (Dresden, 1883), pp. 138-9. *K.J.*, p. 234, gives totals of 7,000 foot and 2,500 horse.

36 *A.ö.G.*, lxxxvi. 226, 229, 232; *Acta*, pp. 199-200.

37 *N.Q.*, 81 ff; Camesina, Supplement, pp. 194-200; Newald, i. 125-6, 175 and ii. 56; Klopp, pp. 283-4.

38 Newald, i. 124.

39 Camesina, Supplement, pp. 197-8.

40 Klopp, p. 283.

41 *N.Q.*, p. 95.

42 *A.ö.G.* lxxxvi. 236.

43 Klopp, pp. 281-2; J. Kukuljević, *Jura regna Croatiae, Dalmatiae, et Slavoniae*, i. (Zagreb, 1862), pp. 350-7.

44 Newald, i. 149 ff; ii. 28.

45 Klopp, pp. 235-6; MS. Relatione particolare (see note 48, p. 204 above).

46 An English newsletter-writer, then at Passau, interviewed Caprara on 15 August. Caprara said that the Emperor's soldiers had ferried him over the Danube. B.L. Additional MS. 41838, f. 215.

Chapter 7: Warsaw, Berlin, Dresden and Regensburg

1 *Acta historica*, vii. 370-2.

2 Bojani, pp. 675-9, 682-3; M. Kukiel, 'Polski wysilek zbrojny roku 1683', *Kwartalnik historyczny*, xlvii. (1933), p. 164.

3   *Acta*, p. 150; *Acta historica*, vii. 369.

4   *Acta*, pp. 161–2; *Acta historica*, vii. 361–8.

5   See pp. 72, 76–7 above

6   Bojani, p. 685.

7   *Acta*, p. 164. See also p. 84 above.

8   Bojani, pp. 696–7, 703; A*cta*, pp. 176–91, 233–4.

9   *Acta*, p. 294.

10 M. Kukiel (art. cit., p. 163) calculates that Leopold's subsidy did not amount to more than seven per cent of the total Polish and Lithuanian military budget in 1683–4; but the subsidy was ready money, and the taxes were not.

11 *Acta*, pp. 151–2, 176–9.

12 Ibid. p. 168.

13 Ibid. pp. 187–9. It is curious that Lorraine's first letter, to which this is an answer, has not survived when a number of copies seem to have been made of other parts of the correspondence, but Sobieski is certainly not answering, in his first paragraph, any document now extant. Even more curious, Lorraine replies later that his original letter has not been properly understood by the King.

14 F. P. Dalérac, *Anecdotes de Pologne* (Amsterdam, 1699), i. 117–18.

15 *Acta*, pp. 181–190.

16 P. Dupont, *Mémoires* (ed. Janicki, Warsaw, 1885), pp. 102, 125; *Acta*, pp. 216, 229, 243.

17 *Acta*, p. 243.

18 Bojani, pp. 703 –4; A*cta*, p. 617; Dalérac, i. 115 ff.

19 *Acta*, pp. 244, 260; Newald, ii. 84.

20 B. Brulig, 'Bericht über die Belagerung . . . 1683', *A.ö.G.*, iv (1850), pp. 425–6; *Acta*, p. 580.

21 *Acta*, pp. 233, 240–1, 303.

22 Dalérac, p. 122.

23 *Acta*, pp. 243, 249, 618.

24 *Acta*, pp. 580–1, 618.

25 *Acta*, p. 618; Dalérac, p. 119.

26 *Acta*, pp. 262–3.

27 Dalérac, i. 125.

28 This journal was issued in twenty-one consecutive numbers, giving an account of the campaign between July and October, 1683. H. Wendt, *Schlesien und der Orient* (Breslau, 1916), p. 146.

29 *Acta*, p. 284.

30 *Acta*, pp. 263, 291.

31 *Acta*, pp. 227, 229, 241, 279, 303.

32 *Acta*, p. 301.

33 See below, pp. 160, 162.

34 *Acta*, pp. 318–21.

35 *Historisches Taschenbuch* (1848), pp. 227, 232.

36 Cf. above, pp. 120–1.

37 Hassel and Vitzthum v. Eckstädt, op. cit., pp. 107–12, 177–8.

38 Hassel and Vitzthurn v. Eckstädt, pp. 113–16; *Historisches Taschenbuch* (1848), p. 238.

39 Hassel and Vitzthurn v. Eckstädt, pp. 117–28; M. G. C. Kreysig, *Beyträge zur Historie derer Chur- und Fürstlichen Sachsischen Lande* (Altenburg, 1755), ii. 413–20.

40 *Historisches Taschenbuch*, p. 246.

41 G. Helbig, 'Kurfürst Johann Georg III in seinen Beziehungen zum Kaiser und zum Reich 1682 und 1683', *Archiv für die Sächsische Geschichte*, ix (1871), 103 ff.

42 *Historisches Taschenbuch*, p. 252; Kreysig, p. 418.

43 G. Pagès, *Contributions à l'histoire de la politique française en Allemagne sous Louis XIV* (Paris, 1905), pp. 71–2.

44 Lossky, op. cit., p. 18.

45 *U. und A.*, iii. 734; xx 775; xxiii. 1022.

46 Ibid., xiv. 1071–80.

47 Ibid., xx. 783.

48 See above, p. 134.

49 *U. und A*, xiv. 1082 ff.

50 Ibid., xiv. 1091–1105.

51 *Weensche Gezantschapsberichten*, i. 367; *U. und A.*, iii. 742.

52 Klopp, pp. 272–4. Cf. *The last resolution of the Most Christian King in relation to a general peace, and the present miserable Estate of Hungaria . . . the 26th of July, 1683* (London, 1683). B.L. Cat.: 105 f. 20 (5).

53 H. Prutz, 'Gottfried von Jena . . . 1679–87', *Forschungen zur brandenburgischen und preussischen Geschichte*, xviii, pt. 2 (1905), pp. 25–106.

54 A French offer of 1st September, 1682, to negotiate a settlement in the Empire had expired on 30th November. Renewed in December, it expired again on 1st February, 1683.

55 *Weensche Gezantschapsberichten*, i. 365.

56 Prutz, p. 71.

57 For Waldeck's activity in the preceding weeks, see p. 123.

58 *Correspondentie van Willem III en van H. W. Bentinck*, ed. Japikse, ii. ii. (1935), p. 599.

Chapter 8: The Relief of Vienna

1 Bojani, pp. 733–46; Klopp, pp. 295–8.

2 *Klopp, Corrispondenza, p. 27.*

3 *A.ö.G.*, lxxxvi. 239.

4 Klopp, *Corrispondenza*, pp. 28–30; *A.ö.G.*, lxxxvi. 247–50.

5 Kreutel, pp. 78, 80.

6 Hocke, pp. 123–4; Valcaren, pp. 66–7.

7 Newald, ii. 66–9.

8 Hocke, pp. 131–2.

9 Kreutel, p. 89. The *kethuda beyi* was an extremely high-ranking official in the Ottoman administration.

10 Valcaren, p. 76.

11 Valcaren, pp. 78–9; ii. 69; Kreutel, p. 92.

12 Hocke, pp. 174–5; *N.Q.*, p. 136.

13 Newald, i. 197–8 and ii. 120–6. The dispatch from which this passage is quoted has been used by some writers to argue that a party of burghers positively wished to negotiate a capitulation with the Grand Vezir. Newald shows that no evidence

supports this thesis, apart from the reported statement of a prisoner under cross-examination by the Turks. Certainly an 'Armenian' doctor resided in Vienna during the siege, but his 'servant' was probably Seradly, bearing a final letter of appeal from Starhemberg to Lorraine which described the events of 4 September. He was caught by the Turks, but somehow destroyed or concealed the letter.

14 *N.Q.*, p. 138. This shrinkage in numbers of effectives – from 11,000 to 4,000 – must be contrasted with the very small civilian losses due to fighting. G. Gugitz, '1683 und die Bürger Wiens. Legende und Geschichte', *Unsere Heimat*, xxv. (1954), pp. 108–20, calculates that only 10 burghers, and 39 other civilians, died in battle or from wounds. Fifteen more, including 3 burghers, were killed by the Turkish bombardment. But many of the soldiers, like many civilians, died from sickness.

15 Hocke, pp. 162–92; Newald, i. 190–6, 207; J. G. W. Reuss, *Wahrhaffte und grundliche Relation . . . Wien* (Vienna, 1683), pp. 25–60; *Glaubwürdiges Diarum . . . von einem Kayserl: Officier* (Regensburg, 1683), pp. D-Dii.

16 Hocke, p. 193. The position of the Kahlenberg, though not its true configuration, is shown on illustration XI.

17 N.Q., p. 94.

18 Ibid., p. 28.

19 Newald, i. 92–4, 114, 158.

20 O. Uechtritz-Steinkirch, *Heinrich Tobias Freiherr von Haslingen* (Breslau, 1883), pp. 12–13; Newald, i. 175. For Haslingen, see also p. 73 above.

21 Rauchbar, *Waldeck*, ii. 258 ff.; *N.Q.*, pp. 31–2, 97–9; Newald, ii. 95 ff.; *Acta*, pp. 329–33, 342–50.

22 'Résolutions prises à Stetteldorf le 24/3 Septembre 1683', Rauchbar, pp. 261–3.

23 Uechtritz-Steinkirch, p. 13.

24 *Acta*, pp. 359, 371.

25 *K.J.*, map no. IIIa.

26 Ibid., p. 237.

27 Klopp, p. 294; C. Staudinger, *Geschichte der K. bayerischen Heeres unter Kurfürst Max Emmanuel 1680–1726* (Munich, 1904–5), i. 167.

28 These were no doubt the forces responsible for the first rockets observed rising from the Wiener Wald on the night of 7 September by watchers in Vienna. See p. 158 above.

29 *Acta*, pp. 288–9; *K.J.*, pp. 240–4; Newald, i. 179.

30 Rauchbar, p. 265.

31 *K.J.*, p. 245.

32 *Acta*, p. 373.

33 Klopp, pp. 303–4, 552; *Acta*, pp. 646–7.

34 Rauchbar, p. 268; *Acta*, p. 374; Dupont, *Mémoires*, p. 135.

35 *Acta*, p. 375.

36 Kreutel, pp. 163–4.

37 The date of this instruction is variously given as 23 August or 4 September (ibid., pp. 86, 160). The second is more plausible.

38 Ibid., pp. 99–100, 161.

39 Klopp, pp. 310–11.

40 Kreutel, pp. 131, 161–3.

41 Kreutel, p. 107.

42 Klopp, pp. 304, 552.

43 *K.J.*, 249 ff.

44 A number of contemporary writers stated that, about this hour, Marco d'Aviano solemnised Mass for these commanders on the Leopoldsberg (or, less probably, on the Kahlenberg), and that Sobieski himself was his server. But no one who might have been present refers to this famous episode.

45 Kreutel, p. 107.

46 *Acta*, p. 592; Dupont, p. 136.

47 Rauchbar, *Waldeck*, p. 268.

48 Vaelckeren, quoted by Klopp, p. 309.

49 *Acta*, p. 375.

50 Hassel and Vitzthurn v. Eckstädt, 161 ff.; O. Laskowski, *Sobieski King of Poland* (Glasgow, 1944), 147 ff.

51 Kreutel, pp. 109–10, 165–6.

52 *Acta*, p. 369.

Chapter 9 : *The Consequences of Victory*

1 *Acta*, p. 385.

2 *Acta*, pp. 376–82; Hammer, p. 415.

3 L. Pukianiec, *Sobieski a Stolica Apostolska na tle wojny z Turcją (1683–1684)* (Vilna, 1937), p. 1.

4 *Acta*, pp. 379–80, 392; Newald, i. 215–6; *A.ö.G.*, lxxxvi. 252.

5 Newald, i. 223; Bojani, pp. 746–8, 753; Pukianiec, pp. 131–2; Hammer p. 413.

6 *Acta*, pp. 366–70, 382; Schnath, *Geschichte Hannovers*, i. 222.

7 *Acta*, pp. 395–407; *N.Q.*, pp. 103, 140.

8 *Acta*, pp. 400, 448.

9 *Acta*, p. 623.

10 But Buonvisi's clear-cut condemnation of Leopold for insisting on this interview is worth notice. Pukianiec, p. 72.

11 *Acta historica*, vii. 386; Klopp, p. 318.

12 Rauchbar, *Waldeck*, ii. 271–85.

13 *N.Q.*, pp. 104–6; *Acta*, pp. 417, 431–4; *K.J.*, p. 274 ff.

14 *Acta*, pp. 410, 423.

15 *N.Q.*, pp. 41, 106, 110.

16 Hammer, 418; C. Contarini, *Istoria della guerra di Leapoldo I imperadore e de' principi collegati contro il Turco dall' anno 1683 sino alla pace* (Venice, 1710), pp. 193–200; Marsigli, *L'état militaire de l'empire ottoman*, ii. 121–3; Kreutel, pp. 111 – 14.

17 Hurmuzaki, *Documente*, ix. 2 (1897), p. 305; *N.Q.* pp. 105, 111; Kreutel, pp. 85, 167; Klopp, p. 557.

18 *Acta*, pp. 411–13; 504–6; Bojani, pp. 774–76; *N.Q.*, pp. 111–14; J. Wolinski, *Z dziejow wojny i politiki w dobie Jana Sobieskiego* (Warsaw, 1960), pp. 168, 182.

19 *Acta*, p. 457; *Kriegsgeschichtliche Einzenlschriften*, 5 (General Staff, Berlin, 1884), pp. 19–21.

20 Hurmuzaki, *Documente, Supplement* I, i. 271.

21 Hammer, p. 423; Kreutel, pp. 122–3.

22 Bojani, p. 779 ff.; Klopp, pp. 249–52; *Acta*, pp. 598–613; Pukianiec, pp. 111–30.

23 Newald, ii. 112 ff.

24 *N.Q.*, pp. 117, 124.

25 *Acta*, pp. 511, 493-4.

26 *N.Q.*, pp. 122-4; *K.J.*, pp. 306, 339.

27 Maurer, *Kollonitsch*, pp. 164-7.

28 O. Brunner, 'Österreich und die Wällachei wahrend des Türkenkrieges von 1683 bis 1689', *M.I.ö.G.*, xliv. (1930), p. 277.

29 *Acta*, pp. 501-3, 519-20; Bojani, p. 882.

30 Hammer, p. 425.

31 H. Kretschmayr, *Geschichte von Venedig*, iii. (Stuttgart, 1934), pp. 340-3; A. A. Bernardy, *Venezia e il Turco nella secunda metà del secolo xvii.* (Florence, 1902), pp. 75-80; Pastor, *History of the Popes*, xxxii (1940), pp. 193-205.

32 Pukianiec, pp. 13-15.

33 Klopp, pp. 371-2, 380-9; Bojani, p. 927 ff.

34 H. Uebersberger, *Russlands Orientpolitik in den letzten zwei Jahrhunderten* (Stuttgart, 1913), i. 36-8.

35 A. Theiner, *Monuments historiques relatifs aux règnes d'Alexis Michaélowitch, Féodor III. et Pierre le Grand, Czars de Russie* (Rome, 1859), pp. 271-8; P. Pierling, *La Russie et le Saint-Siège*, iv (Paris, 1907), pp. 79-83.

36 Some Jesuits also hoped to use their mission in Moscow as a base from which to attempt the overland routes to China via Siberia and Mongolia or Turkestan. This was probably one reason why the Russian authorities soon closed the mission.

37 *Acta*, pp. 497, 513.

38 *Tagebuch des Generals Patrick Gordon*, ii. (Moscow, 1851), pp. 3-13.

39 *Chronicle of the Carmelites in Persia* (London, 1939), i. 420-3.

40 Pukianiec, p. 27.

41 E. Michaud, *Louis XIV et Innocent XI* (Paris, 1882-3), ii. 91.

42 C. de la Roncière, *Histoire de la marine française*, v (Paris, 1934), pp. 74-32; A. Jal, *Abraham Du Quesne et la marine de son temps* (Paris, 1873), ii. 459-69.

43 Mme de Maintenon, *Lettres*, ed. M. Langlois (Paris, 1935), ii. 503-25 and iii. 5-7; M. Langlois, *Louis XIV et la cour* (Paris, 1926), pp. 178-81.

44 See above, p. 148.

45 Bossuet, *Oeuvres complètes* (Paris, 1836), v. 295, 301.

46 C. Rousset, *Histoire de Louvois*, iii (Paris, 1863), pp. 236-44.

47 For the Baltic crisis, see pp. 52, 65-6 above.

48 For William's predicament, see *Négociations de monsieur le comte d'Avaux en Hollande 1679-1688* (Paris, 1752-3), i. 319 ff. and ii. *passim*; *Despatches of Thomas Plot and Thomas Chudleigh*, ed. F. A. Middlebush (R.G.P., Kleine Serie, xxii., 1926); and Lossky, pp. 36-42.

49 *Weensche Gezantschapsberichten*, i. 370; Rauchbar, ii. 285-9, 323.

50 *Weensche Gezantschapsberichten*, i. 371-2.

51 Schnath, *Geschichte Hannovers*, i. 223-6, 240-2, 255; Strich, *Das Kurhaus Bayern*, ii. 532 ff.

52 A. Levae, *Essai historique sur les négociations de la trêve de vingt ans conclue à Ratisbonne en 1684* (Brussels, 1844), p. 202; Srbik, *Österreichische Staatsverträge. Niederland*, p. 230.

53 *Het Staatsche Leger*, ed. Ten Raa, vi. (The Hague, 1940), pp. 94-5.

54 Muller, *Wilhelm III und Waldeck*, i. 256 ff.; Strich, ii. 558-64.

55 *Mitt. des K. K. Kriegs-Archivs*, 1884, pp. 384-8.

56 *Weensche Gezantschapsberichien*, i. 377-8; Strich, ii. 561. For Max Emmanuel's

attitude, see above all *Göttingensche gelehrte Anzeigen*, 198 (1936), pp. 226–7.

57 A. Schachinger, *Der Wienerwald* (Vienna, 1934), p. 311.

58 See above, pp. 99–100

59 Renner, pp. 472–7.

60 For this entrancing topic see G. Gugitz, *Das Wiener Kaffeehaus* (Vienna, 1940), Sturminger, *art. cit.*, pp. 357–8.

61 *Geschichte der Stadt Wien*, iv. 40–72.

Index